God, Torah, and the Meaning of Life

Musings on the things that matter

Rabbi Barry Leff

The Neshamah Center Press
Jerusalem

The Neshamah Center Press

ISBN: 978-965-7508-01-5

The Neshamah Center Press
Jerusalem

For Kiri, Heather, Katherine, Aliza and Devorah. This one really is for you…and for your children and their children.

CONTENTS

INTRODUCTION

Rabbis have an unusual writing job. We are expected to expound meaningfully week after week, connecting Torah to life or current events, and we are given ten to fifteen minutes to do so. Two thousand words a week. On the High Holidays, four sermons a year that might be double that length. Longer than a typical op-ed piece. Shorter than an in-depth essay. As runners we would be competing in those little known intermediate distances: longer than the 100 yard dash, shorter than a 10k or marathon.

For some time now, one of my goals has been to write something longer than those 2,000 word essays: to write a book that would capture my life's philosophy. I've been a spiritual seeker since I was 17; now that I've passed the age of 50, which Pirkei Avot tells us is the age for giving counsel, I figure it's time I shared what I've learned. It's time to write a book.

As I started thinking about writing that book, however, I realized in a way it has already been written. Instead of having been written as a book from the outset, it's been written a sermon at a time. As I started reviewing my writings, it became clear to me that things I've written – ranging from short blog entries to 750 word op-ed pieces to 4,500 word High Holiday "masterpieces" – come together to form a more or less coherent philosophy. They just come together in relatively small pieces, and they have been written over a period of years.

Almost all of the material – except a few bits written specifically for this book – is available online, on my blog or website. So one might wonder, why bother pulling these selections together into a book?

The short answer is I'm afraid of dying.

I write this on the first evening of Chol Hamoed Sukkot, 5770 – October 3, 2009. We have just come through the High Holidays of Rosh Hashanah, the Day of Judgment, and Yom Kippur, the Day of Atonement.

Yom Kippur is called a rehearsal for our deaths – we don't eat, we don't drink, we wear a "*kittel*," which is similar to a burial shroud, and we pray as if our lives depended on it.

The most powerful prayer of the season is Unatana Tokef – we ask "who will live, and who will die?" "Who by fire, and who by flood?" Leonard Cohen famously updated this prayer in his song "Who by Fire" with lines like "who by accident" and "who by barbiturate."

But more than the prayers, age brings a much greater awareness of one's own mortality. Around the time I turned 50, one of my congregants, a cardiologist, pointed out that the mortality tables took a rather nasty turn around the age of 50. I became acutely aware of this when I was first ordained as a rabbi, at the age of 47: the first funeral I officiated at was for a man just one year older than me. He was a man who had been completely healthy up until that point, a bike rider, an Aikido black belt, who just dropped dead of a massive heart attack, leaving a wife and two teenage kids with no life insurance. Obviously he thought he had a lot of time left.

Once you turn 50, it is almost inevitable that you will have friends who pass away from natural causes. In the last few years I've lost friends like Ron Rosen and Emerich Salzberger, and teachers like Rabbi Mickey Rosen and Rabbi Alan Lew, and my step brother Carson Holder. Once you are 50 you can no longer maintain the illusion that you will live forever.

It also occurred to me that if I got hit by a bus tomorrow, the fees on my blog/web site would no longer be paid, the password to my computer might get lost, and all my words of wisdom could disappear into the night. Posterity is not what it once was in the digital age. We no longer leave shoeboxes full of old letters.

So I decided I would bring together a selection of my writings – my "greatest hits" so to speak – which represent the philosophy and theology I have put together, one sermon, one op-ed, one blog entry at a time. Teachings that represent the values I want to pass on to my children and grandchildren.

And they are the real intended audience for this book: my descendants. I want them to know my values – and I hope they will accept many of them as their own, and pass them on. I know values don't so much get passed on by books as by life. I am proud of my children, and know that they already have accepted and live by many of the values I have been trying to teach them. This book collects those values into essays, and it makes available ones that perhaps were not accessible to them when they were children.

I will make this book available to the public, so if anyone else might read it and enjoy it or benefit from it, so much the better. But God willing I will still have the opportunity to write other books, ones that will be designed as books from the start, which may have an easier time finding a wider audience.

The title for this book – "Musings on God, Torah, and the Meaning of Life" – is the organizing principle I have used in collecting these talks and writings. It all starts with God, doesn't it?

A note on gender: God is not a "he." God is not a "she." Sometimes I will "mix it up" a bit and call God "She" just to remind the reader that "She" and "He" are equally incorrect when talking about God.

A Message in a Bottle

Writing a book is like sending a "message in a bottle." You don't know where it will end up, who will read it, what effect it might have. You put your thoughts together, and send them off with a prayer that someone will read them. So here's the message in my bottle:

Being a congregational rabbi is an awesome job. I've had many different jobs over the years: busboy, dishwasher, cook, electronic warfare specialist, restaurant manager, salesman, cab driver, bouncer (in a gay disco!), flight instructor, charter pilot, tech writer, technical instructor, marketing manager, product manager, business executive, entrepreneur, professor, and some I'm sure I'm forgetting. Of them all, being a congregational rabbi was my favorite. It's a tremendous privilege to spend your days preaching, teaching, drawing people closer to God, helping people deal with loss, helping people grow spiritually, comforting the afflicted, afflicting the comfortable, studying Torah.

One of my teachers in rabbinical school, Rabbi Ed Feinstein, said it would only take six months to teach someone the nuts and bolts of how to be a congregational rabbi: how to lead prayers, how to conduct lifecycle events, how to give sermons. So why does it take five or six years of school to become a rabbi? Rabbi Feinstein said it's because we need to "marinate in Torah," so we can learn to think like rabbis. But I found in many ways, the real education of the rabbi comes after he or she leaves rabbinical school – it comes through serving a congregation.

When I started rabbinical school, I wasn't sure what direction my career would eventually take, but I was committed to starting out by serving as a pulpit rabbi, because it seemed to me that being a pulpit rabbi is "where the rubber hits the road" in the rabbinate. It's where you really learn what being a rabbi is all about. Seven years later, I'm convinced I was right in that assessment.

As Rabbi Hanina says in the Talmud, "I have learned much from my teachers, more from my colleagues, and most of all from my students." Similarly, Ben Azzai teaches (in Pirkei Avot), "who is wise? He who can learn from everyone."

I'm an intellectual and philosophical kind of guy. The teaching and preaching part of being a rabbi came very naturally to me. But the real learning for me came not from intellectual insights, but from human connections. One of the most important lessons I learned in the rabbinate is one that I have not spoken about nearly enough – it's about how to open your heart to other people. I didn't learn that in rabbinical school; I learned it from being privileged to be a part of many people's most important life cycle events, from birth through death, and even beyond death, remembering loved ones some time after they have passed on, at unveilings, cemetery visits, and Yizkor services.

Many of the most intense moments in my time as a congregational rabbi had to do with death and dying. It's naturally a very difficult time, and a time when people turn to their religion, and to their rabbi, seeking comfort and guidance. Sometimes we provide that comfort and guidance even to people who are so far gone they don't seem to be aware of our presence. One day when I was in Vancouver I was in my study at the synagogue when I got a call from a congregant asking me to come to the hospital right away, because his father seemed quite near to the end of his life. When I got to the hospital I heard the characteristic "death rattle" of someone nearing the end. I told my congregant that there is a prayer we recite as death is approaching, the *vidui*, or confessional, and I thought we should say that prayer for his father. The family agreed, so I recited the confessional prayer, a prayer which echoes the prayers we say on Yom Kippur, since the tradition says that death and Yom Kippur both atone for our sins. Normally a person would say it for themselves, but if they are incapable, someone can say it on his behalf. I recited the prayer for the dying man, and literally, the moment when I finished the prayer and the family said "amen" was the moment he took his last breath. It was as if he was waiting for that prayer, as if he needed that absolution to be comfortable slipping into death and facing his maker.

The beginning of life is, of course, a time filled with wonder and meaning, and generally (but not always) a joyous time. I was relieved that the first time I officiated at a bris I was able to remain calm and collected, unlike the rabbi in the movie "Keeping the Faith," who passed out cold!

Even though I have five kids of my own, working with kids taught me a lot I hadn't properly appreciated just from watching my own kids. Bar and Bat Mitzvah kids often surprise me with their interpretations of the Torah. They can find ways to connect Torah to their lives that I would not have thought of – real *"chidushim,"* new teachings, which is quite a compliment, considering how long we've been pondering the Torah.

My greatest passion in my rabbinate has been adult education. I learn a lot from teaching, both because I have to prepare for the classes, and also because the students come from varied backgrounds and bring their unique perspectives to studying Torah. One of my greatest pleasures as a rabbi has been working with converts, helping people discover the beauty and wisdom I have found in Judaism.

And what is the essence of the wisdom I have found in Judaism? I would sum it up as follows:

- God is real and religion can help you find God and become a better person.
- The meaning of life is to contribute to making the world a better place. "It's not incumbent on you to complete the task, yet neither are you exempt from contributing."
- We are all created in God's image – this is a fundamental teaching. It should drive how we treat other people.

That's the essence. Ultimately, each person has to find his/her own way to God, and there are many paths to God. No one person, no one religion has all the answers for all the people. The Jewish path is one that has blown me away with its wisdom, compassion, and practicality. I hope that my descendants will stay on this path, and continue the 3,000 year old family chain going back to Mt. Sinai. At the same time, I acknowledge that my path toward God is not the only path toward God.

The best summary of what Judaism is about is the one provided by the prophet Micha: "What does God ask of you, Man, but to do justice, love mercy, and walk humbly with your God." To do justice is to follow the ethical commandments regarding how we treat others; yet at the same time, while we are commanded to do justice, we also need to love mercy toward others and be helpful and forgiving as much as possible. And walking humbly with your God is to imitate God in how we treat other people, and to "walk in the way" of the ritual commandments as a path to draw close to God.

And it's OK to be comfortable and enjoy life while contributing to making the world a better place. As it says in Kohelet, "Live joyfully with the wife whom you love all the days of the life of your vanity, which he has given you under the sun, all the days of your vanity; for that is your portion in life, and in your labor in which you labor under the sun."

PART I: GOD

What is the nature of God? How do we find God's presence in this world? Why do we want to bother searching for God?

Chapter One

Faith

"But the righteous shall live by his faith"

Habakuk 2:4

My faith journey has taken me many different places, physically, emotionally, and spiritually. I studied Buddhism, martial arts, and meditated; I studied psychology, philosophy, and comparative religion. Eventually my search for faith brought me to back to the religion of my youth, Judaism, to rabbinical school and to Israel.

People who have a deep faith in God seem different than other people. They are more at peace, better equipped to deal with the ups and downs that life throws their way. Having faith in God can totally transform your life. But is there a way to cultivate faith in God if you don't already have it? You can. But it's not easy.

Searching for God

This sermon was given on the first day of Rosh Hashanah 5765 – it was the first High Holiday sermon I gave at Congregation B'nai Israel in Toledo. It is a meditation on the search for God.

Is the richest person you know the happiest person you know?

Is the poorest person the unhappiest?

If your circle of acquaintances is anything like mine, the connection between wealth and happiness is tenuous at best.

The Dalai Lama writes "There are two ways to create happiness. The first is external. By obtaining better shelter, better clothes, and better friends we can find a certain measure of happiness and satisfaction. The second is through mental development, which yields inner happiness. However, these two approaches are not equally viable. External happiness cannot last long without its counterpart. If something is lacking in your perspective—if something is missing in your heart—then despite the most luxurious surroundings, you cannot be happy. However, if you have peace of mind, you can find happiness even under the most difficult circumstances."

The Dalai Lama writes from the perspective of Tibetan Buddhism. But the Jewish tradition teaches the exact same thing. In Pirkei Avot it says "*aizehu ashir? Hasameach b'chelko,*" "Who is rich? He who is happy with his lot."

Most people focus on the external path to happiness. We've been conditioned by the media to equate possessions with joy. We've allowed our self-worth to become defined by our job titles, our incomes, the size of our S.U.V.s and the demographics of our neighborhoods.

But if money buys happiness, then why are the richest nations on earth the biggest consumers of Prozac?

And if money buys happiness, why do so many so-called "successful" people feel that something in their lives is missing?

When people decide to look in the internal direction for happiness, sometimes they have no idea where to start—even when the answer is right at hand.

The story is told of a humble shoe maker named Chaim Mendel who lived in the little village of Shnipishtick. One night Chaim dreamt of a great treasure under a bridge in Warsaw. The next night he had the same dream. And again a third night. The dream was so realistic, Chaim couldn't shake it. He resolved to go to Warsaw and look under the bridge for the treasure. His wife and neighbors thought he was crazy, but he wasn't going to be deterred. He packed up a few meager provisions and headed out for Warsaw.

After a few weeks of walking, he finally reached Warsaw. He wasn't quite sure what to do, because if he made a show of obviously looking, he would be sure to attract notice. So he tried to blend in, he walked over the bridge a few times, looking discretely for signs. An officer noticed him and came over and asked, "Just what is it you are looking for?" Chaim decided he would never find the treasure this way, and it would be best to tell the officer the story, and hope he would help him find the treasure and share it with him. So Chaim told him the story. When he finished, the officer said, "foolish peasant, wasting all that time and money to come to Warsaw looking for treasure because of a silly dream. Why, I've had the same dream three nights in a row myself…that in the town of Shnipishtick there's a man named Chaim Mendel, and under his stove there's a treasure. Do you know how far Shnipish-tick is? Do you know how many people named Chaim Mendel must live there? Do you think I would waste my time on such a fruitless journey? Go home, little man, and quit wasting your time."

When Chaim got home, he looked under his stove, and sure enough found a great treasure, sufficient for him and his family to live very comfortably.

A lot of Jews, me included, are like Chaim in the story. We've gone looking for treasure somewhere far away from home.

Jews are disproportionately represented in American Buddhist circles. They're called "Jew-Bu's" – and I used to be one of them. When I was 18 years old and in the Army, I got interested in spiritual things. Despite (or maybe because of) having had a Bar Mitzvah and several years of Hebrew school, it never occurred to me to look at Judaism to fulfill my spiritual needs. I turned to Buddhism: I read every book I could find, I started meditating 15-20 minutes a day. But for me, Buddhism was not the answer. There may be a lot of wisdom there, but my soul, my neshamah, is not a Buddhist neshamah. It's a Jewish neshamah, and I eventually figured out that my path to inner happiness had to be the Jewish path, not the Buddhist path. Years later I started looking, and eventually found MY treasure right at home.

Why is it that so many Jews go looking for spirituality in the East, or in New Age fads, instead of turning to the Jewish wisdom that is their birthright?

It's not because what they are looking for is missing in Judaism. They just don't know it's there. For too many Jews, their Jewish education stopped at the age of 13, and for too many who continued after 13 the curriculum in Hebrew High or confirmation classes failed to fire up their souls with a love of Torah.

What picture of Judaism does a child have? Many kids – and some adults! – get the idea of God as an old man with a long beard who sits on a throne in heaven. The Bible is full of stories that a rational, scientific, intellectual adult could not possibly believe. Some people find they can't believe the world was created in six days, or that God destroyed the world in a flood, so they rejects Judaism. If they can't believe in Adam and Eve in a literal sense, they can't believe in keeping kosher either.

It was a great revelation to me when I figured out that you can believe in the Big Bang theory and evolution AND be a seriously committed and religious Jew. I used to have this sort of secular superiority complex, thinking that if you wanted to be religious, it meant you had to take your rational, scientific brain out and put it on a shelf. NOT TRUE!

We're not required to take the Torah literally. In fact, we're not ALLOWED to take it literally! The great rabbi Maimonides (Rambam) said that if you take the Torah literally you're distorting it and doing it a great disservice. You should not, God forbid, think that because the Torah says that God took us out of Egypt "with a strong arm" it means that God has a real, physical arm. We're supposed to understand that the Torah speaks in the language of people and it uses myth and metaphor to teach us.

Many of the stories in the Bible are completely in line with science if you read them on a metaphorical level. Take the story of Adam and Eve. The Torah says God created Adam, "male and female He created them." Science, via evolution, can explain the mechanism through which God created Adam and Eve. Science, in fact, confirms that we all have a common paternal ancestor, which they have nicknamed "Adam" and a common maternal ancestor they have named "Eve." The scientists also say that Adam and Eve lived 80,000 years apart. Maybe the Torah makes more sense! The important lesson which comes from Torah, and is backed up by science, is that everyone on the planet is family: we are all related to each other, and that implies we should treat each other with respect and consideration. Ultimately we all have the same "*yichus*," the same ancestry.

The stories like Adam and Eve, or Noah's Ark, are myths. A myth is not necessarily false, nor is it necessarily true. According to Rabbi Neil Gilman "A myth should be understood as a structure through which a community organizes and makes sense of its experience." A myth is the way that we explain the world. In the scientific realm, the "myth" of evolution does a good job of explaining how people came to be. In the spiritual realm, the myth of Adam and Eve does a good job of explaining what it means to be *Adam*, to be human.

Science has only recently discovered the idea of a common ancestor; Judaism has had this concept for thousands of years, and has developed a rich spiritual and ethical literature based on the fact that we are all family.

When we read the Torah metaphorically, we can also find a very different picture of God than if we read it literally. One of the things that helped me find my way back to Judaism as a spiritual path was finding a conception of God in Judaism that worked for me. It's a concept of God the observant Jew affirms twice a day in the Shema: *Adonai Echad*, God is One. The profound unity and interconnectedness of everything in the universe is an idea that I thought was strictly a Buddhist concept—until I learned that Kabbalah says the exact same thing, and science agrees. There is a deep unifying structure to the universe that science is only beginning to understand—which Judaism has been talking about for millennia.

Finding a view of God that made sense to me, and learning that to be a serious Jew does not mean running away from science, opened a huge door for me. A couple of books I read served as the officer in the story for me—they showed me that the treasure I was looking for—a spiritual path that would answer my soul's instinctive search for meaning and happiness—was right back at "home," within the Jewish tradition.

Following Judaism as a spiritual path is more than just reading and learning—it's very much about doing. But more than just "doing"—it's about doing with understanding.

Logic suggests that understanding leads to doing: that insight leads to commitment. That's why I'm giving this sermon. I hope that increased *understanding* of Judaism you get from it will inspire you to actually *do* something different.

The Talmud itself agrees that insight leads to action. In the Talmud, masechet Kiddushin it says: R. Tarfon and the Elders were sitting around when someone asked, "Which is greater, study, or deeds?" R. Tarfon answered, "Deeds are greater." R. Akiva responded "Study is greater, for it leads to deeds." Then they all answered and said: "Study is greater, for it leads to action."

However, we also have an example in the Torah itself of the process working the other way around. Of commitment leading to insight. Of doing leading to understanding. After Moses came down from the mountain with the Ten Commandments, the people responded (Exodus 24:7) "*na'aseh v'nishmah,*" we will obey, and we will understand. The Besht, the Baal Shem Tov, the founder of Chasidut, interpreted this as meaning that it is through action, through doing, that we are led to understanding. The Besht takes the teaching from the Talmud and turns it on its head!

For me, after I had that flash of insight, that "Judaism could make sense," I was willing to take on some commitment. It led to my wife Lauri and I being willing to take on some of the mitzvot. To take what Abraham Joshua Heschel called a "leap of action." We were willing to say, "OK, maybe we don't completely "get" the idea of Shabbat, but let's try it and see what happens."

And what we discovered when we tried Shabbat in a serious way completely transformed our lives. Shabbat is one of the fundamental pieces of the Jewish spiritual path.

I hate to admit it, since as a rabbi I want to encourage all of you to come to shul on Saturday morning, but attending synagogue is NOT the most important part of Shabbat.

Shabbat is really a statement about your priorities, and it's about making time for the things we say are important.

Any kind of spiritual work—any kind of seeking inner happiness—takes time. There is no way around it. There are no short cuts. You can sit and meditate, you can spend time in prayer, you can read books, you can study sacred texts, or you can go listen to your guru, but finding inner happiness takes some time. Most of us are so busy during the week chasing *external* happiness that we don't have time to pursue *inner* happiness—real happiness! Shabbat is about setting aside 25 hours a week to spend time with friends and family, at a leisurely pace with no attention paid to the clock. 25 hours a week to read or talk about spiritual matters, to eat good meals and drink good wine. To really experience life that is rushing by so quickly. To find peace in *being*, rather than pursuing happiness by *doing*. My wife Lauri calls Shabbat a 25-hour spa for the soul. I couldn't think of a better description!

Some people are afraid that if they try really observing Shabbat it will be hard on their families—the kids won't be able to participate in soccer or drive to birthday parties. But if you replace soccer or birthday parties with serious quality time with Mom and Dad—time which can be spent walking, bike riding, playing cards, and sharing leisurely meals—the gain is far more than the loss. Our kids love putting on plays and musicals of their own invention for us on Shabbat afternoon. Go ask one of my kids what's her favorite day of the week. She'll tell you it's Shabbat.

And you can become an activist – if soccer games are on Saturdays, try to get them switched to Sundays; start a Jewish league if you need to. If your kids are invited to Shabbat birthday parties, send them to a Jewish Day School where parents honor the Sabbath – or should – by not discriminating against children who don't drive on Shabbat. Our own children love theatre – but all the major children's theatre programs in Toledo are on Saturday mornings. So my wife has helped to start one with a Jewish orientation – on Sunday after-noons here at B'nai Israel. Next on the list are the Toledo Art Museum's Saturday-only children's classes.

You may think, it's easy for you to say – you're a rabbi! OF course YOU can come to shul on Shabbat – it's your job!

But I came to the rabbinate after 20 years in the business world. And when I first became observant I was the Vice President of a semiconductor firm with over $100 million a year in sales. I admit it was tough for me the first time I told my boss I couldn't get to an offsite meeting held on Saturday until over an hour after the sun went down. But you know what? I did it, and the CEO was sympathetic, and it was not a problem.

Too often in our Jewish history – especially in the last century – we've worked *too* hard to fit in, to assimilate, not to make a fuss about our holidays or our laws. It's gotten to be where observant Jews like Senator Joe Lieberman are seen as "exotic" – outside the Jewish mainstream.

The truth is it's never been easier to be an observant Jew. Even here in Toledo we have several stores that carry kosher meat. We live in a multi-cultural society that accepts diversity. Anyone who really does not want to work on Saturday can usually find a way to do it, often by working the days the Christians would like to have off. We don't have to hide anymore. In fact, we shouldn't! Each one of us can strike a blow for Jewish liberation, to make ourselves, our neighbors and our children and grandchildren free to live openly – and observantly – as Jews.

I mentioned how both the Dalai Lama and Pirkei Avot say that happiness comes from having an attitude of being content with your lot. One of the ways we cultivate this attitude in Judaism is through daily prayer. Now you may be thinking that if daily prayer is anything like what I'm experiencing today—hours of Hebrew that I don't understand—what's the point? I don't blame you. But that's NOT what daily prayer is about. You can say all of your prayers in English if you want to—God understands all languages. And while it's nice to use a prayer book, you are also totally free to improvise.

For me, prayer is about two things: connecting with God, and cultivating a certain attitude toward the world. Having a relationship with God is like having a relationship with a person: you're going to be on much more intimate terms with someone you talk to three times a day than someone you talk to three times a year. Prayer can include simply talking to God, pouring out your heart to God like you would to a good friend. If you make it part of your daily routine, prayer can help you feel God as a presence in your life and not just as a theoretical concept.

Prayer encourages us to cultivate an attitude of gratitude—of being happy with our lot. Our tradition teaches us to start our day, first thing, before we even get out of bed, with a short prayer thanking God for restoring OUR souls to US. If you start your day with a reminder that it's good to be alive—and especially if you are in good health—it helps to take the disappointments life throws your way in stride.

All of the different aspects of Judaism—whether ritual commandments like the Sabbath and prayer, or ethical commandments like giving charity or not gossiping —are part of a path to inner happiness. My experience has led me to understand that within Judaism obeying the mitzvot is a path for drawing closer to God. Just as Buddhists meditate to achieve Enlightenment—to draw close to God—Jews do mitzvot.

If we can engage in a process of "mindful obedience," of being aware of what we are doing and why, when we obey the commandments we can transform the most mundane of activities into a path of spiritual growth. A Chabad rabbi friend of mine told me that when he goes to the grocery store, it's a religious experience: because he knows that he is shopping to buy food to sustain his family so they can perform mitzvot and serve God.

The most mundane of activities can be a part of the "shoemaker's treasure." The message of the story of the shoemaker is perhaps a little more involved than it might appear at first. It doesn't really help to just tell people that what they're looking for is at home. If Chaim Mendel had felt completely content, he never would have gone on the journey in the first place. Spiritual progress, like material progress, needs an element of discontent as a spur. Once on the journey, once he was searching, like so many of us are searching for answers to life's most profound questions, he never would have known to look in the right place—which was at home—without someone there to point him in the right direction.

As your new rabbi, I hope that I will have the opportunity to serve as the officer in that story for you. To help you discover where the treasure is. Or if you already know the treasure is at home, in Judaism, to help you uncover it and unlock its secrets.

Shanah Tovah

Finding Faith

This sermon was given at Kol Nidre, 5766 in Toledo. It's an outline of my thoughts on how we can go about finding faith in God – a subject to which I hope to devote an entire book.

A story is told of a Beverly Hills tycoon who was dismayed by his son's decision to study in a yeshiva instead of joining the family business. After several years the son returned home to his father's sardonic question: So what have you got to show for your years of study? "I know that there is a God" replied the young man. Angrily the father leapt to his feet and pointed out the window at the elderly gardener patiently mowing the vast lawns. "He also knows there is a God" shouted the older man. "No father" the boy quietly responded. "He believes there is a God, I know."

You may be wondering, what's the difference between believing in God and knowing there is a God?

The difference is huge. Many people who believe in God, believe in God as an abstract concept. Sort of the way they believe that $E = MC^2$, or the way they believe the theory of evolution. Lots of people believe —yet it does not have much impact on their lives. It's not something that changes their behavior in any discernible fashion.

Believing in God can work much the same way. For example, some people believe in God as explained by Baruch Spinoza and Mordecai Kaplan: God is simply the impersonal force that made the Big Bang go bang. Belief in the God of Spinoza will bring all of the passion and commitment to your life that believing in the Big Bang theory will bring to your life. There is nothing personal about such a God. Simply believing in God does not make someone a religious person—80% of all Jews say they mostly agree that there is a God, and 56% of all Jews are quite certain that God exists—yet only 7% of Jews describe themselves as "religious."

But if you KNOW God exists—just as surely as you know you yourself exist—if you have a relationship with God just like you have a relationship with your spouse or your best friend—your life is totally transformed.

To KNOW God exists—that is to have true faith. The Slonimer rebbe tells us that *emunah*, faith, is the secret of existence, it is the breath of life, it is the life-giving breath of Torah, the mitzvot, and all of Judaism. Belief is in your head – faith is in your heart.

Almost all Jews would agree that the one statement that sums up the essence of Judaism is *Shema Yisrael, Adonai Eloheinu, Adonai Echad,* Listen up Israel, Adonai is our God, Adonai is One. The word *"shema"* is written in the imperative—it's a command, it's insistent. The word *shema* contains the Hebrew word *m'ai,* which is Hebrew for *kishkes,* or guts. The Shema is telling us more than just listen, more than just understand, but get it into your guts – KNOW – that Adonai is our God and She is One.

Maimonides, Rambam, wrote in the Mishneh Torah "The foundation of the entire structure and the pillar of all wisdom is to know that there is a Fundamental Cause (God)." Not simply to believe – but to know. To have faith.

The Slonimer rebbe wrote that faith is the altar of love on which was spilled the blood of millions of Jews. Throughout the Middle Ages, Jews in Europe were persecuted, and they were offered the opportunity to abandon their faith and become Christian to avoid punishment. Millions refused, because of their faith in God—because they *knew* the God of Israel in their guts, not because they merely "believed" that God existed.

What if all those prayers we recite tonight are really true? What if God really does want Jews to follow the Torah? What if all of our deeds really are being recorded for posterity and God does care what we do? What if God really does decide who is going to die and who is going to live?

If you knew those things in your guts—on a deeper level than just believing them intellectually—do you think you would act differently? What would be different? Would you come to shul more often, give more money to charity, go out of your way to be kinder and more thoughtful?

And more than just behaving differently—what would it feel like? Can you imagine what it would feel like to have that kind of faith in God? Faith and trust come together—if you have that kind of knowledge of God, you will also have a great sense of *bitachon*, of trust, that whatever happens God is there for you—somehow things will work out.

The confidence that God is there, God is real, and everything will work out is described in a teaching of one of the great rabbis of the Talmud, Rabbi Akiva. Rabbi Akiva taught: A person should always say: (Aramaic) *Kol d'avid rachmanah l'tav*…"Everything that God does, He does for the good."

To illustrate the point, the Talmud brings a story about Rabbi Akiva. The rabbi was traveling, and when he arrived at a certain town he asked for lodgings and was refused. R. Akiva said: "*Kol d'avid rachmanah l'tav*, everything that God does, He does for the good," and he went to spend the night in a field.

He had with him a rooster, a donkey and a lamp. A wind came and extinguished the lamp, a cat came and ate the rooster, and a lion came and ate the donkey. Once again he said "Everything that God does, He does for good." That night, an army came and took the entire town captive. Rabbi Akiva told his disciples: "Didn't I tell you that everything that God does, He does for good? If I had a room in town, the army would have taken me. If the lamp had been lit, the army would have seen me; if the donkey would have brayed or the rooster would have called, the army would have come and captured me."

What are in many ways even more impressive are the generations of Jews who would say *kol d'avid rachmanah l'tav* without necessarily seeing how it did work out for the best. Rabbi Akiva would have still said "Everything that

God does, He does for the good" even if he had continued traveling in the opposite direction and never heard the news that the town had been taken captive.

Having that kind of faith and trust in God, *knowing* that God cares about you, not only leads a person to greater piety, but it leads a person to a great sense of inner peace and calm. Faith in God, knowing God, will give a person strength to face the tragedies that every life encounters. It doesn't mean that you won't experience tragedies—it just means that when the inevitable tragedies occur you have greater strength to deal with them. And it will make every moment richer and more pleasant—you're never alone if you have a close relationship with God.

And relationship with God is what faith is about. There is no commandment to believe in God. But there is a commandment, part of the Shema, to love God. What's more, the commandment is to love God with all your heart, with all your soul, and with all your might. To have a love of God just as intense as the love you have for your husband or wife, or the love you have for your children.

That kind of love does not come from an intellectual belief—you don't love your children because you believe they are real. You love your children because you *know* them—because you have a very deep relationship with them.

But if you don't have that kind of faith—if you don't have that kind of love for God—can it be cultivated? Or is it just some kind of gift from God, which some people are blessed with, and others aren't?

Thirty years ago, when I was a 19 year old enlisted man serving in the US Army in Ft. Hood, Texas I experienced a case of "faith envy." I was a spiritual seeker: I read vary widely in psychology, philosophy, and religion in an attempt to figure out what the world was all about.

I took a class in philosophy at Central Texas College, and became friends with the professor, Phil. We would sit around his living room drinking

French wine (Medoc), and while our then wives fell asleep on the couch out of boredom we would excitedly explore the ideas of Aristotle, Kant, Hume, and Heidegger.

Phil had spent ten years in a seminary studying to become a Roman Catholic priest. He eventually concluded that being a priest was not the path for him: he wanted to get married and share his life with a woman. So he left the seminary and got married, but he didn't leave his faith. Phil was the first person I met whose intellect I respected who also had a deep and sincere faith and belief in God. I felt my intellect was a huge barrier to faith: how could someone who took science for granted, who believed in Evolution, not the Creation story of the Bible, have faith? I envied his faith. I saw it as a beautiful thing, to have faith in God, in the world, and your place in it. I figured I didn't have it because I lost the "faith lottery." It seemed to me then that faith was one of those things that you are either blessed with, or not. It didn't seem to me that there was anything you could do to get it. Somehow some people just got tapped with the magic wand that made them believers—the rest of us were left out.

I was struggling with the major life questions so much—I wished somehow that magic wand could be waved for me too and I would have that faith. I felt like the kid standing outside the closed candy store, looking in the window and wishing I could get inside.

It seemed obvious to me at the time that you cannot decide to believe. You can decide to act as if something is true. You can decide to intellectually accept something if you think you see evidence for it. But if you don't see compelling evidence you can't decide you are going to believe. You can't simply decide to have faith.

But what I've learned as the result of a long spiritual journey is that you *can* decide you would like to have faith; and that decision can open the door that leads down the path to a real relationship with God.

I'm not claiming to be some kind of *tzaddik,* saintly righteous person. I'm not saying I'm the most pious person in this room tonight. I certainly haven't reached the level of Rabbi Akiva who could say: *"Kol d'avid rachmanah l'tav,* everything that God does is for the good*"* in the face of a disaster, and really, sincerely, truly believe it my guts.

But I have gone from a place of having no faith to having at least a modest amount of faith. I've gone from feeling very distant from God to feeling at least some connection with God. There are probably as many ways to find faith as there are people seeking faith. What I want to share with you tonight are a few things that have helped me in my journey, in the hopes that they may help some of you.

The first step in a developing a real relationship with God is to be open to the idea that God exists.

About six weeks ago I gave a sermon about this first step. For those of you who were in shul that Saturday morning, or who read it when I sent it to the shul's email list, please pardon my repetition—but remember as the Talmud says, one who learns something 100 times is not to be compared to the one who learns it 101 times.

Rabbi Milton Steinberg wrote a novelized account of the life of Elisha ben Abuya, a rabbi of the Sanhedrin who went the opposite direction of the one we're trying to go in—he lost his faith. As Steinberg tells the story, Elisha grew up living in the tension between a secular father who promoted Greek learning and a Jewishly observant uncle who banned studying Greek books. As a young man, Elisha was sent off to study with a great rabbi, and eventually earns the title rabbi himself along with a seat on the Sanhedrin, the Supreme Court of the day. But Elisha is plagued by doubt. He can't simply accept things on faith. He tells his friend and colleague Rabbi Akiva that he is going to embark on an intellectual search for God that will hopefully restore his faith. Elisha was very impressed with Euclid's Elements of Geometry—by the "lucidity of the reasoning and the sureness of its results." Elisha resolves to follow a similar approach to God: he tells Akiva "I am going to start at the beginning, by laying aside all prejudices, all preconceived notions, all my beliefs and affirmations."

The next several chapters of the book tell how Elisha gives up the rabbinate, gives up Judaism, immerses himself in an all out study of Greek math, logic, and philosophy for several years. After years of preparation and training, he finally struggles with the question and starts writing furiously. And he fails miserably. At the end of the day he can't really say anything about God—he can't even deny God. He's right back where he started.

The fundamental problem that Elisha ran into is that you can't go all the way back to nothing. Any system of knowledge ultimately demands that you make certain assumptions. With all the beauty and logic of Euclid's geometry, it rests on five postulates—five ideas that are taken to be true without proof. All other proofs are built on those postulates. Remove the postulates—remove the underlying assumptions—and you can't prove a thing.

The primary postulate for monotheists is found in the Torah in Deuteronomy chapter 4 verse 39: *Hu Elohim bashamayim mima'al v'al ha'aretz mitachat, ein od*, He is God in the heavens above and the earth below, there is no other.

So the first step is to "postulate God." To accept the idea that God exists. Note that at this point there is lots of room for doubt and questions. Even accepting Spinoza's God, God as the watchmaker, God who made the Big Bang go *boom*, is enough to open the door.

And that's all it does is open the door. If surveys are correct, over 80% of us here tonight would claim we believe in God. But how many of us *know* God exists, how many of us have *emunah shleimah*, complete faith, and *bitachon*, trust, that God cares about us?

Once I accepted the intellectual possibility that God exists, I was in a position to go looking for proof that God exists. A book that I found very helpful in my quest for God is Rabbi Elliot Dorff's "Knowing God: Jewish

Journeys to the Unknowable." Rabbi Dorff brings a lot of useful ideas in his book, but there are two in particular I found helpful—the Invisible Gardener parable, and the concept of non-hypothetical discovery.

John Wisdom's Invisible Gardener parable goes as follows: "Two people return to their long neglected garden and find among the weeds a few of the old plants surprisingly vigorous. One says to the other, "It must be that a gardener has been coming and doing something about these plants." Upon inquiry, they find that no neighbor has ever seen anyone at work in their garden. The first man says to the other, "He must have worked while people slept." The other says, "No, someone would have heard him, and besides, anybody who cared about plants would have kept down these weeds." The first man says, "Look at the way these are arranged. There is purpose and a feeling for beauty here. I believe someone comes, someone invisible to mortal eyes. I believe the more carefully we look, the more we shall find confirmation of this."

While you can't decide to believe in God, you can decide to look at the world through God-colored lenses. If you go looking for evidence that God exists, you will find plenty. When we lived in Vancouver we would sit on our deck and watch the sun setting over Vancouver Island across the water—and even our kids would see evidence that God exists, praising God for doing good work.

The other idea from Rabbi Dorff's book that impressed me is the idea of the non-hypothetical discovery. Most people approach their search for God they way they learned to approach inquiry in science class in school. Hypothesis: God exists. They then go looking for evidence to support or disprove that hypothesis. But there is a completely different kind of knowledge we can use—non-hypothetical knowledge, knowledge that does not rest on formulating a hypothesis. When we fall in love, most of us don't formulate a hypothesis and weigh the evidence whether or not we love someone. We just know it in our hearts.

And that's really our goal—not to know God in our heads, the way we would know a scientific fact, but to know God in our hearts, the way we know we love someone.

Rabbi Abraham Joshua Heschel teaches us that the path to knowing God in our hearts is through the ability to feel awe or wonder at the world around us. One of the great disservices of our secular education system is that all too often we take away the sense of awe a child can feel at the world and replace it with rational explanations. Something important is lost when we lose the sense of awe.

Heschel says "Ultimate meaning and ultimate wisdom are not found within the world, but in God, and the only way to wisdom is through our relationship to God. That relationship is awe. Awe, in this sense, is more than an emotion; it is a way of understanding. Awe is itself an act of insight into a meaning greater than ourselves." As Heschel describes it, "Awe is a way of being in rapport with the mystery of all reality."

Being able to feel awe does not mean you have to hide yourself from science. One of my hobbies is teaching people how to fly. As such, I teach people all about the aerodynamics involved in flight, about how the four forces of thrust, drag, lift, and gravity affect the aircraft. I know this stuff so well when I go flying I can look at the window and practically visualize the big "H" for high pressure below the wing and the big "L" for low pressure above the wing—yet I can still feel a sense of awe and wonder that I'm cruising around thousands of feet above the ground.

Postulating God, recovering a sense of wonder at the world around us, and being open to a non-hypothetical discovery of God—being open to "falling in love with God," if you will—prepares our hearts for the Jewish path to cultivating a relationship with God: Torah and the mitzvot, the commandments.

Like anything worthwhile, cultivating a relationship with God takes time and effort. If you have a friend you talk to two or three times a year, you are not going to be as close to him as a friend you talk to three times a day. It works the same way with God: if you only talk to God twice a year, on Rosh Hashanah and Yom Kippur, you're probably not going to have a very close relationship. Which is why the Jewish tradition calls on us to pray three times a day—to check in with God three times a day, just as you might check in with a person you love deeply several times during the day.

Our liturgy throws an amazing amount of stuff at us—some of the words we read in our prayers are beautiful poetry, other words may be things that our minds rebel at or have trouble with. Rebbe Nachman of Breslov teaches that the path to faith is in your prayers you should focus on the things that resonate with you as true. Don't spend so much time on the things that challenge your faith or trouble you—save that for study. But let your prayers be a time to focus on the words that harmonize with your soul, that you find beautiful, that confirm your faith in God.

Another teaching of Rebbe Nachman's that I found helpful was to practice hitbodedut, which is a kind of Jewish meditation where you set aside a fixed time—say 15 or 20 minutes to start—to talk to God the way you talk to a friend. To pour your heart out to God the way you would pour your heart out to your most intimate trusted confidant. This sounds like something simple, but I have actually found it to be a very profound spiritual practice. Most of us don't spend enough time just talking to God.

Any relationship should be a two-way street, and our relationship with God is no exception. If praying is the way we talk to God, how does God talk to us? For Jews the answer is through studying the Torah. Just as we set aside time every day to talk to God, we set aside time every day to allow God to talk to us. Studying Torah does not have to mean just picking up the Bible and reading it—there are many Jewish books you can read where you can hear the word of God coming through to you.

Ultimately, not just study and prayer, but obeying any of the commandments can become a vehicle for strengthening your faith in and your relationship with God. Observing the Sabbath becomes a way to make the time needed to reflect on God and the universe. Observing the dietary laws is a way to bring an awareness of God to mind multiple times throughout the day. Giving charity can be not just a "good deed," but a way to serve God, and therefore a way to strengthen your bond with God.

And that, I believe, is really the purpose of all of those rules we have in Judaism—done with the proper *kavvanah*, the proper intentions, we can continually find opportunities to raise our God-consciousness, to raise our awareness of God's presence in the world, in the most mundane of activities. My favorite example is literally the most mundane of activities—there is a blessing to say after using the bathroom, which emphasizes how miraculously our bodies are created with all of these intricate openings that have to function just so. Anyone who has ever suffered from constipation—or from a heart attack—can certainly appreciate how miraculous it is that everything works so well so much of the time.

It is a miracle that our bodies work so well so much of the time. By saying a prayer, we remind ourselves of that miracle, and we remind ourselves of God's presence behind that miracle. As Rabbi Zalman Schachter-Shalomi puts it "God is real. That's what escaped us in Hebrew school and in books we read."

God is real. Knowing that—not just believing it, but really knowing it—absolutely can change your life for the better.

Today is Yom Kippur, the day the tradition says we are at our closest in our relationship with God. We stand before God purified and forgiven for our sins. We imitate the angels, not eating, drinking, or thinking of other physical needs.

In the Ashrei prayer we say *karov Adonai l'chol kor'av, l'chol asher yikraoo-hoo b'emet*, God is near to all who call, to all who call out to Him in truth.

God is waiting to draw near to us—but nothing happens until we call out to God first.

May God open our hearts to the Divine that is all around us, especially in our fellow human beings, and may God help us live lives that emulate God's traits of kindness and compassion,

Amen

Chapter Two

The Nature of God

"It is the most basic of basic principles and a support for wisdom to know that there is something [namely God] that existed before anything else did and that He created everything that there is. Everything in the skies, on the ground and in between exists only because of the fact that He created them."

Moses ben Maimon (Maimonides or Rambam)

God is the Creator, God powers the world, God loves you. But ultimately, God is beyond human comprehension, and any attempt to describe God is doomed to failure, and is by definition incomplete. Still, human nature is such that we cannot help but speculate on the nature of God to the best of our abilities.

God Loves You

Shabbat Hagadol 5767

God loves you.

But I don't blame you if you don't know it. Most rabbis forget to point this out to their congregations. I did a Google search on the phrase "God loves you." 840,000 hits, and all the ones that come out on the first few pages are from Christian sites, mostly citing sending Jesus as the proof.

But Judaism also teaches that God loves you. In fact, that is the spiritual theme for today. Today, the Shabbat before Passover, is known as "Shabbat Hagadol," the great Shabbat. Last year on this Shabbat I mentioned one of the reasons this day is called Shabbat Hagadol is because it was one of the two days a year when the rabbi would give a major sermon – the theme of today's sermon generally being what I did last year, a review of the laws of Passover.

However, there are other more spiritual reasons given for calling today Shabbat Hagadol. The Slonimer Rebbe points out that every Shabbat is "gadol"—as we say in the Birkat Hamazon, the grace after meals on Shabbat, *ki yom zeh gadol v'kadosh hu lefanecha* "for this great and holy day is before you." So what is it that makes this Shabbat in particular so great that we call it "hagadol," THE great Shabbat of all the great Shabbats of the year?

There is a teaching which says the redemption would come immediately if only Israel would truly observe two Shabbatot, a teaching which is based on a verse in the Torah which says *et Shabtotai tishmeru,* if Israel will observe my Sabbaths...all sorts of blessings will follow. But the Slonimer teaches that *Shabtotai,* my Sabbath's, alludes not to just any two Sabbaths, but to two different aspects of the Sabbath, *shamor* (to guard) and *zachor* (to remember).

Shamor and *zachor* refer to the fact that we have two different versions of the 10 Commandments, one in the book of Exodus and one in the book of Deuteronomy. In Exodus we are told to remember the Sabbath day, and in Deuteronomy we are told to guard the Sabbath day. The rabbis understand guarding as dealing with what are called the *lo ta'aseh* commandments, the negative commandments, things we are commanded to refrain from doing, such as the different forms of work that we abstain from on the Sabbath. To remember the Sabbath, on the other hand, is understood as dealing with the positive Commandments, the things we do to make Shabbat special, such as saying the Kiddush blessing over wine, and having a special meal.

The *lo ta'aseh* commandments reflect the side of our relationship with God that is grounded in *yirah,* fear or awe. It's like a child who refrains from doing something wrong because she's afraid of being punished. The positive commandments, on the other hand, reflect the side of our relationship with God that is grounded in *ahava,* in love, much like a child might run to do something a parent asks out of love for the parent.

These two sides of our relationship with God, *yirah* and *ahava,* awe and love, each have a particular Shabbat in which they are ascendant. In Kabbalah, Jewish mysticism, it is taught that Shabbat is the source of blessings for the entire week. Blessings descend on Shabbat which nourish and sustain the other six days of the week. On Shabbat Shuva, the Shabbat before Yom Kippur, the awe and fear represented by the mighty Day of Atonement is drawn down. Today is the other side of the equation: today we draw down the love associated with the holiday of Passover.

Why is Passover associated with love? Maybe because it is spring and love is in the air, as it says in the Bible, in the Song of Songs, "For, behold, the winter is past, the rain is over and gone; The flowers appear on the earth; the time of the singing bird has come, and the voice of the turtledove is heard in our land; The fig tree puts forth her green figs, and the vines in blossom give forth their scent. Arise, my love, my beautiful one, and come away."

The Song of Songs is associated with Passover, as we always read it in the synagogue on the Shabbat that falls during Passover. The Song of Songs is definitely the raciest book in the Bible, and it is all about love. The opening verses proclaim "The song of songs, which is Solomon's. Let him kiss me with the kisses of his mouth; for your love is better than wine. Your anointing oils are fragrant, your name is oil poured out, therefore the maidens love you. Draw me after you, we will run; the king has brought me into his chambers; we will be glad and rejoice in you, we will praise your love more than wine; rightly they love you."

You might be wondering why such a racy love letter would be included in the Bible. It is because the rabbis understood this poetic work as referring not to the love of a man for a woman, but rather to the love of God, the lover, for Israel, the beloved, and vice versa. The Song of Songs is a favorite of our great Rabbi Akiva, as it says in the Midrash: "For the whole world only existed, so to speak, for the day on which The Song of Songs was given to it. Why so? Because all the Writings are holy, and this is holy of holies."

The Midrash goes on to proclaim "THE SONG OF SONGS: as if to say, the best of songs, the most excellent of songs, the finest of songs. Let us recite songs and praises to Him who has made us a theme of song in the world."

One reason the rabbis so appreciate the Song of Songs is that the love is reciprocal. The Midrash explains "In all other songs either God praises Israel or they praise Him. Here, however, they praise Him and He praises them. He praises them: 'Behold you are beautiful, my beloved (I, 16),' and they praise Him: 'Behold you are beautiful, my beloved, verily pleasant (I, 17).'"

The rabbis took it so seriously that the Song of Songs is to be read as allegory that in the Talmud they say "He who recites a verse of the Song of Songs and treats it as a [secular] air brings evil upon the world."

There is another connection between Passover and the Song of Songs found in the text itself: "Behold the voice of my Beloved comes skipping over mountains, hopping over valleys," reminiscent of the way that God skipped over the houses of the Jewish people on Passover.

God skipping over the houses of the Jewish people and redeeming them from slavery in Egypt is a true sign of God's love. The Midrash tells us that during their days in Egypt the Jewish people had descended to the 49th level of spiritual impurity. There are only 50 levels – to reach the 50th level is to be spiritually destroyed. The Israelites were as unworthy as they could be and yet God still redeemed them from slavery.

This is a demonstration of the unconditional nature of God's love. In Psalm 136 we recite repeatedly, *ki l'olam chasdo*, for God's lovingkindness is eternal. The prophet Jeremiah says "The Lord has appeared to me, far away, saying, I have loved you with an everlasting love; therefore I have remained true to you."

God shows Her love for us in many different ways. That we are here, and alive, is one of those ways. The world is powered by God. The Divine energy powers the universe. Mostly we're so busy, we don't notice. But our prayer book challenges us to pay attention. In the Amidah, three times a day, we thank God for the miracles that are with us daily. The miracles of life, of health, of beauty in the world.

Many people say it's easier for them to find God in nature than in the prayerbook. I suppose at no time of year is that more true than in the spring, when the world is coming back to life. When I went for a run yesterday the grass smelled like spring, I heard birds singing, and saw flowers blooming. It's certainly easier to see the world filled with God's love in the spring, than when everything is cold and gray.

In the blessing before the Shema that we recite in the morning we say *ahava raba ahavtanu,* with an abundant love you (God) have loved us. In the blessing before the Shema that we recite in the evening we say *ahavat olam beit Yisrael amcha ahavta,* you have loved the house of Israel with an eternal love.

God's love for you is unconditional and it is eternal. But that doesn't mean you don't have to follow God's rules. Parental love is also unconditional and eternal but we know we have to set limits for children, that they need rules in order to be able to thrive. The Torah tells us "as a man chastens his son, so the Lord your God chastened you." The Talmud takes this idea even further and speaks of *yisorin shel ahava,* afflictions of love, that troubles befalling people can sometimes be an expression of God's love. Of course, even the pious rabbis in the Talmud would mostly prefer that God showed His affection in a different way!

To go back to our question of why is today called Shabbat Hagadol, I said that if Israel would observe the two sides of our relationship with God of awe/fear and love on two Shabbatot, we would be immediately redeemed and brought into a world of peace and harmony. But why not call Shabbat Shuva, the Shabbat before Yom Kippur, "Shabbat Hagadol?" Isn't the *yirah,* the awe/fear just as great as the love?

As important as *yirah* is, *ahava*, love, is greater. There are many sources which talk of the importance of *yirat shamayim*, awe of God. And yet awe of God is but a steppingstone to the real goal – love of God.

The Torah commands us to love God; it does not command us to be afraid of God. But how can we fulfill the commandment to love God, if we are not certain that God loves us too?

That's what makes Shabbat Hagadol and Passover such a special time. As the Mei Shloach, a Chasidic rabbi taught, Passover is a time when the love of the Blessed God opens up for Israel. In Proverbs King Solomon taught that God says "I love those that love Me." Passover is a time when we remember the loving way God treated our ancestors and it's also a time when we show God that we love Her.

We all know that the Passover story includes our ancestors putting blood on the doorposts of their homes, so that God would pass over their houses and not strike the firstborns living within.

But did God need this sign? Doesn't God know everything? God knew where the Jews lived. God certainly didn't need a bloody door to know how to find the Jews. So there must have been a different purpose for the commandment to put blood on the door posts of the houses.

The blood on the door posts of the houses was to be a statement of faith – a statement of love for God. Even when God asks the people to do something pretty crazy – splashing blood on the door posts of their houses – the Israelites were willing to do it.

By coming together on Monday night at our seders we are doing the same thing. Well, we're not literally splashing blood on our doorposts – at least not at my house – but we're fulfilling an ancient commandment, and we're telling a story that's designed to remind us of God's love for us. And by fulfilling the mitzvah of having a seder – a mitzvah that statistics tell us 93% of all Jews in America take part in – we're telling God "Hey God, we love you too!"

May Passover be a time filled with love—love for your friends and family, love for God, and love for all of mankind. We tell the story of Passover with its reminders of days of oppression and slavery partly so that will remember to be compassionate. The Torah tells us over and over to be kind to the stranger – to show love to the stranger – for you were strangers in the land of Egypt and know what it's like to be down and out.

Today, Shabbat Hagadol, is the day we draw down the blessings and love of Passover. May the prophet Elijah visit your Seder and herald the era of love and prosperity,

Amen. And remember – God Loves You!

Science and Religion

A perennial challenge is how to reconcile what we learn in Hebrew school with what we learn in science class; is the world 14 billion years old, or 5,767 years old?   Bereshit 5767

Bereshit bara El-him et hashamayim v'et ha'aretz, "in beginning God created the heavens and the earth."

Genesis 1:1

The Torah tells us that God created the world in six days. On the first day God said "let there be light" and there was light. On the second day God created Heaven to separate "the waters above from the waters below." On the third day God created dry land and plants. On the fourth day God created the sun, the moon, and the stars. On the fifth day God created birds and fish. On the sixth day God first created the land animals, and then said "Let us make man in our image," and he created Adam and Eve.

The Torah and Tanakh give us detailed genealogies from Adam into the Biblical period which the rabbis in the Talmudic period used to calculate the age of the universe. The Torah tells us Adam, who lived to 930 years, was 130 years old when he fathered Seth; Seth, who lived 912 years, was 105 when he fathered Enosh. Based on this sort of information the rabbis determined that the 172nd year after the destruction of the Temple was the 4000th year since Creation. By the rabbis' reckoning, it has now been 5,767 years since the story of creation told in the opening chapter of Genesis.

Christian fundamentalists, using a very similar approach, come up with dates about 1,500 years older – they make the universe somewhat more than 7,000 years old. The difference is because of variations between the Septuagint, a Greek translation of the Torah the Christians use, and the Masoretic text the Jews use.

Fundamentalists – Jewish, Christian, or Muslim – are people who take the Scriptures' words literally. They believe the universe is actually 5,767 years old. If you ask them "what about the fossils of dinosaurs" you'll get a variety of responses, including "God made them that way to fool with us."

Whether you use the Jewish calculations or the Christian calculations the results are a very long way indeed from what science tells us: that the universe is 14 billion years old, and our planet Earth has been around for 4 billion of them.

What are we to do with this glaring inconsistency? Which is it? 14 billion years, or 5,767 years?

There are several different alternatives. One option is to try and reconcile the Bible with science. To say that both can somehow literally be true. Which is kind of like having your cake and eating it too. In his book "Genesis and the Big Bang," Gerald Schroeder maintains that if science and the Bible seem to contradict each other, one of them is not being understood properly. He says that you can read the story of creation as taking place over six literal days – and still be scientifically sound. He says the key to everything is the theory of relativity and one's point of view.

If you're my age, you'll remember that when we learned about the theory of relativity in science class, they taught us that if you had two people on earth, and one of them got in a rocket ship that traveled at a speed approaching the speed of light for some number of years, he would return to earth and only be a few years older, yet hundreds of years would have passed on earth. Time passes differently when you are moving at different speeds. Normally we are all moving so slow (even a space ship orbiting the earth at 17,000 miles per hour is crawling compared to the speed of light at 186,000 miles per second) that the differences are insignificant.

Schroeder maintains that if we take God's position to be at the center of universe, and the universe expands at a speed initially equal to close to the speed of light and then slowing down, the first "day" from God's perspective – a day someone sitting at the center of the universe would experience subjectively as 24 hours – was actually billions of years in our time.

According to Schroeder, the first of the Biblical days lasted 24 hours, viewed from the "God perspective." But the duration from our perspective was 8 billion years. The second day, from the Bible's perspective lasted 24 hours. From our perspective it lasted half of the previous day, 4 billion years. The third day also lasted half of the previous day, 2 billion years. The fourth day - one billion years. The fifth day - one-half billion years. The sixth day - one-quarter billion years. Schroeder says "When you add up the Six Days, you get the age of the universe at 15 and 3/4 billion years. The same as modern cosmology. Is it by chance?"

There are all sorts of other similarities between the Bible and science. Note that there was light before the sun and moon were created – which is accurate according to the Big Bang theory, which postulates that the universe was completely dark for the first 300,000 years, and then it had expanded enough for light to all of a sudden flash into existence – before there were any differentiated stars.

The order of creation in the Bible seems to mimic the order of creation in evolution – the earth, then plants, followed by fish, birds, land animals, and lastly people (the sun and moon being created AFTER plants is, however, a glaring inconsistency).

There are also a number of fascinating parallels between the elaboration of the Creation story told in Kabbalah, Jewish mysticism, and science. Both maintain that everything is connected. Both have a theory of "broken symmetry," that originally everything in the universe was perfectly balanced, but something happened which caused a shattering of the symmetry which allowed the universe as we see it to come into being.

To those of us who love both science and religion, these attempts to reconcile science and religion are very compelling. Wouldn't it be nice and neat if the Bible were also "scientifically" true? I DO want to have my cake and eat it too!

But as attractive as I find that approach, I believe that theologically it's a dead end. As a path to deeper faith in God, I think trying to reconcile science with the Torah is a non-starter.

Because as fascinating as the coincidences are when they add up, there are too many places where they don't add up. The most recent scientific research now dates the age of the universe at 12.8 billion years, +- 1.1 billion, making the oldest current estimate 13.9 billion years, substantially less than Professor Schroeder's calculation of 15 and ¾ billion years. I suppose Schroeder could go back and find some variable he left out.

How about the life spans given in the Torah for early generations? Abraham living to 170 years is tough enough for us to take; but Adam living to 930? Or Methuselah living to the ripe old age of 969? Schroeder claims it is possible that human metabolisms were very different a few thousand years ago. There is of course no evidence whatsoever for this piece of conjecture – so it's a rather unscientific approach for a scientist at MIT.

Or how about the fact that the Torah says the earth was created before the sun and stars, when cosmologists are united in understanding that stars formed first?

As I said, the attempt to reconcile the Bible with science and claim that both are literally true is, I believe, a theological dead-end.

Option number two in our quest to figure out what to do with the discrepancy between science and religion is to say "choose!" One or the other is right. Decide which camp you're in.

Atheists would say that science is right, and the Bible is nothing but a bunch of ancient legends. Obviously as a rabbi I disagree with that answer.

Fundamentalists say that the Bible is right, and it is science that is flawed.

When we say "fundamentalists," we usually think of Christians or Muslims. But there are also Jewish fundamentalists.

Technical training, sadly, is no vaccine against fundamentalism. Rabbi Menachem Mendel Schneerson, the last Lubavitcher rebbe, studied at the Sorbonne and received a degree in electrical engineering from a French technical college. Yet despite his scientific background, he maintained that science was wrong. In an article he wrote in 1962 he said "In view of the unknown conditions which existed in prehistoric times, conditions of atmospheric pressures, temperatures, radioactivity, unknown catalyzers, etc., etc...conditions that is, which could have caused reactions and changes of an entirely different nature and tempo from those known under the present-day orderly processes of nature, one cannot exclude the possibility that dinosaurs existed 5722 years ago, and became fossilized under terrific natural cataclysms in the course of a few years rather than in millions of years; since we have no conceivable measurements or criteria of calculations under those unknown conditions."

In other words, one response of the fundamentalists to the evidence of science is that the laws of physics have basically changed in the last 5000 years, and the way the world works today is not the way the world worked 5000 years ago; hence science has been led astray.

And Chabad rabbis of today of course accept their rebbe's teachings – they believe the world was created in six twenty-four hour periods 5, 767 years ago. Usually Chabad does not push this approach in their outreach to young people, as not too many university students would buy it. So I was somewhat surprised that I found the above referenced quote on the website of Chabad of the University of Cambridge in Britain. I give them credit for being upfront with what they believe.

In simpler terms, Rabbi Benny Zippel of Chabad Lubavitch of Utah said "Torah does not believe in evolution. Torah believes that during the six days of creation, God created man in God's image."

Many non-religious people buy into the argument of the atheists versus the fundamentalists. Many people assume that those are the only two choices.

Unfortunately, I used to be one of those people. I thought that you had to choose between religion and science. You either believed the universe was 13 billion years old or you believed it was less than 6,000 years old. For a long time I thought that to be a religious person meant you had to ignore everything you learned in science class at school. I thought to be a religious person meant you had to take your scientifically trained mind out and put it on a shelf.

And since my favorite subject in school was science, and Hebrew school certainly was NOT my favorite, no surprise after my Bar Mitzvah, science won out and I was only seen in a synagogue three times in the next 25 years.

What changed? When I started studying Judaism as an adult, I learned that the fundamentalists are wrong. It's not just a black and white choice, Torah or science. Maimonides, one of our greatest sages who lived almost 1,000 years ago says that anyone who takes the Torah literally is distorting the Torah. We have to interpret the Torah, and we have to understand it metaphorically. If you understand the Torah as speaking metaphorically, there is no problem with reconciling the biblical stories with what we learn scientifically. Science and Torah are speaking in different realms.

Science is great at answering nuts and bolts practical questions. How is the world put together? How does the world function? But it cannot provide answers to moral, ethical, or aesthetic questions. In this week's Torah portion it says "And God made the beasts of the earth after their kind, and cattle after their kind, and everything that creeps upon the earth after its kind; and God saw that it was good." Science can now tell us a lot about the process of how God did this act of creation, how one species evolved from another. But science cannot tell us that "it was good." The how questions are the realm of science. The why questions are the realm of religion.

There are scientists who claim that science can provide everything, even a basis for ethics. Dr. Norm Hall wrote "Science has succeeded as a cooperative human effort by asserting the belief that the universe can only be understood through the values of integrity and truth-telling. In the process it has become a system of values, and it has provided humankind with a language which transcends cultural boundaries and connects us in a highly satisfying way to all the observable universe. It has the potential to be used as the basis for a workable and profoundly satisfying system of ethics."

Unfortunately, ethical systems based on science generally seem to be profoundly lacking in, well, ethics. You look at evolution, and the ethics you would derive is "survival of the fittest." Eugenics is a good thing. Hitler based his ethics on "science," to create a better race.

It is not rational, and therefore not terribly scientific, to care about what happens to weak, non-contributing members of society. Science will not tell us we are all created "b'tzelem Elohim," in God's image. Science will tell us we are created very differently and should be treated differently.

No, science and religion need to co-exist. The one needs to inform the other. Just as religious fundamentalists are wrong when they try to deny science completely, atheist scientists are wrong when they try to deny religion completely. And I use the term "atheist scientists" advisedly: surveys show that the percentage of scientists who believe in God, about 40%, has remained relatively constant over the last 100 years. All of our scientific progress in understanding the universe has not led more scientists to atheism. Many, like Einstein did, marvel in the intricacy of God's creations.

And this approach to science and religion, to understand the Torah as speaking metaphorically, to understand that Torah and science teach us different truths, is NOT some kind of Conservative or Reform rejection of the tradition. Many Orthodox Jews believe the exact same thing. While all fundamentalist Jews may be Orthodox, not all Orthodox Jews are fundamentalist. I already mentioned how Maimonides rejected taking the Torah literally. Somewhat more recently, Rabbi Abraham Isaac Kook, the very Orthodox first chief rabbi of Palestine said "the theory of evolution accords with the secrets of Kabbalah better than any other theory. Evolution follows a path of ascent and thus provides the world with a basis for optimism. How can one despair, seeing that everything evolves and ascends? When we penetrate the inner nature of evolution, we find divinity illuminated in perfect clarity. Ein Sof, the infinite God, generates, actualizes, potential infinity."

So why is it that I bought into the false dichotomy of science vs. religion? What is it that kept me away from religion all those years?

I believe the problem is that my Jewish education stopped with my bar mitzvah.

Children are not simply little adults. The psychologist Piaget identified stages of cognitive development that we all go through. When teaching children you simply cannot go into abstract philosophical concepts. They are incapable of learning them. Even smart kids simply haven't developed the cognitive ability to deal with certain ideas.

So in Sunday school we teach the kids Bible stories without a great deal of commentary about the need to understand them metaphorically. We teach them about Adam and Eve, and Noah and Abraham and Moses. We present the stories as written without giving them a bunch of footnotes they would not understand.

Which is why it is such a tragedy if a young person's Jewish education stops at the age of thirteen. He or she will have learned the stories of the Bible, but he will not have learned Rambam's guidance on how we should understand those stories. When the child grows up, he may be left turned off to religion, thinking it's a bunch of fairy tales that make no sense and have no relevance to life today.

If we are concerned about Jewish continuity, one of the most important things we can do is to keep our Jewish teens learning. By the time a young person is in the confirmation class, at age 15, he or she is sophisticated enough to deal with abstract ideas. In confirmation class we talk about ideas like "who wrote the Bible?" "if God is all good, why is there evil in the world?" "what's the point of praying?" and the perennial favorite, "what's the meaning of life?" When the graduates of our confirmation class become young adults they may not remember all the details of what they learned but they will at least remember that Judaism does not paint the world into black and white where you have to choose between science and Torah.

And it's not just the kids who need to keep learning—we all need to. I find it sad that there are many Jewish adults who are very educated and sophisticated with graduate degrees in secular studies, who are 6th grade drop outs when it comes to having a command of the wisdom of the Jewish tradition. Last week at Simchat Torah as soon as we finished reading the book of Deuteronomy, we immediately continued with starting over again at the very beginning of the book of Genesis. No pause, no break. The message clearly being that learning never ends.

We are at the beginning of the New Year on the Jewish calendar. May we all resolve to learn more Torah this year, and to share more Torah with our friends and family. And Torah doesn't just mean the Bible. Go to your favorite bookstore, or go to Amazon and find a book on a Jewish subject that interests you…and read it!

Intelligent Design

A few years ago, there was a controversy about teaching "intelligent design" in school. What follows is an op-ed piece of mine that ran in the Toledo Blade.

Einstein said "God does not play dice with the Universe."

The smartest man to ever live believed in Intelligent Design.

I also believe in Intelligent Design. Intelligent Design says the world is too complex to have happened randomly. Look at a car: thousands of parts, all milled with great precision, many of them critical for the car to function at all. Obviously someone pretty intelligent came up with the design. Extrapolate that idea to the universe. The universe is too intricate to have happened by accident.

Even though I believe in Intelligent Design, I also believe that US District Judge John Jones ruled CORRECTLY a few weeks ago that a Dover, Pennsylvania school district was forbidden to teach Intelligent Design in biology class.

That's because Intelligent Design is not science. It is theology.

Science explains WHAT happens in the world around us, and HOW it happens. We observe a phenomenon, and try to understand what caused it.

Theology is not about WHAT and HOW. Theology is about WHY. Theology is about meaning.

The proponents of teaching intelligent design as science argue that Darwin's theory of evolution is "not a fact" and has inexplicable "gaps." But that's not a good reason to reject it as science.

When Einstein said, "God does not play dice with the universe," he was criticizing the theory of quantum mechanics. He thought it was a bunch of hooey. Today, of course, virtually all physicists believe Einstein was wrong, and quantum mechanics IS valid. That does not mean that the old Newtonian physics is "wrong." It's just incomplete. But that doesn't mean we throw it out: if you're going to play a game of pool, knowledge of Newton is much more useful than understanding Heisenberg's Uncertainty Principle.

Even intelligent designers can sometimes do things that are pretty random, or that fail. Look at the Edsel! Or as God (played by George Burns) put it in the movie "Oh, God!" "Avocados. I should have made the pits smaller."

As a licensed theologian I hate it when scientists muddle in theology. For example, Dr. Norman Hall, a scientist specializing in molecular genetics and cardiac biochemistry wrote, "Science has succeeded as a cooperative human effort by asserting the belief that the universe can only be understood through the values of integrity and truth-telling. In the process it has become a system of values, and it has provided humankind with a language which transcends cultural boundaries and connects us in a highly satisfying way to all the observable universe. It has the potential to be used as the basis for a workable and profoundly satisfying system of ethics."

Sorry, science cannot be used as the basis for a profoundly satisfying system of ethics. That's been tried: Hitler thought he was being very "scientific" in crafting a "Master Race," and thousands of highly-educated doctors, engineers, and scientists helped him commit mass murder. The roots of the ethical lie not in science but in something transcendental—in God, in the realm of theology.

Similarly, scientists are quite rightly upset when theologians try to muddle in science. Scientists are like Sgt. Joe Friday in the old Dragnet show: "Just the facts, ma'am."

Based on the facts, I believe in God and Evolution. God, the Intelligent Designer, chose to create the world through the Big Bang and Evolution. Those theories are certainly incomplete, and they contain gaps. But they represent science's attempt to explain observable phenomenon.

What we see when we look at those gaps is clearly colored by what we want to see. John Wisdom described it well in his parable of the Gardener. Two people look at a long neglected garden. One looks at all the weeds and says "there must not be a gardener." One looks at the flowers and says "there must have been a gardener."

As a person of faith, I look at the world through "God-colored lenses." I see evidence of God everywhere I look. But scientists are trained NOT to look at the world with "God-colored lenses," at least not at work. At work, they put aside pre-conceived notions, deal with the facts and try to explain them. And every so often, for many scientists and doctors, they take a step back from their work and feel awe at being in the presence of God who created such a wonder. But mostly they know enough to keep that awe and sense of wonder separate from their scientific work.

Plugging a variable into an equation which says "insert intelligent designer here" is not going to help us understand how the world works. It will not help us unlock the mysteries of physics and cosmology. That would be a cop-out on the part of scientists trying to understand God's world.

Jewish mysticism (Kabbalah) says that the very first act of Creation that God did was to hide—to engage in *tzimtzum*, which means "contraction." And God did a good job of hiding. The Jewish tradition teaches that God is hidden from our sight much the same way that the soul is hidden from our sight. What's the difference between a corpse and a live person? The presence of a soul, which science will never find.

God is the soul of the universe. Scientists will never find God via the scientific method, but God is what brings the universe to life.

By all means teach Intelligent Design in high school. But teach it in a comparative religion class.

It does not belong in science class. Even if it's true.

The Holocaust and the Problem of Evil

This was delivered at a Holocaust Remembrance Day ceremony in Toledo.

Is it possible for a human being to understand Divine justice?

In this week's Torah reading, Aaron's sons, Nadav and Avihu, are killed by God for a seemingly minor infraction.

The Torah tells us that each of them took his incense pan, put fire and incense in it, and offered *aish zarah,* strange fire, before the Lord. They offered something that had not been commanded or requested. Not necessarily something that they had been specifically told NOT to bring. But they did something they shouldn't have. And what was the penalty for this act of volunteerism?

"And there went out fire from the Lord, and devoured them, and they died before the Lord."

This is one of those many troubling passages in the Torah. How does the punishment fit the crime?

Punishment that seems beyond any logical measure is an issue we grapple with on a holiday that begins Monday night: Yom Hashoah, Holocaust Remembrance Day. This week's Torah portion, Shmini, often falls right around Yom Hashoah, and this has led several commentators to observe a similarity between the parsha and Yom Hashoah: like Nadav and Avihu, many of the six million Jews who perished in the Shoah were consumed by fire.

But I would suggest the real similarity between parshat Shmini and the Shoah is NOT the fire – rather it is the theological challenge to our sense of justice. Nadav and Avihu did not do anything that seems to merit a death sentence. Neither did the Jews who perished in the Shoah. Both this week's parsha and the remembrance of the Shoah challenge our understanding of God's justice.

Many of the rabbinic commentators on this week's parsha go looking for additional sins that Nadav and Avihu had committed which add to the severity of their crime. Some say that they were too eager to take over from Moses and Aaron, that they were plotting against the leadership. Others say, based on the fact that a warning to priests to stay away from wine or strong drink before serving in the Temple comes right after the account of their deaths, that they were drunk when they were offering this "strange fire," and that was their crime.

No one has tried to say that the victims of the Shoah were sinners—at least, not in this life. However there are those who say they were sinners in previous lives. In September 2000, while I was living in Israel, former Sephardi Chief Rabbi Ovadiah Yosef created a huge stir when he gave a sermon in which he said "The six million Jews, all those poor people who were lost at the hands of those evil ones, the Nazis, may their names be blotted out - was it all for nothing? No. This was all the reincarnation of earlier souls, who sinned and caused others to sin and did all sorts of forbidden acts. They returned in reincarnation in order to set things right, and received, those poor people, all those torments and troubles and deaths under which they were killed in the Holocaust. They were all reincarnated souls. This is not the first time in their lives that their souls have appeared. They came to do atonement for their sins."

What Rav Yosef said is perfectly in keeping with teachings from the Jewish mystical tradition, Kabbalah, which does hold with reincarnation and the idea of a later life atoning or fixing something that went wrong in an earlier life. But the idea of saying that there was that level of sin among the victims is completely abhorrent. There was a huge public outcry in Israel against this very hurtful teaching of Rabbi Yosef.

The Holocaust forces us to reexamine our theology. Richard Rubenstein – a Conservative rabbi, scholar, and former university President wrote "The thread uniting God and man, heaven and earth, has been broken. We stand in a cold, silent, unfeeling cosmos, unaided by any purposeful power beyond our own resources. After Auschwitz, what else can a Jew say about God?" As you'll see, I disagree with my distinguished colleague and I still believe in a God who cares, despite Auschwitz. But Rabbi Rubinstein's book "After Auschwitz," published in 1966, was one of the earliest scholarly works to point out that the Shoah forces us to re-examine what we believe.

There is a long standing tradition in the Jewish tradition to blame ourselves for disasters that come our way. The Talmud says that when Nebuchadnezzar destroyed the Temple the first time, in the 6th century BCE, he was "the rod of God," punishing the Jews for lapsing into idol worship and abandoning the ways of God.

When the Romans destroyed the Temple a second time a bit over 600 years later, the rabbis didn't see a level of sin that would have justified such a punishment. So they developed the idea we talk about on Tisha b'Av, that the Temple was destroyed because of *sinat chinam,* because of gratuitous hatred between Jews.

I don't think I could have a personal relationship with a God who would use the Nazis as a tool for punishing Jews who had sinned in an earlier life. I wouldn't want to have anything to do with such a God. How could I possibly pray to a God who would do such a thing? How could I possibly rely on such a God? How could I call God my fortress, or my rock, my savior?

Instead, I take comfort in the theology of Maimonides. Rambam said there are three kinds of evil or suffering in the world. The first are bad things that happen as a side effect of the way God created the world – this would include things like earthquakes and cancer. The second type of evil is the evil people do to each other—like wars and murder. The third type of evil is bad things people do to themselves – abusing drugs, eating too much, etc.

For Rambam, the evil of the Holocaust is a by-product of free will. God does not create evil. This kind of evil happens because God gave us this wonderful incredible gift of free will, which gives us the opportunity to choose. Sadly, too many people choose to follow an evil, wicked path, and hurt or kill other people.

This does not mean that the good guys bear no responsibility at all – I think the rabbis of old were on to something important when they sought meaning in disasters. But I think we have to understand the connection more metaphorically than directly.

The teaching that says the Temple was destroyed because of baseless hatred between Jews is true, although not necessarily for the reasons given in the Talmudic story. According to the story of Kamtza and Bar Kamtza baseless hatred led to someone turning someone else over to the Roman authorities, setting in motion an unfortunate chain of events. I would suggest instead a broader form of baseless hatred that caused the destruction. There was a huge amount of distrust – perhaps even hatred – between opposing camps among the Jews in the days of the revolt against Rome. The zealots insisted on trying to take on the Roman government; many other, wiser heads, thought that was a bad idea. There was no unity within the Jewish community. There were many different sects and groups, each with their own ideas on what to do. Perhaps if there had been greater unity among the Jewish people at the time, calmer heads would have prevailed and the revolt would never have happened and the Temple would never have been destroyed.

Hitler succeeded because no one stopped him. Not the millions of Germans who accepted his demands for blind obedience – Goering said "I have no personal conscience; Adolf Hitler is my only conscience." And not the British, whose Prime Minister Neville Chamberlain kept thinking the Nazis would be content with Austria—or Poland, or Czechoslovakia. Not even the Americans. We all remember America's role in beating the Nazis. Less remembered is that two days after Britain, France, Australia and New Zealand declared war on Germany in September, 1939, the United States declared itself neutral. It took another two years before the United States decided to enter the fray – in September, 1941, American ships and planes started firing on German war vessels. Three months later the Japanese attacked Pearl Harbor – and a few days after that, Germany declared war on the United States. How might history have turned out differently if America had joined the war in 1939 instead of in 1941? How many millions of lives might have been saved?

One of my teachers from rabbinical school, Dr. Zev Garber, says "The message of the Shoah for the generation after and for future generations is not survival alone. There is something more important than survival, and that is preventing moral bankruptcy." As long as children anywhere in the world are being taught to be morally bankrupt, to blindly follow demagogues into the cesspool of hate, our children's and grandchildren's future is not secure.

In this analysis, the sinners aren't the people who died – it's the people who lived, and didn't stop Hitler. People who would judge those who perished – like Rabbi Yosef – should perhaps instead be judging themselves and the ones who didn't take action to stop what was going on in Germany in the 1930s.

Hitler, of course, was not the first one to kill Jews. But Hitler had a frightening new twist.

In the past, when Jews were persecuted, they were generally offered a way out at the same time: convert. When Ferdinand and Isabella took control in Spain, they offered the Jews three choices: convert, leave, or die. Most left, some converted, a few died.

In medieval Europe, the oppressors were continually trying to get the Jews to convert to Christianity. Some Jews took the easy way out and converted. But most Jews refused. The majority were proud to be Jews, and they insisted on staying Jewish, sometimes even dying rather than eat a piece of pork.

Hitler's twist was to take the conversion option away. He didn't care what you believed. If you had a Jew too close in your family tree you were destined for the gas chambers. Even people who had converted to Christianity

– or whose parents had converted to Christianity – were killed for being "Jewish."

For someone to die rather than convert is a death that we call a "Kiddush Hashem," a sanctification of God's name. The people that the Nazis murdered weren't even given the opportunity to die a death of Kiddush Hashem. They weren't given any choice. The ones who would have converted to Christianity died right next to the ones who would have chosen to die rather than to let a piece of pork touch their lips. The dignity of being able to give one's life for Kiddush Hashem was taken away from the poor unwilling martyrs of the Shoah.

This is one reason to prefer using the Hebrew term Shoah over the Greek-derived term Holocaust. Holocaust is the Greek word for a burnt-offering, a sacrifice that was completely burned on the altar. Shoah, on the other hand, means "catastrophe," or "calamity." The victims of the Shoah did not willingly offer themselves as sacrifices, as the Midrash says Isaac offered himself when Abraham raised the knife to take his life. Willing or not they were killed. They weren't given a choice.

There is no theologically satisfactory answer to the issues raised by the Shoah. After all, even if we say that evil comes from people, there have been times when God has chosen to intervene miraculously to save us. Just last week we told the story of the Exodus at Passover, when God redeems a bunch of powerless slaves from mighty Egypt; the Maccabees defeated the far more powerful Seleucids; many hold that Israel's victory over the Arab armies in 1948 and 1967 was also nothing short of miraculous. How does God choose when a situation deserves a miracle and when it doesn't?

There are those who say that the Shoah was the price we paid for the State of Israel. In the decision of the Knesset to establish the 27th of Nisan as The Day of the Shoah and Ghetto Revolt Remembrance Day, Mordecai Norouk, in the name of the House Committee of the Knesset said "perhaps by the merit of their blood spilled like water, we achieved a state and the beginning of redemption."

But somehow tying together the Holocaust and the State of Israel—with the implication of suffering and reward—is also unsatisfying on many levels. Who asked the six million—who asked us—if it was worth the price?

There are some theological questions that we can wrestle with and wrestle with but can never come up with a completely satisfying solution. When we wear ourselves out from trying to make sense of the senseless, the only response we are left with is the same response that Aaron had when he was told of the death of his sons.

Vayidom Aharon. And Aaron was silent.

Sheep and Divine Providence

There's a saying "no good deed goes unpunished." My car was stolen while I was leading Yom Kippur services (5769), as a volunteer, at a kibbutz in Northern Israel. It was returned ten days later, broken and filled with stolen sheep.

Sheep?

OK, I get the point that God is sending me a message. My car was stolen davka ON Yom Kippur, when I volunteered to lead services at a kibbutz in the Galilee. And then the police found the car, on, of all days, Simchat Torah, a day which is one of the most joyous days on the Jewish calendar, when we sing and dance with the Torah as we complete our annual cycle of reading the Torah.

I might try and chalk that up to "free will" and coincidence.

But the car was found full of sheep.

Live, stolen, sheep.

The thieves were using our car to rustle sheep. In a way I'm grateful – if they were using the cars to run drugs or steal something like computers they could have harmed a lot more other people using my car as a tool. On the other hand – can you imagine what the carpet in the car looks like (smells like) after a bunch of sheep were left in the car for what looks like a few days? I assure you, it smells as bad as you imagine it would.

And not just full of sheep – the reason the cops were able to find the car is it had a broken axle and body damage. The hapless thieves were driving our American "mommy-van" cross country stealing sheep at a high rate of speed. And smashed it up. I don't know if they hit a tree or a ditch or what, but they damaged the car, and abandoned it. Full of sheep.

Those of you who have been reading my blog for the last 16 months have seen the words "only in Israel" appear in this space more than once. I hate to overuse a cliché, but this is truly an "only in Israel" occasion. I certainly never heard of anyone in America having their stolen car recovered loaded with stolen sheep.

Lauri figured this story is so strange it would make a great movie. I agree. What that car has been through – a journey over the ocean, waiting patiently to be retrieved from customs, the run around with getting it licensed, which was like something out of Kafka – including new $1500 headlights and watching the guy make the license plates – to the indignity of being stolen and filled with sheep messing the carpet – would all make a great connecting line for several vignettes.

The scene with the thieves could be hilarious. We could show the thieves trying to steal a sheep on a motor scooter and deciding they needed to upgrade to something more spacious. Bouncing across a field loaded with sheep, yelling at the sheep to stay out of the way of the driver.

All joking aside, I'm still trying to figure out the theological implications of this strange story.

When Yom Kippur was over, and I got to thinking about the significance of my car being stolen on Yom Kippur, my reaction was not to blame God, but rather to chalk it up as an artifact of free will. The scoundrels who stole a car on Yom Kippur, I figured, were not somehow fulfilling God's will, but rather were exercising – in a particularly odious fashion – the free will that the Creator endowed them with.

But I was just reading some stories of the Baal Shem Tov, the Besht, and there was one that seemed very much on point. The Besht decided to visit the Holy Land: he was convinced that if he and a certain tzaddik living in

Jerusalem were together, they could bring the Messiah. He ignored omens that he shouldn't go, and left his home with his daughter and an assistant for the journey to the Israel. Along the way he got another powerful sign of Heavenly displeasure: his learning fled from him. He ignored this omen as well. Along the way all their money was stolen and they were left abandoned on some island; the Besht understood this as a message, but he wasn't going to be deterred. They got back on their way, and when a great storm hit the boat and swept his daughter overboard, it was then he gave up, realizing he couldn't fight God's will: he promised to give up and go back home if God would only give his daughter back. His daughter was saved, the seas calmed down, and he went home; the tzaddik he wanted to meet passed away three months later.

Now I could see reading the storm as Divine displeasure, but the Besht also saw the bandits who robbed him as part of a Divine message to him—he wasn't content to say it was just the bandits exercising their free will, because in the Chasidic world view, everything comes from God, good and bad alike. And to some degree I would agree; after all, the bandits are also "powered by God" and if God really didn't want them doing what they had started doing, He could intervene.

So if I were to read the theft of the car on Yom Kippur as a divine message, how do I interpret it? What was the message?

I think it was a test. When Lauri came in and asked "did you move the car" just as I was about to lead the morning Amidah on Yom Kippur, it was a test to see if I would become more focused on my material needs than on my spiritual needs and the spiritual needs of the congregation. I passed the test – I shrugged and went back to my prayers, and there was really no discernible effect on my *kavvanah* (focus). If the car was gone, there was nothing I could do about it, and certainly not on Yom Kippur, so I just kept praying.

It was really hard work – nothing to do with the car, just leading all those services, and feeling responsible for the group that was there. I'm not a great singer, I'm not trained as a hazzan, and despite my efforts at studying and practicing ahead of time, I know the melody wasn't always perfect, and neither was my Torah reading. But there were a few peak moments in there, when I did feel connected to God, when I really did pour my heart out to God, and I was really and truly praying. My imperfections helped me have the contrite spirit that the chasids assure us is what is really pleasing to God.

So when I found out the car was recovered on Simchat Torah, it made it seem as if the test had a specific time limit. God wanted to know how I would deal with the loss of my car – which was far and away my family's biggest non-financial asset – between Yom Kippur, the Day of Atonement, and Simchat Torah, the Day of Rejoicing.

I was not upset by the loss of the car (well, not TOO upset, anyway...). Can I describe it as faith in God without seeming guilty of excessive pride? I knew somehow I would find a way to meet my transportation needs. I have a job, I have options. Losing the car was going to be somewhat inconvenient and would involve some expense, but it wasn't going to change my life.

I wish when the car was stolen I could have been like Rabbi Akiva and said "*kol d'avid rachmanah l'tav*," "all that the Compassionate One does is for the good." Even after he had his lamp broken, his donkey ran away, and he was turned away from the inn, Rabbi Akiva was able to say "all that the Compassionate One does is for the good." Or I wish I could have been like "Nachum gam zu" who would always say "*gam zu l'tovah*," "this too is for the best," no matter what happened. It's still very difficult for me to see the hand of Providence in disasters and to have faith that everything is God's will and somehow this is also for the best. And this was just a car; God forbid something bad happened to someone I loved, it would be even harder to see that as 'also for the best.' But I was at least able to accept it with equanimity, and if I couldn't quite say "it's also for the best," at least I could say "it could have been worse."

As much as I believe in free will, it seems very unlikely that of all the cars at the kibbutz, the thief picked the rabbi's car; and they stole it davka on Yom Kippur, and it was returned davka on Simchat Torah—full of sheep. Very strange set of coincidences if it was just coincidence.

When Yaakov was tested by wrestling with the angel, he prevailed, but was injured in the process. Something like that happened here as well; we got the car back, but it was damaged in the process. So I may have passed the test, but I was also damaged in the process. But at least unlike Yaakov, my damage was only financial and is nothing we can't recover from.

Actually, now that I think about it, the story about the Besht says he accepted God's will and went home – but it does not say he was happy about it, or even that he said "*gam zu l'tovah.*" Maybe that's part of our free will as well; we ultimately may have to accept God's will, but we don't have to be happy about it!

Accepting the idea of Divine Providence doesn't necessarily mean simply accepting all bad things without complaint or flinching – after all, the Besht would pray fervently to get Divine decrees changed in order to avert individual or communal suffering.

There are definitely times in my life when I have felt the hand of Divine Providence. Yet I'm still likelier to attribute Divine Providence to positive things in my life than to negative ones. But maybe that's not bad – after all, I'm giving God credit for the good stuff, but letting Him off the hook for the bad stuff. Maybe when my time comes to be judged I'll be able to point that out and say God should reciprocate, and give me credit for the good, but overlook the bad!

Chapter Three

Finding God's Presence

"And Jacob awoke from his sleep, and he said, Surely the Lord is in this place; and I knew it not."

Genesis 28:16

If we accept the premise that God is real, how do we find God's presence in the world? Especially when events occur which make it feel like God is missing, or hiding?

Some find God through prayer, others through intellectual contemplation and effort, others in nature, others still in their fellow man. I had a neighbor in Portola Valley who spoke to God when he rode his bike. Many parents report feeling the presence God at the birth of a child. We often seek God at times of pain or anguish. Feeling the presence of God is comforting; the withdrawal of God's presence is frightening, as the Psalmist says, "Answer me speedily, O Lord; my spirit fails; do not hide your face from me, lest I be like those who go down into the pit."

Responding to Tragedy: Finding Comfort in the Wake of 9/11

The very first year I led High Holiday services was 2001 – the year the High Holidays started with the infamous 9/11 attack on the World Trade Center and the Pentagon. This was my 1st day of Rosh Hashanah sermon for 5762, presented to Congregation Beth Shalom in Tucson.

On Tuesday, September 11 our lives changed.

We continue to struggle with the confusion of feelings and questions we have. We feel pain, we grieve, we are sad, we are angry, we want justice; some would add revenge. We want to know who, and why, and how. We want to know whether such a thing could happen again. We want to know what our government's reaction is going to be. We want to know if we can ever feel safe again.

I had originally planned to speak about Israel today. I was going to talk about how some of my experiences in Israel during the last year had shaped my views on how to respond to the situation there.

Obviously, as concerned as we remain about Israel, the events of last week have overwhelmed our ability focus on other things. Yet despite the obvious political connections, the events of last week have another profound connection with Israel. My family and I have recently returned from a year of living in Israel. We know what it feels like to live with the stress of being under attack. Now all of you, and all Americans, have a taste of what it feels like to live in Israel. To live in a place where your life is profoundly altered by cowardly terrorists. I don't need to describe what it feels like to make phone calls to find out if your loved ones are OK after hearing of a suicide bomber: many of you have had the tension of that experience yourself. I suspect that there will not be nearly so many American calls for "restraint" after a suicide bomber attacks Israel. There have already been reports that the US government is reconsidering its policy against assassination of terrorists.

How do we make sense out of these events? How do we recover our sense of equilibrium? How do move ahead? Last night I spoke about how we cannot blame God for this tragedy. It is pointless to ask how God could allow this to happen. God gave us the most precious possible gift: free will. He gave that gift of free will to all of us, including those who committed this horrible crime against us and against humanity. In last week's Torah portion it says "I set before you life and death, choose life." We choose life—they choose death.

As Jews we turn to God and we turn to our tradition at a time of tragedy like this. We need some help, some guidance, in how to deal with tragedy. In a little while we will recite the Musaf Amidah, which contains the famous medieval prayer of Unetaneh Tokef. The most famous line of Unetaneh Tokef, which we sing together, and which we have embroidered on our Torah reading table cover at Bet Shalom, proclaims "*Teshuvah, tefilah,* and *tzedekah*--repentance, prayer, and deeds of kindness--can remove the severity of the decree."

Note that it does not say "change the decree." It says remove the severity of the decree. What has been decreed, has been decreed. What has happened has happened. We cannot pray hard enough and find that it was all just a bad dream, and see the buildings back in place and lives restored. One of the most horrible things we could imagine has happened. It may have looked like a bad action movie, but it was real life.

However, our actions can remove the severity of the decree. We can find a way to deal with it. We can find a way to ease the pain, a way to help ourselves recover and a way to help others.

I'm going to address each of the three actions—repentance, prayer, and deeds of kindness—moving from the inside out, from the most personal and individual to the most communal.

The most personal, individual action can be prayer. Yes, we come together as a community to pray, but you can pray alone. When you pray you come before God as an individual, using either your own words or the words in the siddur, or a combination of the two.

Last week on Tuesday I found myself unable to pray in the morning. We are commanded to pray three times a day, and I do my best to fulfill this commandment and pray three times a day. Yet last Tuesday I found myself absolutely unable to pray. The pictures I saw on TV, the implications of what I was seeing, were simply too shocking, too mind-numbing, too completely absorbing. I could find no words in my heart, and I was sure I wouldn't have found them in the siddur, to express what I was feeling at that particular moment.

In the Talmud we are informed that you should not pray if you cannot have the proper *kavvanah*, the proper focus. Later authorities have said that we don't know how much or how little is enough, so to be on the safe side we should always pray even if we think we don't have enough *kavvanah*. In general I agree with this rule; however, last Tuesday morning, there was no doubt in my mind whatsoever that I did not have the concentration required to pray.

By later in the day, after some of the initial numbness and shock wore off, that feeling had changed completely. Instead of feeling I couldn't pray I felt I needed to pray, and I needed to pray together with other Jews. I went to a minyan in my neighborhood in Los Angeles, and found many others who felt the same way—a place where we sometimes struggle to have ten Jews together for a minyan was filled with Jews who needed to come together to pray. When we recited Mourner's Kaddish, we all rose to recite Kaddish on behalf of thousands of people killed that horrible day. We were all in a type of mourning, and praying together was very comforting.

As the week has gone on, I have found that at different times certain of the words that are so familiar have suddenly jumped out at me with new images attached to them. Praying with the siddur can help us find words to express what we feel. Sometimes we find that King David was able to say it better in a psalm than we could say it ourselves.

Sometimes the words in the liturgy move us to think about the situation in which we find ourselves. In Psalm 30, which we recite every morning just before Baruch Sheamar, it is written: "I will extol you, O Lord; for you have lifted me up, and have not made my enemies rejoice over me." I was troubled when I recited this verse one morning last week. I read "have not made my enemies rejoice over me," and I couldn't help but think of the images on television of Palestinians handing out candy and rejoicing when they saw the pain and destruction in America. Yet this forced me to think a little further, and remind myself that God did not cause my enemies to rejoice. The enemies were rejoicing because of an act of Man, not an act of God. And God has lifted me up, because I have been able to find some measure of comfort in turning my heart to God at this difficult time.

King David was no pacifist, and his battle cry, expressing our anger, can also be found in the Psalms. The Psalm for the day on Wednesday—the day following the attack—is Psalm 94, which starts out with the cry "God of vengeance, Lord, God of vengeance appear!" The Psalmist had feelings just the same as ours: the end of the psalm proclaims "They gather themselves together against the soul of the righteous, and condemn the innocent blood. But the Lord has become my fortress; and my God, the rock of my refuge. And he shall bring upon them their own iniquity, and shall cut them off in their own wickedness; the Lord our God shall cut them off."

In addition to finding inspiration in the siddur and in words of Torah, we can simply cry out to God in our own ways and in our own words. Rebbe Nachman taught that it is good to pour out your heart to God, like you would to a good friend. You don't need a book in your hand and you don't need to understand Hebrew to be able to pray.

We Jews are often uncomfortable with spontaneous prayer. We are so accustomed to our fixed, and lengthy, liturgy that we sort of automatically assume that praying is something we do with a book in our hands. The book is there to be a tool, an aid to prayer, not a barrier. One of the most moving prayers in our scripture is also the shortest. When Miriam was stricken with *tzuras*, a terrible skin condition, Moses did not recite a lengthy formula. He simply cried out, *"El na, refa na lah."* God, PLEASE heal her.

Similarly at times like this, we need both kinds of prayer. We need those fixed prayers and beautiful liturgy where we can find passages that move us or comfort us; and we also need to make that individual heartfelt pouring out to God. Please God, take care of the souls of those killed and comfort their families.

You may wonder at finding "*teshuvah*" (repentance) on the list. Most of us would not subscribe to the theology that we are somehow personally responsible for all the bad things that happen. On one level, we do have a significant responsibility: we have failed to create the kind of world where such things cannot happen. We have failed to eradicate evil—whether through love and example, or weapons of war, we have not yet succeeded in ridding the world of evil. We also have not until now taken the expensive and inconvenient steps needed to add to our security against terrorists. We need to redouble our efforts to eradicate this evil from our midst.

However, teshuvah means more than repentance. Teshuvah literally means return. This is classically understood as a return to God; however teshuvah can also be a return to our loved ones.

Some of the most heart-wrenching tales from this terrible week have been the final phone calls. Such as calls people on hijacked planes made to tell their loved ones what was going on. Tales of heroism in the skies as well: Jeremy Glick on American Airlines flight 93 with his two month old son, called his wife and told her they had been hijacked, but he also reported that the passengers had voted to attack the terrorists. It would appear that this decision of the passengers and crew aboard the doomed flight resulted in the crash of the plane in a forest instead of into a target like the White House. As the father of several small (and a few not so small) children, the tale that touched me most was of a man on the 80th floor of one of the World Trade Center buildings; he called his wife to say he didn't think he was going to make it out, he loved her, and to take care of their two small children, ages one and three.

Nine days ago, at our Selichot services, we watched the movie "The Straight Story." Based on the story of Al Straight, the movie tells the tale of an elderly gentleman who learns his brother, who he hasn't talked to in ten years, has had a stroke. Having medical problems himself which have resulted in the loss of his driver's license, Al hops on a riding lawnmower for an incredible 360 mile journey of teshuvah, of reconciliation.

All too often we wait until a disaster strikes to do teshuvah, to return.

The ten days between Rosh Hashanah and Yom Kippur are a period for heightened examination of our lives, a time to make amends; we have the image of the decree that will be sealed on Yom Kippur, and closed at the end of Sukkot. The recent events remind us of how real the closure of the book can be, and how sudden.

What would you do, trapped on that plane or in that building? Who would you call and what would you say? How much regret would you feel at the calls you didn't have time to make?

Life is too short, and its ending too uncertain, to put things off for another day. Call the parent, or sibling, or child who has become estranged. Go home and hug your child and your spouse. If you are still at war with your ex-spouse, declare a truce, for the sake of your children and your own peace of mind. A few years ago, at this time of year I did teshuvah with my ex-wife, and asked for her forgiveness; it was a very powerful and healing experience.

Studies have shown that most of the conversation between a parent and child on a typical day is in the form of criticism and giving orders. "Pick up your toys!" "Why didn't you pick up your toys?" "Why do I have to ask you a thousand times?" Instead, go home and tell your children how much you love them, how special they are. Talk about the day they were born, and your favorite memories of them. If, God forbid, something happens to either of you today, let their memory of you be of a hug and a smile, loving words instead of harsh ones.

In Pirkei Avot, The Ethics of our Fathers, Rabbi Eliezer advises "repent one day before your death." The point of his message, so tragically testified to by the events of last week, is that you don't know when you will die: therefore, you should do teshuvah today.

Teshuvah can serve to reduce the harshness of the decree both before and after a disaster. For those who take R. Eliezer's message to heart, and try to live in a state of perpetual teshuvah with their loved ones, if tragedy strikes it will not be compounded by a lot of unfinished business and unreconciled feelings. For those of us here, doing teshuvah now can bring us closer to our loved ones, closer as a community, and ultimately closer to God. The Midrash says that it was the powerfully close community that resulted from the teshuvah our ancestors did between Rosh Hashanah and Yom Kippur that made it possible for us to receive the Ten Commandments on Yom Kippur.

The last of the three actions called for by Unetaneh Tokef is *tzedakah*. I went with a somewhat liberal translation of tzedakah as deeds of kindness. Tzedakah is more often translated as charity; the same basic word in different forms and contexts can mean justice, righteous, a person who is correct, or a saint. Giving tzedakah is both the correct thing to do, and the righteous thing to do. It is obvious how acts of tzedakah can help remove the severity of the decree; some people may be suffering, but if we give of our time, our selves, or our money, we can work to ease their pain, to remove the severity of the decree. Bringing the perpetrators to justice (*tzedek*) would also help to ease some of the pain as it would help prevent such tragedies from afflicting others in the future.

However, ultimately, there can be no real "bringing the criminals to justice" in this case. If the person behind all this and all of his followers were caught, tried, and executed, we would still not have real justice. The lives of a handful of terrorists cannot compensate for the loss of thousands of people, for the pain that so many survivors will have to live with for the rest of their lives. There is a story of how the nations of the world will have to do teshuvah, and it specifies what they will have to pay for what they took from Jerusalem; in place of copper, silver; in place of silver, gold. But in place of Rabbi Akiva there is nothing they can bring; they cannot do real teshuvah for the sin of killing Rabbi Akiva.

While tzedakah as justice will help ease the severity of the decree when we see the criminals who did this brought to trial or killed, it is probably more important to focus on the tzedakah we can do ourselves: charitable acts.

I was very touched by some of the stories of kindness being shown to strangers in New York. I heard that shoe stores were giving away free sneakers to women wearing high heels who had long walks home because of the shutdown of public transportation. That's not the kind of thoughtfulness that immediately comes to mind when we think of tough New Yorkers. But I think New Yorkers are like Israelis: they both have a tough, macho exterior, but underneath they have hearts of gold.

Tzedakah is one thing we can all do in a way that can make a real difference to others. We can give money, especially to organizations that help the victims of terrorism. The Jewish Federation of Southern Arizona has set up a special fund to support the victims of terrorism here in the US and in Israel. Information can be found at the back of the room.

We can also give of ourselves; we can give blood, we can volunteer our time. We can talk to others and convince them to give.

We will continue to struggle with our feelings, our fears, our stress in the wake of this incredible tragedy for quite some time to come. If we can remember the prescription of Unetaneh Tokef—that "Teshuvah, tefilah, and tzedeka--repentance, prayer, and deeds of kindness--can remove the severity of the decree"—perhaps we can find the path to healing our own psychic wounds while working to heal the all too physical wounds of thousands of fellow Americans, and hundreds of fellow Jews in Israel.

May the New Year bring us a just and lasting peace in the Middle East, and an end to terrorism everywhere in the world. May Isaiah's prophecy be fulfilled: Nation shall not lift up sword against nation; neither shall mankind learn war anymore.

The Power of Being Commanded: Na'aseh v'nishmah

Judaism is a spiritual discipline – as such there are actions and disciplines we accept upon ourselves before fully understanding them – they are the path to achieving understanding. This talk was delivered on Shavuot, 5766.

Shavuot is called *zeman matan Torateinu,* the time of the giving of our Torah. That's what we called it earlier this morning in our Amidah prayer.

Why don't we call it *zeman kibalnu Torateinu,* the time when we accepted the Torah?

Years ago, some of the shtetls in Eastern Europe were too small and too poor to afford a full time rabbi. So there were itinerant rabbis, preachers and teachers who would travel from town to town, sharing words of Torah, bringing the light of God's word to the outback and beyond.

Nowadays, Torah is everywhere. Even here in Toledo, a town with fewer than 4,000 Jews, we have six rabbis. Chabad has been producing so many rabbis it seems like any town which has enough Jews to have a minyan has a Chabad. The University of Judaism has doubled the number of Conservative rabbis being ordained in America every year. Some of my colleagues are worried about what we're going to do with this glut of rabbis on the market. Incredible words of Torah – written, audio and even video – are available anywhere there is an internet connection 24 hours a day. Torah is "given" everywhere.

But is anyone listening?

Shavuot is called *zeman matan Torateinu,* the time of the giving of the Torah, because our tradition says God gave the Torah to Moses at a particular time and place. Tradition says 3,318 years ago yesterday Moses went up to Mt. Sinai and came back down with the Ten Commandments. But the receiving of the Torah – that's an event that is personal and individual. We accept the Torah anew every day.

When we Jews say "accept the Torah," we mean accept being bound by the commandments of the Torah. And that's the subject I want to explore this morning. Why should we, people living over three thousand years later, accept the commandments?

Many different reasons have been given for why we should obey the commandments. Some people obey out of a fear of Divine punishment—you want to stay out of Hell, you obey the rules. Some people obey because it's what defines us as Jewish, as part of a covenant between Man and God. Some people obey because our ancestors made a promise to God and we are continuing to fulfill that promise. Some people obey out of a sense of "owing" God, for all the good things God has done for us. In fact this morning's Torah reading gives this as a reason for obeying. Deuteronomy 16:12 says "And you shall remember that you were a slave in Egypt; and you shall observe and do these statutes." God reminds us He brought us out of Egypt, so we owe Him, and we should observe the commandments.

Other people obey because it flows out of their faith in God. They believe in God, so they obey His commandments.

This, in fact, is the attitude of most non-Catholic Christians. One of the differences between Protestants and Catholics is that Protestants believe that obedience has nothing to do with getting into Heaven—that comes exclusively through faith, whereas Catholics believe obedience still has a role to play in salvation. For Protestants obedience simply follows from faith.

The famous 19th century British preacher C. H. Spurgeon said "We preach the obedience of faith. Faith is the fountain, the foundation, and the fosterer of obedience. Men obey not God till they believe him. We preach faith in order that men may be brought to obedience. To disbelieve is to disobey."

In a more contemporary vein, Pastor Paul Mizzi says "Faith is the unseen root; obedience is the seen fruit."

Our Muslim brothers and sisters would appear to agree with this approach; after all, Islam means "submission to God." Abul A'la Mawdudi wrote "And it is a matter of common sense that this obedience cannot ensure in full measure unless man knows certain basic facts of life and reposes firm faith in them....First of all, one should have unshakable belief in the existence of God, for unless a man has a firm and unalloyed faith in God's existence, how can he render obedience to Him?"

The message from both Islam and Protestant Christians is "Faith first. From faith will flow obedience"

A lot of Jews would seem to have a similar attitude. And this explains why they don't obey the commandments. They are waiting to have faith. They may be telling themselves when I have real faith, then I'll obey the rules. Some years ago a friend of mine told me he'd start keeping kosher when God came and told him he wanted him to keep kosher. In the meanwhile, he would keep eating the shrimp cocktails.

My friend didn't consider the message in the Bible to eat only fish with fins and scales sufficiently personal or sufficiently compelling. But his attitude is pretty typical – in essence, it says "convince me of the wisdom of what you want me to do, and then I'll do it."

That is the normal way we learn things. When I'm teaching someone a new maneuver in flying, the first thing I do is explain what the maneuver is, I explain why we do it, and I explain how we do it. I ask the student if he or she has any questions. Then in the air I demonstrate the maneuver, and then have the student perform the maneuver. Afterwards I ask the student to critique it himself before I share my advice on how to improve. So for example, there is a maneuver all student pilots do called "flying a rectangular pattern." I explain to the student that we do this maneuver so that he will learn how to compensate for the effect of the wind when you want to follow a particular ground track, which is an important skill in getting an airplane where you want to go and getting it lined up with the runway when you want to land. I then explain how we select what we call a "crab angle" to compensate for the effect of the wind. When the student shows he understands what it's about we try it. The doing comes after the explaining, and an important part of the understanding and the motivating is an appreciation for why a particular maneuver is part of the process of learning to fly.

This is nothing new. In Madregat HaAdam, a work of Mussar (ethics), R. Joseph Horowitz explains that in the normal course of events, when someone makes a request of them, they first consider the request and decide whether or not they want to do it, and they are cautious, lest the request be something that will cause them harm, or it will be something impossible for them to live with.

All of which makes our ancestors reply when Moses came down the mountain with the Torah somewhat perplexing. They said:

Kol asher diber Hashem na'aseh v'nishmah.

Everything that God has said, we will do and we will hear/understand.

The EXACT opposite of the normal process: they agreed to follow the commandments without even understanding what it was that they were being commanded to do.

The Talmud expresses shock that our ancestors agreed to obey first: "R. Eleazar said: When the Israelites gave precedence to we will do over we will hearken, a Heavenly Voice went forth and exclaimed to them, Who revealed to My children this secret, which is employed by the Ministering Angels, as it is written, Bless the Lord, ye angels of his. Ye mighty in strength, that fulfill his word, that hearken unto the voice of his word: first they fulfill and then they hearken?"

What's so powerful about this secret?

To appreciate the power of this secret, we have to first understand the purpose of the religious life. Why be religious at all?

The goal of most religions is to achieve a state of being connected to God. All religions claim to be a path, if not THE path, to connecting with God. The believer knows that having a real relationship with God can transform your life like nothing else.

The Slonimer Rebbe says the goal of every Jew should be to achieve *devekut*, a cleaving to God, a powerful connection with God. *Na'aseh v'nishmah*—agreeing to obey before hearing the rules—demonstrates this, because the essence of *na'aseh v'nishmah* is that even in dark times, when we don't understand the will of God very clearly, when our understanding is limited, we still put *na'aseh*, we will do, before *nishmah*, we will understand. We still cleave to God, we still accept God, even if we don't totally understand God.

An insistence on having it all explained in an understandable way before taking on a particular mitzvah is symptomatic of a distant relationship with God.

If someone you love says "do me a favor?" what's the answer?

"Of course, what is it?"

We don't need it explained first. We agree first because we trust and love the other person. We want to do things for them. The Slonimer Rebbe says that at Sinai our ancestors accepted the commandments from a place of love, the way children love their parents.

So if we say *na'aseh*, we will do, what do we need the *nishmah* for? Madregat HaAdam says that by saying *na'aseh*, we are agreeing to perform God's will even before we understand it. The *nishmah* we pursue is to understand what it is that God is asking of us—not so that we can decide whether or not to do it, we've already agreed we'll do it—but rather simply so that we'll know what to do.

Too many modern Jews get caught up in making decisions about each individual mitzvah. Should I keep kosher or not? Should I keep kosher at home but eat whatever out? Should I keep the Sabbath? How should I keep the Sabbath?

And what about those rules that seem pretty obscure. Like *shaatnez*, the prohibition of mixing wool and linen. What does God have against wool and linen? Do I really have to follow that one?

Yes, you really have to follow that one.

I may go down in history as the only Conservative rabbi to ever tell his congregants they have to pay attention to *shaatnez* – usually we're so focused on the big two of getting people to keep kosher and observe the Sabbath we don't speak much of other ritual commandments.

But *shaatnez* has important symbolic value—particularly because it seems so random and inexplicable.

When I look at a label to make sure it does not contain a mixture of wool and linen, I am reminded that I accept the idea of being commanded by God to obey the mitzvot. I am reminded that I accept the idea of God being greater than me. I am reminded that I accept being bound to obey the rules God gave us in the Torah. I have a brief moment of increasing my daily "God-consciousness," all from following a seemingly random rule of the Torah.

We accept these rules as a package because we believe God loves us and the rules God gives us are for our own benefit. When my doctor gives me a prescription for a particular medication, I don't have to run to the internet to decide whether or not I'm going to take it– I trust my doctor to have given me something for my benefit.

But even here, there is nothing wrong with asking a *nishmah* question, a question seeking further understanding. After I get my prescription I may look on the internet for advice about a particular medication, or more details on things to watch out for. Not because I'm questioning the instruction, but rather for clarification. Similarly, we accept God's commandments, but can still look for clarification after we have accepted them.

The *nishmah* – the seeking understanding – can become complicated when we see things in the Torah that seem to contradict themselves. That's why the rabbis have struggled so much with the Torah over the centuries. In today's Torah reading we read about the remission of debts in the seventh year. This sounds like a wonderful innovation for poor people – it gives them a chance to get out from under their debt load every seven years. Of course, there is one obvious problem: who's going to lend money to someone in the sixth year? God recognized this, and the in this morning's reading we were cautioned "Beware that there be not a thought in your wicked heart, saying, The seventh year, the year of release, is at hand; and your eye be evil against your poor brother, and you give him nothing; and he cry to the Lord against you, and it be sin to you."

Unfortunately, people did refuse to lend money to poor people as the year of release approached. So the great rabbi Hillel established the *prozbul* two thousand years ago. The prozbul was a mechanism whereby a beit din, a rabbinic court, would take custody of a loan so that it would not be released in the seventh year. He instituted this so that people would continue to lend to poor people even when the seventh year was approaching.

The Torah explicitly commanded something: the debts are to be forgiven in the seventh year. But the rabbi saw that this explicit commandment was preventing a more important principle of the Torah from being fulfilled, the principle of taking care of the poor – so he changed the rule. He used *nishmah* to try and really understand what the Torah commands us—what God wants us to do.

Accepting being commanded means our default response to God's rules must be to obey. There is no good reason not to follow the commandment against *shaatnez*, so I follow it. It's not such a huge inconvenience. If there is a commandment that seems problematic, or seems to contradict other principles in the Torah, like the remission of debts resulting in making it worse

for poor people, the tradition tells us it is OK to wrestle with those commandments. We have been interpreting those commandments for millennia, because
we believe that when we engage in interpretation we are seeking God's will.
We've already agreed we'll do God's will; we're just trying to figure out what it
really is when we spot a contradiction.

Following the commandments is the way that Jews bring God into their
lives. Whether it's by making time for God on the Sabbath and holidays, or by
remembering to thank God with a blessing for the good food She has given us,
or by reading the label on a sports coat to see if it contains shaatnez, the
commandments are ways to bring God into our lives.

And a relationship with God is like a relationship with a person. You
have a deeper relationship with someone in your immediate family that you talk
to several times a day than you have with someone you talk to three times a
year. The more time you spend with God, the deeper your relationship will be.

And THAT'S the power of the secret of our ancestor's putting *na'aseh*
before *nishmah*. Faith does not lead to obedience – the world is full of people
who claim to believe in God who don't follow His rules. It's the other way
around. Obedience leads to faith. We follow the rules not as a reflection of our
close relationship with God, but as a reflection of our DESIRE to have a close
relationship with God.

Abraham Joshua Heschel said that Judaism does not call on people to
take a leap of faith – it calls on people to take a leap of action. Bring your
doubts, bring your questions, but follow the mitzvot – and along the way you
may find your doubts disappearing and your questions being answered.

Today is Shavuot, the day we celebrate *zeman matan Torateinu*, the time
of the giving of our Torah. Will today also be the day for our accepting the
Torah?

In everything we do we ask for God's help – and obeying the commandments is no exception. Earlier this morning—in the prayer before the

Shema—we asked God to help bring us to obey His commandments. It's a prayer worth repeating:

Avinu, Our Father, merciful Father, compassionate One; have mercy on us and give our hearts understanding and wisdom, *lishmoa, lilmod u'l'lamade*, to heed, to learn and to teach, *lishmor v'la'asot ulkayam*, to keep and to do and to establish all the words of Your Torah *b'ahava*, with love,

Amen.

How to Pray

It's not easy to pray. Many Jews are uncomfortable with prayer, are uncomfortable with the prayer book (siddur) and feel distanced from God. This Rosh Hashanah sermon was given in an attempt to give people some ideas on how to pray.

One thousand, nine hundred and thirty four years ago today, on the first of Tishrei, on this holiday, Rosh Hashanah, our ancestors—physical and spiritual—gathered on the top of a small hill with a grand name in the middle of Jerusalem. There, on the top of Har Tzion, Mt. Zion, in the Temple that had been recently expanded and beautified by Herod the Great, a ritual that was already more than a thousand years old was acted out.

A huge crowd gathered—tens of thousands of people. The priests acted out an elaborate ritual, sacrificing one young bull, one ram, and seven lambs, with meal offerings and wine offerings. Some of the more sophisticated among the crowd might have wondered why God, the Master of the Universe, wanted us to offer up a bar-b-que. But our ancestors did it anyway. They showed their love of God by giving up something of value, not really knowing what God might need or want.

Ten months later, on the ninth day of the month of Av, disaster struck: the Romans destroyed the Temple, the holiest place in Judaism, the ONLY place where the Torah allowed us to offer sacrifices that atone for our sins. Jews were forbidden to even return to the LOCATION of the Temple. There would be no sacrifices offered on Rosh Hashanah in the year 70.

The nation was in shock. The heart of the Jewish religion at that time was offering sacrifices. What was to be done?

Over the course of the next few years, the rabbis came up with a totally radical and innovative solution, which redefined Judaism and the way that Jews relate to God. The rabbis decided if we couldn't offer physical sacrifices, we would offer spiritual sacrifices. If we couldn't offer sheep and pigeons, we would offer words. The rabbis decided to replace the sacrificial animals with prayer, and they fixed the basic form of the main prayers that we recite today, and every day.

In a way, the rabbis' scheme succeeded brilliantly. And in a way, it has failed miserably.

It succeeded because here we are almost 2,000 years later, re-enacting that Temple ritual. We gather in our temples, our synagogues, our shuls. Our cantor takes the role of the Cohen Gadol, the High Priest, making offerings to God on behalf of the assembled multitude. Our choir takes the place of the Levites who served and made music in the Temple. There was a sense of mystery on that day long ago as the priests went through the elaborate rituals; there is a sense of mystery today, because most of us don't understand the language of the ritual.

The rabbis' scheme to substitute words for sacrifice succeeded. But is it really prayer that we are offering today? Or is it just a ritual, a sacrifice of time, reading empty words, but nothing more?

Are you really praying to God today? Or are you just reading to yourself? What does it mean to pray? What is prayer, as distinct from mere reading? Psalm 102 describes one kind of prayer beautifully: "A prayer of the afflicted when he is overwhelmed and pours out his complaint before God." Prayer is about pouring your heart out to God. Today's Haftorah, Hannah's prayers for a child, are so moving that the rabbis in the Talmud used Hannah as a template to teach us how all of us should pray. The most beautiful and moving prayer in the entire Torah is a simple one that Moses offers on behalf of his sister Miriam when she was afflicted with *tzuras. "El na rafa na la,"* "Please God, heal her!"

The urge to pray comes from the urge to pour out one's heart before God. The origins of prayer are not only in requests, in asking for things, whether material or spiritual. The origins of prayer are in crying out. As Heschel describes it, "[prayer] is a cry; an elementary outburst of woe, a spontaneous call in need; a hurt, a sorrow, given voice. It is the call of human helplessness directed to God. It is not asking, but coming with one's burden before God. It is like the child's running to the mother because it hurts." Prayer is not just about asking for things—it's about having a relationship with God. If your child falls down and gets hurt and comes running to you, it's not so much for the "Barbie Band-Aid" as it is for the comfort of being close to a parent. Being held, being told it will be OK.

You tell a spouse how you feel—frustrated, lacking, lonely—and you not only feel closer to your spouse, but you also feel comforted just having someone listen. If you are having a good time, things are going well, and you are happy, you also want to share that with your spouse. That's what prayer is about. To know that God is listening, that God is there, that God cares.

So how did our prayers go from "a spontaneous call in need," to "please turn to page 252?" Even before the destruction of the Temple, there were fixed prayers. Tradition says that the Amidah, the central prayer of Judaism, goes back to the days of the Men of the Great Assembly in the 5th century BCE. Two thousand years ago there was a greater emphasis on community than on individualism. I speculate that the rabbis felt there were certain communal needs that were so important, they wanted everyone praying to God for them. And when the Temple was destroyed in the year 70, they strove to combine that spirit of crying out with the ritual that had been carried out in the Temple.

We all have that urge to cry out to God, at least occasionally. Everybody is a spiritual seeker at some point in their lives. Maybe it's when confronted with disaster, or challenges. At times, we all seek transcendence, something greater than ourselves. We all wonder about God, we all have times when we feel distant from God but wish we weren't. The word "spiritual" itself speaks to the issues at the heart of prayer. Now some people cringe when they hear the word spiritual. It sounds kind of New-Agey, dilettante, something for dabblers. But I really like the word. Spiritual is a combination of spirit and ritual. And that is something VERY Jewish. All "spirit," no ritual, no context, could provide a passing pleasant feeling, but it will not provide a sense of meaning and purpose in your life. All ritual and no spirit and your soul is deadened and you are distanced from God.

Yet all ritual and no spirit is where much of the Jewish world is today. And that is where the rabbis failed when they substituted prayer for sacrifice—or perhaps it is where we, the people praying, have failed. The result is the same, however. I not infrequently have people talk to me about their problems with prayer. They are disappointed because prayer doesn't do anything for them. As a people, we have forgotten how to pray. How did this sorrowful state of affairs come about?

There's a story which I think explains what happened: there was a king who loved music. So he directed his musicians to play for him every morning. The musicians performed to obey, but they also loved and respected the king, and they valued the chance to be in his presence. Every morning they played for the king with enthusiasm and delight. For many years things went well—the musicians enjoyed playing, and the king enjoyed listening. The musicians eventually passed away, and their sons sought to take their place. But the sons had not mastered the art, nor had they kept the instruments in proper condition. They didn't know the king so well, and they no longer loved him so much. They blindly followed the fathers' custom of arriving each morning to perform, but the harsh sounds were so offensive to the king he stopped listening.

That's where we are today. We don't know the king so well, and our instrument, the prayer book, seems to be out of tune, and we don't know how to play it anyway. So instead of coming to the synagogue and having our souls soar in communion with God, we come and schmooze with our friends and look forward to lunch. We sit back and appreciate the aesthetic of the ritual, but as observers, not participants. Just look at the language the Jewish community uses in describing what we do on the holidays: we go to shul. We talk about "synagogue attendance." We don't talk about praying.

We Jews have gotten so disconnected from prayer that even some of our rabbis and scholars don't "get" prayer.

I earlier mentioned Psalm 102 which proclaims "A prayer of the afflicted when he is overwhelmed and pours out his complaint before God"—a verse which speaks of prayer as an expression from within, as a response to a person's personal circumstance. Yeshayahu Leibowitz, z"l, a great Israeli scientist and philosopher, points out that this is in direct opposition to prayer as we have it in the prayer book—direct opposition to what we are doing here today. Speaking of the prayer book prayers, Leibowitz says "It is obligatory and fixed. Consider what these two properties imply. As obligatory, it is not what a person desires but what is demanded of him; not prayer initiated by him, but one imposed on him. As fixed, it does not vary with the changing circumstances or states, objective or subjective, in which the praying individual finds himself. Hence it does not reflect the state of mind or situation of the praying person." Leibowitz claims that since no two people have the exact same needs at a given time, it's impossible that fixed prayer was *designed* to meet the spiritual needs of the person. The person who was married the day before and the person who buried his loved one the day before for the most part recite the same prayers. What's the sense in that? So for Leibowitz, the sole purpose of prayer is to prove that you are *kabbalat ohl shamayim*, you accept the yoke of the Kingdom of Heaven. You put aside your personal preferences to obey the commandment to pray in this fashion. Therefore it is meaningless to even ask questions like "was your prayer spiritually moving?" or "is prayer effective?" That's not the point. The point of prayer is simply to make a statement about your relationship with God.

What most of us find to be a great problem—a lack of a personally transcendent spiritual experience in prayer—Leibowitz finds to be a good thing.

He claims it reflects Judaism's total indifference to the individual! If so far today you have not been moved to tears in prayer, Leibowitz says, "don't worry! It's not SUPPOSED to do anything for you!"

What a ridiculous statement! Look, in Judaism we have enough mitzvot which are mysterious. Mitzvot that have no obvious purpose—such as the prohibition on wearing garments that contain a mixture of wool and linen. What the heck is wrong with wool and linen? But to take a commandment whose purpose IS obvious—prayer, which clearly is about communicating with God, in some way—and deny it, is such a shame as to be almost criminal!

Today is a perfect example of the problem we face in really praying. Very few Jews in North America understand Hebrew. I'm quite certain that fewer than 10% of the people here today understand the words we are saying. Which means the service is largely incomprehensible, and at four and a half hours in length, it seems interminable. The fact that some people WILL have a powerful spiritual experience today is far more surprising than the fact that most people do not. It's no surprise that most people come late, stay a little while—mostly for the ritual surrounding the Torah service and the sermon which is in English—and leave.

So what's to be done? In the effort to balance spirit and ritual to achieve something spiritual, we need to focus on the spirit. This, by the way, is not a new problem: in the Talmud, over 1500 years ago, the rabbis already debated the need to have spirit, (which they call *kavvanah*, or intent) before the ritual prayers (which they call the *keva*, which means "fixed"). Some rabbis insisted that you must have the spirit before engaging in the ritual. Some rabbis wouldn't pray for three days after returning from a trip, because they felt the burdens of the journey prevented them from having the proper spirit. Obviously, those rabbis lost the argument, and the ones who said we have to perform the ritual, whether or not we have the spirit, won out. But we need to go back to demanding of ourselves that we bring spirit to our ritual, that we have *kavvanah*.

For many of us, instead of opening our hearts to prayer, Hebrew school had the effect of silencing our natural instinct to prayer. It's like the story of a simple shepherd, who every day would offer his personal prayer to God: "God, I love you so much, that if you were here, I would give you half of my sheep. If it was raining and you were cold, I would share my blanket with you." One day a great rabbi was walking by the field, and he heard the shepherd praying. He ran up to him, and said "do you call that praying? Are you kidding? What would God do with your sheep? Of what use would a blanket be to God? Here, let me show you to pray properly before you further desecrate God's holy name!" The rabbi then got out a siddur, and gave a brilliant lecture on the structure and meaning of the various prayers, and explained what to say when to the poor illiterate shepherd. As soon as the rabbi left, the shepherd sat there dumbfounded. He didn't understand a word of it. But he knew the great rabbi was quite upset that his prayers were not proper. So he stopped praying.

For too many of us, that's where the story ends…fortunately for the shepherd, there IS more to HIS story…

Up in Heaven, God noticed the silence, and said "what happened to the beautiful prayers of my humble shepherd?" He decided to send an angel down to find out what was wrong. The angel found the shepherd, and the shepherd told him the whole story of his meeting with the rabbi. The angel said, "What does that rabbi know? Would you like to see how we pray in Heaven?" The shepherd instantly agreed and the angel whisked him off to Heaven, where he saw a Heavenly Host standing and proclaiming: "God, I love you so much, that if you were here, I would give you half of my sheep. If it was raining and you were cold, I would share my blanket with you." The shepherd happily went back to his prayers, and God happily listened.

If the heart of prayer is this kind of simple crying out to God, why do we need a fixed liturgy at all?

At its best, the fixed service can help us in our efforts to connect with God. Writing good religious poetry is truly an art. Just as not all of us are concert musicians, not all of us can write Psalms as moving as the ones attributed to King David. Just as hearing a beautiful concert can elicit certain feelings which reflect something in our own souls, saying beautiful words of prayer can do the same.

While we may all recite the same words in our prayers, they will resonate with us differently on different days. I have found that often a set prayer can express a feeling better than my own words. If I want to thank God for being with me, I might say something like "thanks, God, for being there for me." Yet when I recite Psalm 30, which reads "Lord, I cried out and You healed me. You saved me from the pit of death. Sing to the Lord you faithful, acclaiming his holiness. His anger lasts for a moment; His love is for a lifetime" I feel the words of King David do a better job of capturing what *I* feel than my own simple words.

The prayer service is one long guided meditation. It is designed to take us, in stages, through different aspects of our relationships with God, Israel, and Mankind. We prepare ourselves for prayer with a warm-up, by reciting psalms. We establish our relationship with God and recreate the revelation at Mt. Sinai when we say the Shema. The Amidah is the peak of the service, when we strive to achieve *devekut,* a cleaving with God. And we then have the closing part of the service, including Aleinu, as a way of gently taking leave, of cooling off, after an intense spiritual experience. The structured service takes us on a spiritual journey.

So how do we use the fixed liturgy as a way to talk to God?

Being aware of God's presence is the most fundamental principle in prayer. It's the point of prayer. The Talmud relates that when R. Eliezer was dying, he told his students, "when you are praying, *da lifnei mi atem omdim,* know before whom you are standing." As you recite your prayers, if you can keep in mind that you are in the presence of God, the words will have an entirely different feeling.

But how do we achieve that knowledge? Many books have been written on that subject, and all I can do this morning is give a few hints from within our tradition.

The Talmud tells us that a person should enter two doors into the synagogue, and then pray. What is meant by two doors? The distance of two door-widths. One of the Chabad rebbes explained that this means when you enter the synagogue, you should truly enter—leaving your worries, concerns, and distractions outside. When you come into the synagogue, use the physical transition as a reminder to make a spiritual transition—that you are now present in the House of God, and you are here to pray, to talk to God.

And how can you talk if you don't know what you are saying? If you don't fully understand Hebrew, make frequent use of the translation. The Hebrew language and the music may be majestic, but it won't be true prayer if you don't know what you are saying. The Talmud tells us that a person can pray in any language he understands, as God understands all languages.

Understanding the words helps, but by itself it's not enough. If it were, there would be no such thing as a secular Israeli. The Kotzker rebbe tells us that "a little with spirit, with *kavvanah,* is better than a lot without." Ten minutes of REAL praying, opening your heart to God and pouring out your dreams and fears before your Maker, will do more for you spiritually than four hours of sitting and being bored – OBVIOUSLY. Find something in the prayer book that speaks to you—whether it is a prayer, a psalm, or a reading—and stay with it, think about it, apply it to your life. Find words of religious poetry in that book that express what YOU feel.

I said earlier that prayer is about creating a relationship with God. Can you have a deep relationship with someone if you only talk to them once or twice a year? Remember when you were first in love, and needed to call (or email, or IM) your beloved at least three times a day, just to check in? That's why our tradition tells us to pray three times a day, every day. The path to intimacy comes through spending time together. One of the ways we spend time with God is through prayer.

Making prayer a daily thing can have a profound effect on your connection with the words. Rabbi Chaim HaLevy Donin said in his book To Pray as a Jew, "if I didn't pray three times a day because I was commanded to, I wouldn't know how to pray when I needed to." If you pray three times a day with the traditional liturgy, you will say the Amidah over 1000 times in one year. You develop a familiarity with the words, with the themes, that allows them to work as a guided meditation. But I do not recommend STARTING with saying the Amidah three times a day. I recommend starting with a heavier focus on the spirit than on the ritual. A great starting point is to say the Shema twice a day— even if it's just the six words of *Shema, Yisrael Hashem Elokeinu, Hashem Echad.* If you say them twice a day, and really focus on the meaning—Hear, O Israel, Hashem is OUR God, Hashem is ONE—it can serve as a way to remind you of God's presence in the world and in your life.

I also recommend a practice that the great Chasidic rebbe, Rebbe Nachman of Braslav prescribed. Rebbe Nachman tells us "It is very good to pour out one's thoughts before God, like a child pleading before its parent." He recommends simply talking to God, sharing with God what is in your heart in your own words as a spiritual practice. This is a form of Jewish meditation called *hitbodededut,* which literally would mean to be alone with yourself. R. Nachman suggests spending an hour a day in *hitbodedut.* If you don't have an hour, try it for ten or fifteen minutes. I've found it to be a very profound experience. In addition to setting a time for talking to God, you can cry out to

God whenever the spirit moves you: it can be a plea, like Moses' plea on behalf of Miriam, or it can even be an argument or challenge, like Abraham challenged God when told that God was going to destroy Sodom and Gomorrah.

I said earlier that prayer is about developing a relationship with God. A relationship implies a two way communication. When we pray, we talk to God. How do we hear God's reply? For Jews, the answer is studying Torah. When we study the wisdom of our tradition—whether it is in the Torah, in the Talmud, or in the words of contemporary teachers—we are straining to hear the word of God. It has been said "my cantor helps me talk to God, and my rabbi helps God talk to me."

When I find it difficult to talk to God—if I'm distracted, or distant, or agitated—I find it comforting to know that even someone on as high a spiritual level as King David sometimes had trouble praying. There is a line that we recite at the very beginning of every Amidah which King David said when he was having trouble praying: "*Hashem, s'ftai tiftach ufi yagid tehilatecha,*" God, open my lips and my mouth will recite your praises. Sometimes the best way to start praying is to ask for God's help in praying.

Shanah Tovah

Linking the Physical and the Spiritual

The ideal in Judaism is not to separate from the physical – rather it is to elevate the physical. Naso 5765.

There are no Jewish monasteries. As much as we Jews love Torah, there are no places where Jews go to take a vow of poverty, forsake wine, women, and song, and live in seclusion. Jews are supposed to be engaged in the world around us, not separated from it.

There's a rabbi in the Talmud, Ben Azzai, who loved studying Torah to the exclusion of anything else in his life. He didn't have time to get married and raise a family; he was consumed with studying Torah. His colleagues told him "Some preach well and act well, others act well but do not preach well; you, however, preach well but do not act well!" You give great sermons about the importance of obeying the commandments, like "be fruitful and multiply," but you don't follow them! Ben Azzai replied, "What can I do? My soul is in love with the Torah, the world can be carried on by others." His colleagues chastised him. They said anyone who does not try to have children is like someone who sheds blood! Obviously, they don't mean it literally: but it shows the importance attached to being a part of the world, not set apart from it. What if the Messiah is destined to be descended from you and you refuse to even try and have children?

The closest we come to a monk is the *nazir*, which is described in this week's Torah portion, Naso. The Nazir takes a vow not to drink wine or eat grapes or grape products, or drink other strong drink; he vows not to cut his hair, and not to become *tamei*, ritually impure, through contact with a dead person. Note that being celibate is not part of the mix, neither is renouncing any other worldly pleasures. Unless otherwise specified, the period for being a nazir is thirty days. There is one example given in the Bible of a life-long nazir, and that's Samson—but he's a special case.

In some places, such as the midrash Bamidbar Rabbah, the nazir is called *kadosh*, holy. In other places the nazir is called a *chotei*, a sinner. We can readily see why a nazir might be called *kadosh*—here he is taking a vow to elevate himself, to separate himself in a special for service to God. But why should he be called a sinner?

When a person completed the period of their naziriteship they had a ritual to complete. The Torah says "And this is the Torah of the Nazirite, when the days of his separation are fulfilled; he shall be brought to the door of the Tent of Meeting; And he shall offer his offering to the Lord, one male lamb of the first year without blemish for a burnt offering, and one ewe lamb of the first year without blemish for a sin offering, and one ram without blemish for peace offerings."

Among the offerings the nazir brings is a sin offering. Here's the answer to our question: he has to bring a sin offering, so he must be a sinner. But what's his sin?

The Talmud tells us that the reason the nazir has to bring a sin offering is because he denied himself wine – one of God's blessings to man. In Pirkei Avot it says "All that the Holy One, Blessed is He, created in His world, He created solely for His glory (Avot 6:11)." When we refuse to drink wine, it is as if we are refusing to partake of some of God's good bounty that he has provided for us! It seems like an attitude of ingratitude, not appreciating the good things God is providing. The rabbis tell us that "it's enough what the Torah forbids." You don't need to add to what the Torah forbids and deny yourself wine.

If that's the case, why do we have the option for being a nazir at all? It seems just a little strange to give someone the option to do something, and then call him a sinner for doing it.

We can often find connections between disparate subjects by looking at the way the Torah is laid out. The section about the nazir comes right after the section for the sotah. The sotah was a woman who had been secluded with a man other than her husband. The husband got jealous, but he couldn't prove that his wife had done something wrong. The Torah calls for the woman to be subjected to a degrading ritual, involving drinking water mixed with dirt from the floor of the temple, and exposing her hair, and tearing her clothes, which was supposed to prove whether the wife was innocent or guilty of infidelity. The priest announced that if she was guilty her thigh would sag and her belly would swell and she would die—and she had to respond "Amen." The commentators say that the reason the teachings about the nazir come right after the passage about the sotah is that when someone saw the disgrace of the sotah, he would swear off wine and strong drink. Obviously, she must have been drinking if she committed such an indiscretion! It would be like someone today deciding to give up drinking entirely after watching someone get in a car accident because they were driving while drunk.

The Rama, a medieval Torah commentator, says that God doesn't mind if someone drinks wine in a responsible manner. He says that the nazir vow exists for those who are afraid that they are going to sin because of drink—in other words, it's for people who have a drinking problem. Someone who is an alcoholic needs to refrain from wine completely. Alcoholics Anonymous insists that participants refrain from wine and strong drink 100%. An alcoholic generally can't manage "social drinking." For someone with an alcohol problem, one drink all too often leads to another leads to another leads to another. Such people need to abstain from all hard drink—and that's why we have the vow of the nazir.

Maimonides, Rambam, teaches that the ideal is the "middle way," to enjoy things in moderation; but sometimes, for example when someone is sick, he may need to go to one extreme or another. Someone seriously overweight may need to go on a very low calorie diet for health reasons, even though in general, moderation is what is best.

There are times when someone may need to refrain from wine and alcohol because of a problem, but they are still considered a "sinner" in a sense because they need to forgo a permitted pleasure. Rambam tells us that when we die we will be held accountable for all permitted pleasures that we denied ourselves! God wants us to enjoy the good things of this world.

You might be thinking this whole discussion does not apply to you. Perhaps you are part of the vast majority of adult Jews who drink responsibly—a glass of wine with Friday night dinner, but nothing to excess—just where it seems we are supposed to be.

The problem is that simply being a responsible drinker is not enough.

According to the way Jewish mysticism understands the world, our mission is to bring holiness into the world. I think of it as a spiritual path where what we are trying to do is to elevate our "God-consciousness," our awareness of God in our lives and in our world. The Slonimer rebbe teaches that the goal of serving God is to join the things of below—of this world—to the things above, to God. They teach that even when we are engaged in mundane activities in this world, we should do them in the name of heaven. The proper spiritual path is to take the things from this world and elevate them and sanctify them to the Holy One.

Chovat Halvavot, The Obligations of the Heart, a mussar (Jewish ethics) text takes this teaching to another level. According to Chovat Halvavot there is no such thing as something that is merely "permitted." The world is divided into two sides—*mitzvah* and *aveirah*—the commanded and the sin, the good and the bad. If we are not doing something in a way that is a mitzvah—if we are not elevating things in a positive way, we are doing something bad. There is no neutral. It's like biology: if you're not growing you're dying, there is no sitting still. The same principle applies in business.

Does this mean that the ONLY time one should have a glass of wine is when it's part of an "official celebration," a *seudat mitzvah*, like Shabbat dinner?

No. Enjoying God's bounty with a glass of wine with dinner is fine. How do we make it a mitzvah, how do we make it an activity whereby we are joining together the things of this world with the world above? By remembering to say a blessing beforehand. When we make a bracha, when we pause for a moment to say the *borei pri hagafen* blessing before drinking a glass of wine, when we pause a moment to say the *motzi* before eating bread, we are giving ourselves a reminder of God's presence, and we are joining together the things of this world with their spiritual source, with God.

And if you can't remember the exact formula of a blessing to say, it doesn't matter. In the Talmud Yerushalmi, tractate Brachot, R. Meir says that even if someone makes something up, like *baruch sh'barach hachofetz hazeh mah naeh hu,* "Blessed is the one who created this nice stuff," he has fulfilled his obligation to say a blessing.

There are commentators who say that the nazir's sin is being a show off—by not cutting his hair, not drinking wine, as if he's saying "look how pious I am!" This reminds me of a story. One Yom Kippur the rabbi cries out "I am nothing but dust and ashes," and falls on the floor. The cantor then cries out "I am nothing but dust and ashes" and falls to the floor. Then Goldstein in the back stands up, and cries out "I am nothing but dust and ashes!" The rabbi turns to the cantor and says, "Look who thinks he's nothing but dust and ashes!" Koehler, Ecclesiastes, says *al tiyeh tzadik harbeh,* don't be overly righteous. From looking at the sotah, however, we also learn don't be "underly righteous." Be moderate. And remember to thank God, and through thanking God and thinking of God we elevate the physical things of this world to a higher level.

As the lyrics to the Police song go, "We are spirits in the material world." But we are not disembodied spirits. The best path is to connect the physical with the spiritual.

Shabbat Shalom.

PART II: TORAH

This section will explore the nature of Torah, and the ethical and religious teachings we glean from Torah.

Chapter Four

The Nature of Torah

"Ben Bag Bag said: turn it (the Torah) and turn it again, for everything can be found within it; and look into it, and become grey and old in it; don't move away from it, for there is no better standard of conduct than the Torah."

Mishnah, Avot 5:22

The Torah is the "Constitution" of the Jewish people – it is, as Rabbi Joel Roth describes it—the "grundnorm" for the Jews, the basis for our legal system, in fact the basis for our beliefs overall. The next few essays elaborate on my belief that the Torah is a holy partnership between God and Man which contains the answers to life's important questions.

The Gift of Torah
This was a talk presented on parshat Yitro 5765, at the Kabbalat HaSiddur for the third grade Hebrew school class.

The most precious gift from God to the Jewish people is the Torah.

When we put the Torah away, we sing a song calling it a "tree of life to all who cling to it." The mystics say that the Torah sustains the entire world and that it contains all the secrets of the universe, of the worlds above as well as our world.

In this week's Torah portion, Yitro, we read the story of God giving the Torah to the Jewish people. Moses climbs the mountain, God descends to the mountain, and there, in one of the most important moments in the spiritual history of the world, God gives Moses the Ten Commandments, engraved on two stone tablets, symbolizing their eternal significance.

It is said that the Torah is God's most precious possession. If you were going to lend your most precious possession to someone, you'd probably want some kind of security, some kind of pledge, so that you know they would take good care of it. When someone who is poor wants to borrow money from the bank, the bank will often require a co-signer. A guarantor that the loan will be paid.

There is a midrash (Shir haShirim Raba 1:3) that says when God was ready to give Her most precious gift, the Torah, to the Jewish people, She also wanted a "guarantor." God said "I'm giving you my precious Torah, bring me a good guarantor, and I'll give it to you." The people of Israel said, "we'll give you our ancestors, Abraham, Isaac, and Jacob, Sarah, Rebecca, Rachel, and Leah, they'll vouch for us and be our guarantors." God said, "what kind of guarantors are they?"

"You're promising to give me something which is already mine. They are already committed to me. You give your ancestors, who have already lived and died serving me, and you haven't given me anything." So the people tried again. They said, "how about the prophets?" God said "the prophets! Forget it. I've got some real problems with some of those prophets. Look at what it says in Jeremiah, 'the prophets prophesied by Baal,' a false idol. I'm not going to take the prophets as your guarantor." So the people tried again. "Master of the Universe, our CHILDREN will be our guarantors." God responded, "now you're talking! Your children will make a great guarantor. For their sake, I will give you the Torah."

What makes children acceptable to God as a guarantor, as a promise, when our ancestors and our prophets were not?

God is giving us His most precious possession-the Torah. The only worthy guarantor, therefore, would have to be OUR most precious possession—our children.

But there is another reason. Why does God want a guarantor for the Torah? It's because what God wants is that the Torah will continue.

Torah is NOT something that's all God. Torah represents a connection between God and Man-as symbolized by the connection between God and Moses at Mt. Sinai. The care that God wants taken is that we will keep that connection alive. God wants to know that Torah will continue to be a bridge between God and Man. And if Torah is going to be a bridge between God and Man, our ancestors can't guarantee that this will be the case-it's not enough that your great-grandfather was a rabbi. Our prophets can't guarantee Torah will continue to be a bridge between God and Man—people have ignored prophets ever since they started prophesying. The only thing that can assure that Torah will continue to connect the Jewish people to God is our children.

The last Lubavitcher Rebbe, Menachem Mendel Schneerson, z"l, said that we relive this Midrash all the time here in America. At a farbrengen, a Chasidic gathering and discourse, he said "You go to a Jew who is not observant—a little traditional but not very religiously observant. And you ask him, "So what about the Torah? You're a Yid. Do you learn Torah?" He says, "Torah? I have a father who's eighty years old and he's in a religious nursing home and he has a *shiur* (lesson) three times a day. Isn't that enough? My father's such a religious Jew." And he'll point to his dining room and he'll show you a picture of his *zeide* (grandfather) in Europe with a long white beard.

When you tell him that this is good for his father, but what about him? Then the American Jew says, "Well, what about my Rabbi? You should see my Rabbi. He can daven Minchah by heart, without a siddur even. He's such a *tzaddik*, so righteous. And I've seen him rattle off verses from the Torah. I pay his salary. And my father in the old-age home, I pay for him there. So I have a portion in my father's Gemara (Talmud) in the nursing home and I have a portion in my Rabbi's sermons. He's so learned, he gives such nice sermons, and I pay my dues."

Neither the father's Gemara nor the rabbi's sermons works for assuring that Torah will continue to connect Jews with God in the future. If no one picks it up from your father or your rabbi, that will be the end of the line. For Torah to continue to be alive, for Torah to continue to nourish the Jewish people as it has for thousands of years, it needs to be handed down, *ldor vador*, from generation to generation. You need to take it yourself—and now I'm talking to the parents, not the children. Each of us needs to be engaged in Torah. Studying Torah doesn't only mean reading the parsha of the week, or trying to study some Talmud. If you read "The Jewish Book of Why," or Joseph Telushkin's "Jewish Literacy," or Anita Diamant's "The Red Tent," or Rodger Kamenetz' "The Jew and the Lotus" you are studying Torah—you are learning and growing in your knowledge of Torah, and through Torah your knowledge of God.

Today we have our third grade class here for the ceremony of "Kabbalat Hasiddur," the receiving of the siddur. This Shabbat is especially chosen for Kabbalat Hasiddur because it is the Shabbat where we read about the giving of the Torah. By giving our children their own siddurs today, we are proving to God that our children are our guarantors-that we are fulfilling our ancestors' commitment, and our commitment, to pass on the tradition to the next generation. As we recited in the Shema a little while ago, "and these words which I command you this day, you shall take to heart. You shall diligently teach them to your children."

If we take these words to heart ourselves, and strive to grow in Jewish learning and observance, our children will also take them to heart, and they will pass it on to their children, and we will find that today has been simply one day in a long chain going back to Moses at Mt. Sinai and stretching forward to as long as the Jews exist as a people.

May we as a community continue to fulfill the words we said earlier this morning in the Amidah: "*l'dor v'dor nagid godlecha*," from generation to generation we will tell of Your greatness.

Amen.

Who Wrote the Bible?

Usually I don't give all that much thought to "Biblical Criticism" and the debates over when different strands in the Bible were written. I'm much more interested in what the rabbis have to say about what's in the Torah than I am about who wrote what. But sometimes the scholars come up with some useful teachings. Delivered Bamidbar 5762.

As a general rule, I am NOT a big fan of the critical-scholarly approach to Bible studies. The scholarly approach for the most part is interested in dissecting the Torah and trying to figure out when different pieces were edited, and by whom, and it looks for analogs in other cultures, etc.

It's not that I disagree with the so-called "documentary hypothesis"— the idea that the Torah was edited by a number of different people over many years. I don't. It's just that for the most part those scholastic contemplations are not terribly relevant to my reading of Torah.

I do not read Torah the way I would read a history book. I do not look to the Torah to tell me with a great deal of historical accuracy what actually happened on any particular day. Instead, I read the Torah looking for the eternal truths about people, especially the Jewish people, and our relationship with God, and how God wants us to conduct our lives. As such, the collected wisdom of our sages, who have commented on the Torah for the last several thousand years, are generally of much greater interest to me. I am more interested in the MEANING of the Torah than the HISTORY of the Torah.

Conservative Judaism is a pluralistic movement. Within the movement we have some people whose theology is close to Reform: Torah is the work of people, perhaps "divinely inspired," but definitely the work of people. There are also people in the Conservative movement who have a view of Torah that is close to what is typical of Orthodoxy: God gave the Torah to Moses at Mt. Sinai, and it contains the literal word of God.

I do believe in a certain mystical sense that God contracted God-self, and God is found in the Torah. I also believe, on an intellectual level, that the

Torah records the history of our people as legend; most episodes in the Torah probably have some basis in truth, but have been elaborated on by story tellers up until the final editing. I do believe that there was a special encounter between God and the Jewish people through the spiritual giant Moses at Mt. Sinai over 3,000 years ago.

This week's Torah portion provides an example of a way in which the critical scholarly approach can be valuable in enhancing our understanding of the Torah. This week we read parsha Bamidbar, the first parsha in the book of Numbers. The Torah records that 603,550 men of fighting age went out from Egypt.

This is a very challenging number. 600,000 fighting men would extrapolate to a total population of over 2 million people wandering around the desert. A rather incredible number, very hard to believe. Surely 2 million people wandering around the desert would have left some kind of archeological record. How could they all have been supported in the desert? Questions like this lead some to say the Exodus never happened.

A critical approach to the text however, can lead us to a way out of this quandary. As Gunther Plaut points out in his commentary on the Bible, the word *"elef,"* in modern Hebrew, the number 1,000, can also have another meaning. It is not unreasonable to translate *elef* as troop, or platoon. The same word with different vowels, is *"ahloof"* which means chief, or in modern Hebrew, general. Instead, we could read the text as originally saying there were 600 platoons—perhaps with ten men to each—for a total of about 6,000 fighting men, and a total entourage of perhaps 20,000 people. Later editors of the Torah, taking *elef* for thousand, not troop, made some editorial changes to make other verses consistent with this reading.

Twenty thousand people in the desert is a far more believable number. Twenty thousand nomads, living a low-tech low-impact lifestyle, might not have made big troves of easy to find archeological artifacts. Six thousand troops is consistent with what scholars say would have been a reasonable size fighting force in that day and age.

There are those who totally avoid the critical scholarly approach. They say that analyzing the Torah in this way will lead people to lose faith in the validity of Torah, to lose faith in God.

I disagree. Knowing that there is a reasonable explanation to bring the numbers in this week's parsha into line with a more reasonable and believable figure strengthens my faith in the Torah. It strengthens my faith that the Torah contains a record of our people based on actual events, even though the details may vary, as in any story told over and over again for a period of a few thousand years.

May we all succeed in growing our faith in the Torah, especially this week as we approach the holiday of Shavuot when we celebrate God giving the Torah over to the Jewish people. Whether or not all the details recorded around this event are accurate—whether it happened with lightning and thunder and Moses fasting for 40 days—is not nearly so important as the fact that it happened. God gave us the Torah, and that is plenty of cause for celebration.

Shabbat Shalom

5,422 Pages of the Babylonian Talmud

If you want to understand Judaism, it's more important to study the Talmud than to study the Torah. The Talmud is a vast work – even most rabbis only study selections. This is a talk I gave after completing the seven and a half year long cycle of reading the entire Babylonian Talmud in the spring of 2005.

Over three thousand years ago, there was a gathering of the Jewish people to study Torah. This week's Torah portion, Vayakhel, opens with the words:

> "And Moses gathered all the congregation of the people of Israel together and said to them, These are the words which the Lord has commanded, that you should do them."

This past Tuesday night I was at another gathering of the people of Israel. I was in New York City, at Madison Square Garden, fulfilling a promise I made to myself seven and a half years ago, before I had even decided to become a rabbi.

Seven and a half years ago I was living in the San Francisco Bay Area, working as an executive for a high-tech company. We were relatively observant, and were regular shul goers, but my Hebrew abilities were pretty marginal. Sure, I could recite the prayers, but I didn't really understand what they meant. I had started going to a once a week Talmud class given by a Chabad rabbi, and I took an online Introduction to Talmud course offered by JTS, but I certainly couldn't study a page of Talmud without an English translation in front of me.

I read an article in the local Jewish newspaper about this huge celebration that was held in Madison Square Garden where thousands of Jews were gathered together to celebrate completing the study of the entire Babylonian Talmud. They had all completed a program called the "Daf Yomi." In the Daf Yomi program you study a daf (two sided page) of Talmud every day, and in seven and a half years you can complete the study of the entire Talmud. I read about that celebration, and having recently celebrated Simchat Torah and enjoying the feeling of completion that comes when you read the whole Torah, even in translation, I decided I was going to give it a shot. I decided that I was going to start doing this Daf Yomi program, I was going to study a page of Talmud every day, and in seven and a half years I was going to go to Madison Square Garden to be a part of the next celebration.

So on Tuesday night, I was there. Having studied 5,422 pages of dense Aramaic, I was enjoying my reward of being a part of that crowd celebrating the completion of the study of the Talmud. What I would like to do this morning is share with you some of the things I learned and some of the things I felt at this amazing gathering of Jews.

First, by way of background, a word on why the Talmud is so important. Why do we make such a big deal over the Talmud? It's because it is really in many ways the heart of Judaism. If you want to know what Judaism is all about, and you are only going to turn to one source, that source would not be the Torah—it would be the Talmud. For the Talmud contains the rabbis understanding of how we apply all those teachings in the Torah. The Torah tells us to observe the Sabbath—but the Talmud tells us what that means and how to do it. All the things we do to make Shabbat Shabbat: lighting candles on Friday night, saying blessings over wine and bread, blessing our children, enjoying a nice meal with friends and family—these are all things we learn NOT from the Torah, but from the Talmud. The Talmud has law, legend, superstition, and a unique way of approaching the world. In the Talmud you learn how to argue well, and you learn to respect other opinions. One of the things I love about studying Talmud is that it feels like "intellectual archeology." When I study a page of Talmud I feel like I'm sitting in the study hall with these great rabbis listening to both their legal arguments and their personal anecdotes.

On Tuesday I got some more anecdotes to add to my personal Talmud. My feeling of connection to other Jews started right when I got on the subway at 72nd street—there were a few "black hats" sitting near me, discussing which subway stop to get off for Madison Square Garden. When we got to our stop at Penn Station it was already quite an interesting sight to see—hundreds of Orthodox Jews all walking in the same direction, all streaming toward the Garden. The only other time I've been part of something like that was on Shavuot in Jerusalem, where, at 4 in the morning, Jews from all over the city are walking toward the Western Wall after being up all night studying.

Madison Square Garden was full—it was a sold out house. 30,000 Jews. Not only were there 30,000 of us at the Garden, but we were linked electronically via satellite with large screen displays with similar gatherings in other places—Continental Arena in Newark, as well as gatherings in places like Chicago, Detroit, Los Angeles, and for the first time since the Holocaust, Jews in the home of the Daf Yomi idea, Lublin, Poland, also celebrated the *siyum* (completion). All together there were 100,000 Jews all studying the same piece of Torah together at the same time, linked in person and electronically.

The story told in this week's Torah portion – that Moses gathered the people together and told them what God commanded, in other words they studied Torah together – took place at Mt. Sinai. One of the speakers at the siyum, the Bostoner Rebbe, observed our gathering of 100,000 was the biggest crowd to be together all studying the same piece of Torah, since that gathering at Mt. Sinai. Now there's an amazing idea!

Madison Square Garden was turned into the world's largest Orthodox synagogue, with men on the main floor and lower levels and women up in the balcony. We started with saying the afternoon prayers. The intention and focus of the prayer leader was amazing: he was clearly on the verge of tears several times during the repetition of the Amidah, he truly had his whole heart in the words he was saying as he was praying for our communal health, prosperity, and ingathering from exile. Saying "Amen" together with 30,000 other Jews is definitely something to experience.

I was reminded of the teaching from Proverbs (14:28) "In the multitude of people is the King's Glory" which is elaborated on in the Talmud

(Brachot 53a) where we learn that it's better that people should pray together, rather than each one pray for himself, because "In the multitude of people is the King's glory."

The Daf Yomi program is a relatively recent innovation. It was started by Rabbi Meir Shapira, the rabbi of Lublin, Poland, in 1923. Jews had been studying Talmud since before it was written down; Rabbi Shapira's innovation was to suggest a schedule whereby Jews all over the world would study the same page of Talmud on a given day, which would allow someone who was traveling to find other people to study with who were studying the same page of Talmud. The idea caught on, leading to the most recent completion of the cycle.

In 1923, Europe was the great center for Jewish learning. In those days before the Holocaust, the vast majority of the world's great scholars in Jewish learning were in Europe. The celebration of the siyum was made in honor of the 6 million Jews who perished in the Holocaust, and especially to honor the Torah scholars and learning that was lost. In honor of the European roots of the Daf Yomi, several of the speakers at the siyum spoke in Yiddish. I had to buy one of the $10 headsets over which they provided a simultaneous translation to understand what they were saying. R. Chaskel Beser said in his introduction that when he first came to America 60 years ago they called it a *"treife medina,"* an "impure land." He said he never imagined there would be 100,000 Jews in America all celebrating completing the Talmud.

There are some Jews who believe that the days of the Messiah, the era of great peace and harmony, will be preceded by a very difficult period, the "birthpangs of the Messiah." Not unlike what we went through with the Holocaust. There is a teaching in the Talmud which says one famous rabbi said he did not want to see the Messiah, because he did not want to have to live through the preceding painful period. R. Chaim Stein from the Telshe Yeshiva in Cleveland said that the creation of the Daf Yomi program was a Jewish preparation for the difficult days ahead in the Holocaust. R. Stein said the way we prepare for difficult days is by studying Torah and doing acts of kindness. He said it is the responsibility of every Jew who survived the Holocaust to help rebuild Torah, to learn and study, and rebuild the learning that was destroyed by the Nazis.

R. Stein started doing the Daf Yomi in 1938. He was given the honor of doing the actual siyum, the actual teaching completing our studying the last page of the Talmud.

We're now going to do our own siyum, we will study the last teaching in the Talmud. I'm very glad so many of you were able to come today to help me celebrate!

And the completion of the Talmud is your party too. Just as many of you are here to help Alexx celebrate a milestone in her Jewish learning—her bat mitzvah—the completion of the Daf Yomi cycle is a celebration for all Jews as well.

One of the speakers, Rabbi Hershkowitz, shared an interesting story. He said someone approached him a few days before the siyum, saying he was thinking of going, but thought that perhaps he shouldn't because he didn't study the whole Talmud so it's not his party. The rabbi said, "no, of course you should go (if you can get a ticket). This is a celebration for all Israel. The ones who didn't complete help the ones who did celebrate. We are all "*machatunim*" (parents of the bride and groom)."

So here we go, completing the Talmud:

The last teaching in the Talmud (Niddah 73a) says:

"The Tanna debe Eliyahu [teaches]: Whoever learns halachas, Jewish teachings, every day is assured that he will have a place in the World To Come, for it is said, *Halikoth* — the world is his; (Chabakuk 3:6) read not *halikoth* but *halakoth*."

The Tanna brings proof from a verse that by learning some halacha, something about Jewish law every day you are assured a place in the world to come. In a way this passage is the foundation for the great reverence that Jews have traditionally placed on learning—which may be one reason why we are so over-represented in professions that rely on learning, like law, medicine, and science.

R. Stein tied this to a teaching from the Tur, a 14th century code of Jewish law: After beginning the day at services in the synagogue followed by a period of Torah study, we are to go off to work, "because Torah without a livelihood will eventually come undone and turn into sin. For if we have nothing to eat, poverty will soon bring us to violate God's word. Nevertheless, we ought not to make our livelihood primary but secondary. The study of Torah should be the center of our lives as it was for the early pietists, who made their livelihood secondary and the study of Torah primary and both flourished" (Orah Hayyim 156).

The ideal for a Jew traditionally has been to combine Torah with *derech eretz*, to combine learning with making a living—but you should remember that learning is the thing that's really important.

It's difficult to make time to study every day. During the last seven and a half years I've learned to squeeze in a few minutes of learning Talmud on coffee breaks, at lunch, on occasion even when stuck in traffic. All too often I do some learning at 11:30 at night when my mind is not at its sharpest.

But our rabbis teach that this is the path not only to eternal life, but to a better life in this world. Now there are some people who say, well, I'm too busy now, I'll study ...and insert your favorite future time here: when the kids are all back to school, when I get the next promotion, when I make partner, when I retire. But to that the great rabbi Hillel said, "do not say I will study when I have leisure, for perhaps you will never have leisure."

Reverence for study and learning Torah is something that binds all Jews together. Several of the speakers pointed out this was a great celebration of *Clal Yisrael*, of all the people of Israel. They spoke about how there were Ashkenazi and Sefardi Jews, Chassidic Jews, Jews from all over the world celebrating together. One harsh note for me, however, was when R. Shmuel Bloom, the Exec VP of Agudath Israel said "we have Jews who go to Agudath synagogues, who go to Chasidic synagogues, who go to OU synagogues all together." Not mentioning at all that there were also Jews there—at least one—who goes to a Conservative synagogue!

But in a way I can't blame him—mine was a lonely grey hat in a sea of black hats.

There are three times as many Conservative Jews than Orthodox Jews in America. Torah is just as much our legacy as it is their legacy. Torah is the spiritual heritage of all Jews, regardless of what kind of synagogue you go to. Yet the Orthodox managed to fill Madison Square Garden with people who studied the entire Talmud. We could probably fit all the Conservative Jews who studied the entire Talmud in the last seven and half years comfortably into our chapel, let alone this sanctuary.

Seven and a half years ago, reading about other people completing the Daf Yomi inspired me to do the same. I'm hoping that my sharing the story of completing the Daf will inspire you to do the same. The last seven and a half years have been a time of amazing learning for me, and I hope the next seven and a half years will be a time of amazing learning for all of us.

R. Hershkowitz talked about how he never finishes a lesson with the end of a chapter—he always leaves a little something over, or starts something else. You should not be content that you finished a chapter—or that you finished the whole *shas*, the whole Talmud. You need to start over, keep going.

I hope that Alexx today feels the way I did on Tuesday night. Not a feeling of "wow, I did it, I'm done," but rather a feeling of "nice milestone—now let's keep learning." Because for a Jew, learning is a lifelong enterprise. It's just like exercise and diet. If you go on a diet and start working out every day, you can feel good when you reach your goal. But if you quit working out, you're going to get fat again. Reaching your goal does not mean you're done and finished and can sit on your tuchas.

So having just finished the Talmud, let's start over.

The very first teaching in the Talmud, Brachot 2a, says "From when do we recite the evening Shema?" Rabbi Hershkowitz brought a teaching from the Yerushalmi, the Palestinian Talmud, which focuses on the word "korin," recites. The word is written in the plural form. Why is it written in the plural form? To teach us that everyone must recite the Shema for himself—it's not enough to have someone else say it for you.

It's the same way with Jewish learning. You can't have someone else do it for you. Not your spouse and definitely not your rabbi. We all need to do our own learning and take ownership of it. If you want to start studying the Daf Yomi, Artscroll has a great English translation of the whole thing, with explanatory footnotes that make it possible to study on your own. You can buy it a volume at a time—and you'll go through a volume every six weeks or so. There are also great resources available on the internet.

Another speaker, Rabbi Frand, said last time there were 50,000 people celebrating the siyum, this time there were 100,000. He said a big part of the reason why is the inspiration of this event. Studying the Talmud is not elitist anymore. He said when people see their friends doing it, they get an attitude of "if you can do it, I can too." Nothing encourages people like the knowledge that other people are doing it too, there's a real ripple effect. I did it, I at least got started, when I was a lay person, just like you. You can do it too. God willing, in seven and a half years there will be a lot more "gray hats" at Madison Square Garden.

If studying the whole Talmud seems too ambitious for you, pick something else. If you read a chapter of the Tanakh, the Hebrew Bible every day—something which takes about five or ten minutes—in two and a half years you will have read the whole thing. Or pick up a contemporary Jewish book and read a little something from it every day.

May God strengthen us in our efforts to learn and to teach and to grow. May the Torah we learn inspire us to deeds of charity and kindness and to more learning.

Amen.

Chapter Five

Ethics: Taking Care of Others

"And the Lord said to Cain, Where is Abel your brother? And he said, I know not; Am I my brother's keeper?"

Genesis 4:9

Most secular legal systems are very concerned with individual rights. The United States Declaration of Independence begins "We declare these rights to be self evident…" Judaism takes a very different approach. As a religion, it is not so concerned with rights – it is much more concerned with responsibilities. God never answers Cain's question; however, we all know what God's answer would be, don't we?

Giving Charity

I was surprised at how controversial this sermon was – many people are uncomfortable with giving money to beggars. It was delivered at Ki Tisa 5765, a refinement of a similar talk I gave previously in Richmond.

"And Aaron said to them, Take off the golden ear rings, which are in the ears of your wives, of your sons, and of your daughters, and bring them to me. And all the people took off the golden ear rings which were in their ears, and brought them to Aaron."

Exodus 32:2-3

"Speak to the people of Israel, that they bring me an offering; from every man that gives it willingly with his heart you shall take my offering."

Exodus 25:2

In this week's parsha, Aaron asks the people to make a donation for the Golden Calf…and they give. In the Torah portion we read a few weeks ago, the people were asked to make a donation for the Tabernacle, the "portable Temple"…and they gave.

In the Yerushalmi Talmud, Bar Acha comments on this: "It's impossible to understand the character of this nation: they were asked to give for the Golden Calf and they gave; they were asked to give for the Tabernacle, and they gave!"

Is this a bad thing? Jews are among the most philanthropic of people—we're big givers! Is it so bad if we're sometimes a little indiscriminate?

Here in Toledo we don't seem to have a lot of panhandlers. At least not in the parts of town that I frequent. Maybe the homeless people prefer bigger cities like Cleveland or Detroit where there are more resources…or maybe they move south to Florida for the winter: I would if I were homeless! However, we've all traveled to places like New York where there are panhandlers all over the place.

When you go to a place like New York where there are many panhandlers, how do you treat them? Do you avoid giving money to any of them? Or do you give to all of them? Are you likelier to give to a woman? To someone with a child? To someone with a sign like "Need help. Willing to work. God Bless." How about a sign that says "Hungry, need food?" What if the person looks like they have a drug or alcohol problem?

Many people act very judgmental in a situation like this. They either give to the one who is willing to work because it seems that at least he's trying. Or they give to women but not men, or refuse to give anything to someone who looks like he might use it on drugs or liquor (or as my daughter Katherine suggested in our discussion during services, some look like they are spending their money on body piercings!).

Our tradition, however, teaches us not to be so picky. According to the Rambam (Maimonides), "Anyone who sees a poor person asking for money who turns his eyes away and doesn't give him *tzedakah* (charity) transgresses a negative commandment, as it is written, do not harden your heart, and do not close your hand from your poor brother."

It is important to note that in formulating this commandment, Rambam tells us that not only does a person fail to fulfill a positive commandment to give tzedakah, but rather he violates a negative commandment, which is a more serious thing.

As a general rule, there is no penalty (at least not in this world!) attached to failing to fulfill a positive commandment. You are supposed to light Shabbat candles, but if you don't, even in the days when the Jewish courts had jurisdiction over every aspect of Jewish life, you wouldn't have been penalized or punished.

Violating a negative commandment is a different thing entirely. Unless otherwise specified, the penalty for violating a negative commandment was to receive lashes. Rambam taught that turning your eyes away from a poor person is a serious enough transgression to merit lashes.

You might argue, well, what if you're poor yourself? What if you need help yourself? Do you still have to give?

The Talmud answers this question for us as well. In tractate Gittin, 7b it says: "Even a poor man, a subject of charity, should give charity."

What if you don't have any change? What do you do then? Rambam tells us if you don't happen to have any money in your pocket, you should at least give the beggar a smile and a kind word. When I see people looking for work, and I don't have work, sometimes I'll tell them that I'm sorry I don't have any work for them.

As you evaluate whether to give money to different kinds of people, it might enter your mind to consider whether it makes any difference if you think the beggar is Jewish or not. Again, the Talmud in tractate Gittin provides some guidance: "Poor Gentiles should be supported along with poor Jews; the Gentile sick should be visited along with the Jewish sick; and their dead should be buried along with the Jewish dead, *mipnei darchei shalom*, for these are the ways of peace." There is, however, also a teaching that if your money is limited, it is OK to prioritize how much you give to different people, with family taking precedence over strangers, Jews over non-Jews, people from your town over people from another town, etc. But you still should give at least a little something to everyone.

We have been invited by the Multi Faith Council of Northwest Ohio to participate in a Habitat for Humanity build, a program through which volunteers donate time and money to actually build a house for a poor family. I am working with a few people who are interested, and I hope we will have critical mass to participate. As we learned from the Talmud, we need to contribute to the non-Jews in our community as well. In the past I know there was some question about participating in a build if the Muslim community is involved because of our political differences with them, and their refusal to condemn terrorism. But if we refuse to participate in building a Habitat house because of that, who are we penalizing? The Muslim community or the poor family that the Multi-Faith Council is trying to help? If you are interested in participating in a Habitat build, please contact me.

But, back to beggars. What if you think the beggar is being lazy? Is it OK to question why he doesn't have a job? Why doesn't he take advantage of the many resources the government provides? What if you think he might use your money to buy booze or drugs?

Rabbi Shmelke of Nicholsburg tells us, "When a poor man asks you for aid, do not use his faults as an excuse for not helping him. For then God will look for your offenses, and He is sure to find many of them. Keep in mind that the poor man's transgressions have been atoned for by his poverty while yours still remain with you."

We're not appointed the judge over every poor person who comes our way. It's not your job to determine whether every beggar you meet truly deserves your support or not. But, you might counter, it's one thing to give money to a real poor person who might misuse it…he is at least poor. But what if he's a fraud? We've all read stories in the paper of people who beg because they can make a lot more money than minimum wage if they're good at it.

Rabbi Chayim of Sanz makes an important point about fraudulent charity collectors: "The merit of charity is so great that I am happy to give to 100 beggars even if only one might actually be needy. Some people, however, act as if they are exempt from giving charity to 100 beggars in the event that one might be a fraud."

Of course, if you know for a fact that someone is a fraud, that he is not really poor at all, you are not obligated to give him money. Personally, I've never met a beggar who I was sure was a fraud. A few I might have suspected…but as Rabbi Chayim tells us, being suspicious is not a reason to refrain from giving.

One of the biggest challenges in giving tzedakah to beggars is that our tradition also tells us that it's not enough just to give…rather we need to give gladly. In the eight levels of tzedakah, Rambam tells us that the lowest level of charity is one who gives to the poor person unwillingly; that someone who gives gladly and with a smile is at a higher level.

I grew up in New York City. Kids in New York are trained to be tough. We are trained from an early age to look away from all the creepy characters inhabiting the streets of New York. We are taught to look ahead, walk fast, and keep going. With some effort I've been able to train myself to be much freer with my small change. But the part about acknowledging the other person, about giving a scruffy beggar a smile along with a quarter or fifty cents was a LOT harder.

Why does it make a difference how we give? Why shouldn't it be enough to just give something and be done with it?

From the perspective of the poor person, it's about helping them maintain their dignity even when they are in desperate circumstances. It's not easy to be impoverished, and a smile and acknowledgement as a human being can be very important to helping a poor person's self-esteem. The Torah is concerned with the dignity of poor people. Farmers are commanded to leave a corner of their field, and to leave behind forgotten sheaves, or areas they missed in harvesting for poor people. Why not tell the farmer to simply harvest everything and give a piece of it to the poor? Because it is better for the poor person's dignity to harvest it himself.

There is, however, another reason why it matters how we give.

Giving tzedakah serves two purposes: the first is to support the poor who are needy. The second purpose of giving tzedakah, however, is to refine our own characters. To make us less selfish…less judgmental about the faults of others…more giving…to make us see the flaws in the world around us. To remind us that we are obligated to do something, even if it's small.

If you live in a place like New York where there are a lot of beggars on the streets, you don't have to give a lot to each one. Give what you can. Carry a roll of pennies or nickels if you can't afford a roll of quarters in a place with so many poor people. But giving a small amount will both do a little something to help the other person, and it will do a little something for opening your heart and helping you become a kinder more giving person.

Next time you see a beggar, don't turn your eye…thank him in your heart for providing you an opportunity to do the mitzvah of giving tzedakah!

Why Did Carson Die? Universal Health Care as a Jewish Value

In 2009, the debate over universal health care was raging strongly in the United States as the Obama administration tried to push through major changes in the American health care system. Sadly, my step brother Carson Holder died of pneumonia because he had no health insurance. This was originally posted on my blog, and is dedicated to Carson's memory.

A few months ago, I received the sad news that my step brother Carson died.

Carson was a few years older than me. I got to know Carson pretty well in the early 1980s when he came up from Southern California to where I was in the SF Bay Area to build a house for me. He was a real craftsman. He took care of the whole project, hired all the subcontractors, etc., but still did a huge amount of work himself, everything from rough carpentry to electrical to plumbing to finish work and paint. He got the project finished more or less on budget and on schedule, which is pretty remarkable for building a house. Especially considering he had a klutz like me "helping!"

He was kind, funny, and a good guy to have a beer with. When something didn't work out right, he didn't swear and curse, he just fixed it.

Carson died of pneumonia -- a disease which in someone his age who is otherwise healthy is normally quite readily treatable.

In a way, what Carson really died of was lack of health insurance. He was a casualty of America's broken health care system.

Carson did not have any health insurance. He was only working intermittently, and without a steady employer to pay for it, he certainly couldn't afford to buy insurance on his own. So despite being ill, he didn't go to the doctor. Eventually it got so bad he dragged himself to the emergency room. And while sitting there in the emergency room, he got freaked out about how much the visit to the hospital was going to cost, so he walked out of the emergency room. And died a short time later.

As my teacher Rabbi Elliot Dorff points out in his article "Why We Must Support Universal Health Care," the Jewish tradition teaches "in addition to paying for his own health care, a man assumes an explicit obligation in marriage, according to Jewish law, to pay for the medical care of his wife, children and other relatives if they cannot care for themselves."

So where was Carson's family? Where was I?

Certainly family is ideally part of the "social safety net." Carson's death shows that family can make a pretty rickety support structure. I hadn't spoken to Carson in a number of years; when he passed away he was living in Southern California and I live in Jerusalem. Carson had a lot of difficult personal issues to deal with over a long time, and he had become estranged from much of his family. You can't help someone if you don't know they need help.

Carson died because he was "working poor." If he was older -- 65 and eligible for Medicare -- he would have had health insurance, and would have gone to the doctor sooner. Would probably have avoided the need for a trip to the emergency room at all. If he was a child he would have been covered. If he had been REALLY poor -- indigent -- he would not have had to worry about the bill, the hospital would have had to treat him anyway.

Those opposed to universal health care often cry "socialized medicine!" as if it's some kind of plague, and crying out those words will ward it off. But America already has one of the largest socialized medicine programs in the world. Something like 80 million people are covered by Medicare / Medicaid -- more than are covered by almost any other national health insurance plan. And that doesn't include all the truly indigent people who get emergency treatment for free.

The free treatment of indigent people, of course, also contributes to emergency room crowding, and raises the costs of health care for everyone else

-- it's inefficient. Being treated in an emergency room costs society more than a visit to a doctor's office. But indigent people aren't guaranteed a visit to the doctor's office, so they wait and go to the emergency room instead.

People complain that they don't want matters of life and death decided by some government bureaucrat. However, right now, today, those matters of life and death are decided by insurance company bureaucrats, and those insurance company bureaucrats are no kinder than the government. In fact, a major survey by Calpers shows that people are happier with government provided Medicare than they are with basic private health insurance. The WORST Medicare plan ranked better than the #2 private insurance plan in terms of customer satisfaction. The best Medicare plan was rated much better than the best basic private insurance.

So why was Carson left out in the cold? He was a working age guy. America still clings to a 1950s vision of society, when, at least in our imagination, anyone who wanted to could get a job, and with the job would come health insurance. So if you didn't have health insurance it's because you were lazy, or at least incompetent. Something was wrong with you if you didn't have a job (and insurance).

The times have certainly changed. Millions of Americans, including millions who have jobs, have no health insurance. My oldest daughter, age 27, is unemployed and has no health insurance. Thank God she's relatively healthy. If she were to get in a car accident, I wouldn't be able to afford to pay her bill -- so she'd lose her few possessions, like her car, become indigent, and get the rest of her health care for free.

Doesn't it seem like there ought to be a better way?

Business is often opposed to universal health care and other liberal ideas. Yet as a business man, I really don't understand why. If the government had been taking care of health care, GM might not have needed to go bankrupt. Many small businesses are struggling to keep up with ever increasing health insurance premiums; it would make their life much easier if there were a government sponsored plan at a reasonable cost. In Israel employees pay on average less than 4.8% of their income for health insurance. Many small businesses in America find health insurance premiums running 10 or 15% or even more of their salary expense. In 2008, the average cost for a family insurance plan was over $12,000. Rabbi Elliot Dorff has written extensively on Jewish sources that call for universal health care. But for me, the most compelling source is a very simple one. The Torah commands us "Do not stand idly by the blood of your neighbor." We cannot just sit around and watch people die. We are commanded to care for our brother. When Cain asks God, "Am I my brother's keeper?" God doesn't reply -- but we do know what God's answer is, don't we? "Yes, as a matter of fact you ARE your brother's keeper!" And he is yours.

There are many people who would say "Universal health insurance is a great idea, but who's going to pay for it?"

The problem is not that America would need to spend more money to cover everyone. America would have to spend money more wisely to cover everyone. America already spends nearly twice the amount per capita on health care than almost any other country in the world -- over $7,000/year, most other industrialized countries spend about $3,000/year. America's excess spending does not lead to any noticeable improvement in life expectancy statistics: to the contrary, America's life expectancy is on the low side for industrialized nations.

A few months back the New Yorker ran a fascinating article, "The Cost Conundrum: What a Texas town can teach us about healthcare" which shows that quality of health care and cost of health care do not have much of a relationship. Rochester, Minnesota, home of the world renowned Mayo Clinic provides world class health care at a cost less than half of McAllen, Texas.

Universal health insurance should go hand in hand with a major overhaul of many features of medicine in America, including tort reform, which the

Democrats have been traditionally somewhat reluctant to take on. But it's a necessary component to pay for covering everyone: if we only gave tests to people who really needed them, instead of giving unnecessary tests in the practice of "defensive medicine," we could make our health care dollars go a lot further.

America already spends more dollars per capita of public money -- government money -- than most other countries. Yet America only covers elderly, disabled, and some poor people on that money. For the same spending per head or less, other countries cover everyone.

I think it's scandalous that a country as rich as America can't manage to provide a basic necessity like health care for all of its citizens. The United States is the only industrialized country in the world that does not provide for universal health care.

Too many Carsons have died. I'm ashamed and embarrassed that I wasn't able to prevent his death. Let's work together to prevent more.

The best thing you can do is to write your Congressman and ask him to support universal health care. Feel free to share Carson's story, or your own health care nightmare.

Terri Schiavo and Advance Medical Directives

In 2005, Terri Schiavo lay in a coma – a "persistent vegetative state," according to her doctors – and her family was torn about whether to stop artificial nutrition and let her die. President Bush interrupted a vacation to return to Washington to sign legislation designed to keep her alive. Ultimately the courts ruled that her husband, Michael, was right, and Terri would have wanted treatment discontinued – despite the objections of her parents. She died in March 2005 after artificial nutrition was discontinued. An Advance Medical Directive can help prevent such debates. This was delivered at parshat Tzav, 5765.

"And the fat of the beast that dies of itself, and the fat of that which is torn by beasts *(treifah)*, may be used in any other use; but you shall in no wise eat of it."

Leviticus 7:24

Fifteen years ago, Terri Shindler Schiavo was a vibrant and lively 26 year old woman. She loved music—she even wrote to John Denver to ask if he would play at her wedding—and was fond of animals. She had been happily married to Michael Schiavo for five years.

And then in an instant, life as she knew it came to an end. Terri had a sudden heart attack, brought on by a potassium imbalance. She went unconscious, fell into a coma, and has been comatose ever since.

All of the activities we associate with the joys of living—going for walks, talking with friends, reading a book, going to a movie, eating a meal with friends—have not been part of Terri's life for the last fifteen years.

Her higher brain functions have essentially shut down. For several years, her husband Michael worked for her rehabilitation. He studied nursing so he could take better care of her. He had Terri flown to California for experimental surgical treatments, sleeping on a cot in her room.

After a few years of those efforts, Michael came to realize Terri's situation was hopeless. The doctors diagnosed her as being in a Persistent Vegetative State (PVS). There is only one person known to have recovered from PVS, ever; and he had only been in that state for 20 months. Michael came to the conclusion that Terri was never going to be able to regain normal conscious-ness. He decided that the artificial measures, feeding Terri through a tube, that were keeping her alive should be discontinued, and his wife should be allowed to die. He believes this is what she would have wanted.

Terri's parents, Bob and Mary Shindler, disagree. They dispute Terri's diagnosis—they claim she is responsive. They dispute Terri's wishes: they believe as a Catholic, Terri would have agreed with the teachings of the Catholic Church on the sanctity of life, totally regardless of the quality of that life.

Both sides feel so strongly that they are defending what Terri wants that they have pursued every possible legal device, including multiple appeals to the Supreme Court of the United States, and the passage of an extraordinary bill in Congress over-ruling the traditional separation of states powers to allow a Federal court to rule on an appeal.

This is an extremely complicated and emotional situation. The rhetoric has been extremely impassioned. Pat Buchanan had the nerve to compare what Michael Schiavo is doing to his wife to what the Nazis did to prisoners in the Holocaust. Such comparisons are truly absurd, odious, and an affront to the memory of those who perished at the hands of the Nazis. If Terri Schiavo were capable of eating, there are plenty of people who would feed her. The situation is not the same.

I'm NOT going to talk this morning about what the courts should have done, or whether it was proper that Congress passed a special bill. I have my opinions, but I don't think the Torah has a lot to say about whether Federalism is a good thing or a bad thing, or the roles of the various branches of the US government. But this sad case does raise a few questions we need to think about.

What if, God forbid, such a thing were to happen to your loved one, what would you do? Where would you turn for guidance?

The Shindlers are Catholic. They are trying to follow the teachings of their church. The Vatican does not usually comment on individual cases, but they made an exception for Terri Schiavo because of all the publicity. The Vatican's position is as follows:

> "By any decent count, Mrs. Terri Schiavo can be considered a living human being, deprived of full conscience, whose legal rights must be recognized, respected and defended. The removal of the feeding tube from this person, in these conditions, can be considered direct euthanasia."

The Catholic Church's position is that even if it was Terri's desire not to be fed, she would be committing a mortal sin to refuse the feeding tube. A typical Catholic Church approved advance medical directive reads "In no circumstances would I wish basic care, including (if appropriate to my condition) the assisted administration of food and fluids, to be withdrawn with the aim of ending my life." Note it says "in no circumstances." No matter how much pain the person is in, how unlikely recovery, or how far gone already.

The Vatican statement said removing the tube would be "Direct euthanasia." In other words, the Catholic Church says that removal of the feeding tube is an act of murder.

What would the Jewish tradition say about removing the feeding tube?

The first issue we need to consider is what is Terri's status? Is she alive, dead, or in some kind of in between state?

Judaism does not view life as a digital phenomena, on or off. Life is not something that begins precisely at the moment of conception and ends precisely at the moment breathing stops. The Jewish view is that life is something we come into gradually in stages and we exit gradually in stages.

Terri is not dead. Even though traditionally death was defined as cardio-pulmonary death, the vast majority of rabbis today accept brain-death as death. However, since her brain stem is still functioning, Terri does not meet the usual criteria of brain death.

This week's Torah portion, Tzav, has rules and regulations about all different kinds of sacrifices. Amongst all the rules is one that refers to an animal that is a *treifah*, which literally means "torn." We cannot eat or offer as a sacrifice an animal that is a *treifah*. The same word in Yiddish usage, *treif*, came to mean anything that is not kosher.

However in halacha, in Jewish law, there is another usage for the term *treifah*. A person who has a terminal illness is called a *treifah*. An animal that had been ripped open by something like a wolf was called a *treifah*, and in some ways was considered almost as if dead already even if it was still moving around—death was inevitable.

The Jewish tradition holds that saving lives is one of the very highest of values. We disregard any of the commandments except for three to save a human life. For someone who is otherwise healthy, we would go to extraordinary lengths to save them. However, once someone is a *treifah*, once they have a terminal illness, their status changes somewhat. If you came across two people drowning and could only save one, and you knew one was a *treifah*, was suffering from a terminal illness, you would be justified in choosing to save the one that was NOT a *treifah*. Traditionally, someone is defined as a *treifah* if they have less than a year to live. One problem of course, is that we all know people who the doctors said had way less than a year to live who made a recovery—I recall a case two years ago when the doctors said a congregant of mine was within 24 hours of death, and he made a recovery and is still with us, alert and living an almost normal life.

The next stage in the dying process is called the *goses*. A *goses* is someone who is in the process of dying, which halacha defines as within three days of death. It is halachically permissible to do things like turn off a ventilator for someone who is a *goses* because medical intervention is no longer seen as preserving life, but rather is seen as dragging out the process of dying. As my teacher Rabbi Elliot Dorff put it, God only has so many ways of taking us: with artificial hydration, nutrition, and ventilation, we can be seen as trying to foil the will of God that a person's time on this earth is up.

We are all mortal and will pass away. The Jewish tradition considers it an honor to be present when a person passes from this world to the next. I have had the honor to be present numerous times when a person has passed on. When someone is on a ventilator, unconscious, and their organs are shutting down, it is usually pretty clear when the end is imminent. Families I have been with have been comforted to know that it is OK within the Jewish tradition at that point to turn the ventilator off and allow the person to leave this world without dragging out the dying process.

Prior to the removal of the feeding tube, Terri Schiavo was certainly NOT a *goses*, within three days of death. If you consider nutrition through a feeding tube an artificial measure sustaining life, similar to someone who could only live with a ventilator, one could argue that she is a *treifah*, someone who would die within a year without extraordinary medical intervention.

But even if she does not have the status of either a *goses* or a *treifah*, it would be permissible for her husband to remove the feeding tube. It would also be permissible to leave it in.

It is generally accepted that people have a right to refuse medical treatment if they feel it will not help cure their condition. In Terri Schiavo's case, an important question then is whether feeding someone through a feeding tube counts as "nutrition" or "medication." There are rabbis with different opinions on the issue.

I go with the opinion of Rabbi Dorff, who wrote that "artificial nutrition and hydration is medicine because it does not have important characteristics of food -- specifically, it does not have taste, temperature, or texture, and it comes into the body through tubes rather than through the mouth which then chews and swallows it. Therefore, I think that we should intubate (insert a tube) or extubate (remove a tube) according to whether it is in the best interests of the patient."

So from a Jewish perspective the question regarding whether or not to keep a feeding tube in Terri Schiavo would be whether it is in the best interests of the patient. Her own wishes make a big difference—a person can refuse medical treatment if they think it is not helping.

There have been arguments about the facts in the case and the status of Terri Schiavo. The Florida courts have ruled in accordance with the doctors who say she is in a persistent vegetative state (PVS). People who are in a PVS because of loss of blood flow to the brain, like Terri, never recover, so administering artificial nutrition is not benefiting her—it is only keeping her in a state from which she will never recover consciousness. As Rabbi Dorff says, "As Jews, we have a strong mandate to heal, but when we cannot, we must recognize and accept the fact that we are mortal (this goes back to the Adam and Eve story). As Kohelet says, "There is time to be born, and a time to die." To deny the reality of death is both psychologically unhealthy and religiously perverse."

Millions of dollars in medical expenses, legal fees, and gas for Air Force One could have been saved if Terry Schiavo had filled out an Advance Medical Directive, a living will.

In an advance medical directive you fill out a form which stipulates how you want these issues to be dealt with.

Often older people will fill out a medical directive because they start seeing mortality staring them in the face; the more funerals you go to, the more aware you become of the fact that some day it will be your turn. Young people, like Terri Schiavo, rarely think to fill out such a directive.

But the truth is, we ALL need to fill one out. I've been in car accidents, a motorcycle accident, and an airplane accident. Any one of them could have turned out much worse than it did. I was given a powerful reminder of the need for all of us to fill out a medical directive last month. I was out running one morning and slipped on an icy sidewalk on the UT campus. My legs went right out from under me, and I came down very hard, flat on my back. I hobbled home, called my wife Lauri, and had her come home and take me to the emergency room where they gave me some powerful pain killers and muscle relaxants—I had given myself whiplash. I was quite fortunate: a few visits to the chiropractor and a few sessions of my yoga class and I was as good as new. But I also realize that with that fall my head probably came within a couple of inches of striking the pavement hard enough to put me in a coma. And I did NOT have an advance medical directive filled out!

I believe in practicing what I preach, so yesterday Lauri and I filled out our advance medical directives. We did it together, discussing the different issues. It's not a fun session. It's uncomfortable to sit with your loved one and consider things like whether you would agree to having a limb amputated if you were unconscious and had a life threatening infection. But I'm very glad we filled it out together, because even with me being a rabbi and she being a lawyer, there were issues we needed to discuss and think through.

The Conservative Movement's Rabbinical Assembly has prepared a document called "Jewish Medical Directives for Health Care." I believe this issue is so important I am going to mail a copy of the document to every member of B'nai Israel, and on the evening of Tuesday, April 12, I will lead a session for anyone interested in going through the form and answering questions about filling it out. If you would like a copy right away, before receiving your copy in the mail, please contact the office. The document is also available online at http://www.mishkon.org/documents/jewishmedicaldirectives.pdf . If you have filled out a standard secular living will, you might want to consider replacing it with this one, which reflects specifically Jewish teachings on these issues.

In the Mishnah Torah Rambam (Maimonides) explains there is no "coming to be" without a "passing away." Psalm 49 affirms "For all the glory that they cherish, men die, even as the beasts that perish." Whenever that day comes, you can help prevent needless anguish and strife amongst your loved ones if you make your wishes known in writing ahead of time.

May it be God's will that no one needs to look at your advance medical directive until you are 120!!!

Chapter Six

Human Rights

"And God said, Let us make man in our image, after our likeness;"

Genesis 1:26

There are many human rights values we learn from the Torah – several of them grounded in teachings from the first few chapters of the Torah. We are all created in God's image – and we are all descended from a common ancestor. From a few fundamental verses come the radical ideas that we are all related to each other and we all have a spark of God within. If we accept those two ideas, how can we not be concerned with the human rights of everyone?

The Values of Torah

Delivered on Parshat Naso, 5766 in Toledo. What do we do when the values of Torah conflict with rules in the Torah?

The rabbis of two thousand years were a real bunch of radicals.

When they were confronted with something in the Torah that conflicted with the values and ethics they learned from the Torah itself, they resolved the issue by deciding in favor of the values over the explicit law found in the Torah.

If the Torah said something that was deeply troubling, or that didn't work, they either interpreted the troubling passage out of existence or they found a way around it.

This week's Torah portion, Naso, contains an example of this.

This week's reading contains one of the most troubling rituals in the Torah. The Torah tells us that if a spirit of jealousy comes upon a man, and he suspects his wife of infidelity, he can bring her to the priest and force her to undergo a degrading ritual designed to determine whether or not she had committed adultery.

The Torah tells us if a man suspected his wife of having gone astray, and he was caught up in a *ruach kinah*, a jealous spirit, he was to bring his wife to the priest.

The woman was told to bring an offering of barley—the lowest category of offering, the most plain, most worthless possible offering. The priest would then take the woman, loosen the hair of her head—the Talmud tells us he would also expose her breasts, in public, for everyone to see—very much against the values of modesty. He would then take a mixture of water and dust from the floor of the Temple. The priest would tell the woman that if she had gone astray, drinking the bitter water would cause her belly to swell and her thigh to fall, and she would die. She was forced to say "amen" to this curse. The priest would write the name of God on a piece of paper, dissolve it in the water, and make the woman drink the water.

In other words, the woman was being told that if she was guilty of infidelity she would die a gruesome death by the hand of God, after being shamed in public.

One might argue that if a woman had gone astray and slept with someone else she was getting what she deserved. I wouldn't argue you that, mind you, but some might. But how about the innocent woman?

The Torah says "And the spirit of jealousy comes upon him, and he is jealous of his wife, and she is defiled; or if the spirit of jealousy comes upon him, and he is jealous of his wife, and she is not defiled (Numbers 5:14);"

If a spirit of jealousy comes over a man "and she is not defiled"—she is innocent of the charges—she has to go through this ritual, ostensibly designed to clear her name.

One could take the approach of being an apologist for this strange ritual – and say that it provided a way to purge the ugliness of jealousy from a relationship. If the woman didn't die, the husband had to keep his mouth shut, and the Torah tells us the woman would get pregnant. End of story.

But why should an innocent woman be made to suffer through this degrading and scary ritual just because her husband was overcome by a sense of jealousy?

The rabbis two thousand years ago asked themselves that same question. To start with, the Mishnah puts in place a lot of procedural barriers to make it more difficult to subject a woman to the procedure. While the Torah makes it sound like any guy who is suddenly overcome by a fit of jealousy can send his wife through the procedure, the Talmud specifies that the husband must first warn her not to be secluded with a particular man, and she must then ignore than explicit warning. The rabbis argue at great length about whether the warning and or the seclusion need to be witnessed by one or two witnesses, or just the word of the husband.

But ultimately, procedural barriers were not sufficient, and the Mishnah tells us

> "When adulterers multiplied the ceremony of the bitter water was discontinued and it was R. Johanan b. Zakkai who discontinued it, as it is said, I will not punish your daughters when they commit whoredom, nor your brides when they commit adultery, for they themselves etc."

After an entire tractate of the Talmud deals with all of the arcane details of this strange ritual, at the end of the day we are told the rabbis discontinued it because it wasn't fair: it punished the women, but not the men who were guilty of the same crime.

The Torah gives us an explicit procedure to follow with detailed instructions. Yet those radical rabbis analyzed it, and they found the procedure to be out of synch with the values they learned from the Torah: values such as every person is created in the image of God, and deserves to be treated with respect. Values such as "justice, justice, you shall pursue." Values such as "there shall be one form of law to you." Finding this explicit commandment in the Torah out of synch with the values we learn from the Torah, the rabbis voted in favor of the values instead of in favor of the explicit commandment of the Torah. Pretty radical!

There are many other examples throughout the Torah where the later rabbis used the values they derived from the Torah to trump something written in the Torah itself. The Torah commands us to stone to death the "rebellious son." The rabbis could not imagine how such a thing could be done, to put someone to death who has not yet committed a capital crime. They put so many restrictions on it that it was made impossible to administer. One rabbi argues that there never was a rebellious son put to death in accordance with this law in the Torah – it's only there for us to accrue merit through studying the passage.

The rabbis were uncomfortable with capital punishment, so they put so many restrictions around implementing capital punishment that the Talmud concludes "a Sanhedrin that executed one person in seven years – and some say one in seventy years – is called a 'bloody court.'"

We read the Torah's commandment "an eye for an eye, a tooth for a tooth," and it sounds barbaric. The rabbis of old agree – they insist, that despite the seemingly very clear statement in the Torah that the *pshat*, the plain or simple meaning of the text, is that it calls for monetary compensation when a person injures another. They say that anyone who says the verse means you should poke out the eye of someone who pokes out your eye is distorting the Torah!

Last Shabbat among the different things we read was the command-ment of the remission of debts during the *shmittah* year, the seventh year, when the fields were to lie fallow and Jewish slaves were to be released.

Of course, one problem with having a general release of debts in the seventh year is that when year six comes along, people will be reluctant to make loans, since they figure they might not get paid back. The Torah in fact explicitly warns against having that attitude: "Beware that there be not a thought in your wicked heart, saying, The seventh year, the year of release, is at hand; and your eye be evil against your poor brother, and you give him nothing; and he cry to the Lord against you, and it be a sin to you."

Despite that explicit warning in the Torah, human nature is human nature, and people stopped making loans when the *shmittah* year was approaching. The rule in the Torah that was designed to make life easier and more bearable for poor people – the rule about forgiving debts – was in fact making life HARDER for poor people. So the great radical rabbi Hillel devised a way around the Torah. He instituted what is known as the *prozbul,* a mechanism whereby the debt is transferred from a person to a *beit din*, a rabbinic court, and the debt is NOT wiped out by the seventh year.

Here was an explicit rule in the Torah – debts are to be forgiven in the seventh year – and yet a rabbi came up with a way around the rule because it wasn't accomplishing the goal of the rule, and the result was not in keeping with the values he learned from the Torah.

So where are the radical rabbis of today? The rabbis who strive to live lives informed not just by the details of the Torah, but by the values of the Torah?

Earlier this week I had the great *zchut*, the great merit, of attending what was one of the most unusual, and most illuminating, board meetings I have ever attended.

I have over the years served on three corporate boards, a university board, a trade association board, and a synagogue board; in addition, in my capacity as rabbi, I have been a non-voting participant on two additional synagogue boards.

Boards are usually all business. That includes the synagogue boards with which I've been involved. Yes, the synagogue board starts the meeting with a d'var Torah. But then it's off to budgets, committee reports, personnel issues, and perhaps at a special occasion like a board retreat a review of our vision and mission statements.

Earlier this week I participated in Rabbis for Human Rights' once per year in person board meeting. We talked about business – I probably talked about business more than anyone else in my role as chair of the development committee and soon to be Treasurer – but we also integrated spirituality into our meeting.

We started our day on Tuesday with an hour of serious text study with an Orthodox rabbi on issues of human rights, which transformed into a discussion of why we seem to have trouble getting Orthodox rabbis in America involved in human rights issues. We had a meditation that led into the afternoon prayers. We had a guided visualization before saying the motzi about the chain of suppliers who had brought the food to our table. We took a meditation break in the middle of a long afternoon discussing human rights issues like torture. We closed with a chant from Psalm 145, each board member making a statement about what they commit themselves to regarding our cause while everyone made physical contact with others representing our connectedness.

I know that to any of you who serve on community or other boards this may sound just over the top touchy feely. And the meeting was in New York, NOT California! Nevertheless, we did also discuss budgets and fundraising, our programmatic priorities, we heard committee reports, and we revised our bylaws and elected new members to the board– in other words, all the normal business of a board. But all that spiritual stuff helped us remember that God was a presence in the room with us, and even when we were discussing budgets we were doing holy work.

Rabbis for Human Rights is a group of rabbis who are concerned not only with the detailed halacha of the Torah, but also with the values of the Torah. The Torah tells us that everyone—Jew and Gentile—is created in the image of God. The Torah tells us "you shall not stand idly by the blood of your neighbor." The rabbis of the Talmud tell us *"dina d'malchuta dina,"* the law of the land is the law. So how could the Jewish community stand by idly while the American government abuses prisoners in Guantanamo Bay, in violation of international law? How could we stand by while people are held for years without being charged with any crime, with no access to their families?

To be opposed to this kind of treatment of prisoners does not mean one is "soft" on terrorism. I think it's great that Al-Zarqawi was killed in a recent airstrike. I favor taking aggressive action against terrorists. However, even in a time of war – I would say especially in a time of war – we need to be faithful to the values that make us the "good guys." Rabbis for Human Rights North America has been prominent among Jewish groups opposing abuse of prisoners.

Rabbis for Human Rights is an organization dominated by Reform and Reconstructionist rabbis, with growing representation from Conservative rabbis. We have no representation on our board whatsoever from Orthodox rabbis in North America. Why not?

The Orthodox colleague who came and spoke to us shared an important insight. He said Orthodox Jews live their lives dominated by halacha. They strive to follow halacha in all its details. There are detailed laws about the separation of meat and dairy. But regarding something like protesting abuse of prisoners, there are no detailed halachot to follow. Following the VALUES of the Torah has too often become totally secondary to following the details of the halacha. Even though there is a principle in the Torah which says we should remember to be kind to the stranger, and the Talmud tells us we support the poor of the Gentiles along with the poor of Jews, since there is no detailed halacha that tells us how much money we should give to non-Jewish victims of a tsunami, all too often in the Orthodox community they give nothing.

There is also a sense in the Orthodox community that issues of social action and social justice have somehow been taken over by Reform Jews, and to

participate with Reform Jews would be to lend them credibility. Some Orthodox rabbis are afraid that if they participate in organizations with the Reform or
Conservative they will lose credibility among their flock or among their colleagues for daring to "recognize" us.

I see a similar schism in ritual issues. Because of the demands of the
times we live in and because of our understanding of the values we derive from
the Torah, the Conservative movement has made changes that the Orthodox
consider very radical, and not permissible – allowing mixed seating and allowing
women to not only count for a minyan but to even lead services and be rabbis.
Why are Conservative rabbis so much more radical in these and other areas?

I've been having an email exchange with an Orthodox Jew on this subject. It's because the Orthodox rabbis have great humility. They feel they have
nowhere near the knowledge, insight, and piety of the rabbis of old. Hillel
could do something radical like institute the *prozbul*. But in our times, we are
not so great, and all we can do is follow the decisions of the great rabbis who
came before, perhaps applying the details to the times we live in, but certainly
not coming up with any radical changes ourselves.

Humility is certainly an important Jewish value. Moshe Rabbeinu, our
greatest teacher, was also said to be the humblest man that ever lived. So isn't it
chutzpadik, isn't it a sign of lack of humility, to think we could come to a
different conclusion halachically than the great rabbis of yesteryear?

Humility is a very important and valuable trait. However, we should
not allow it to paralyze us, or to cause us to lose sight of the values of the
Torah. The Torah commands us "If there arises a matter too hard for you in
judgment…you shall come to the judge who shall be in those days, and inquire."

The Talmud actually cautions us against paralysis by humility. The
Talmud teaches (Bavli Rosh Hashanah 25b) "'It says also: Moses and Aaron
among his priests and Samuel among them that call on his name (Psalm 99:6).'
We see therefore that the Scripture places three of the most questionable

characters on the same level as three of the most estimable characters, to show that Jerubaal in his generation is like Moses in his generation, Bedan in his generation is like Aaron in his generation, Jepthah in his generation is like Samuel in his generation, [and] to teach you that the most worthless, once he has been appointed a leader of the community, is to be accounted like the mightiest of the mighty. Scripture says also: And you shall come to the priests the Levites and to the judge that shall be in those days. Can we then imagine that a man should go to a judge who is not in his days? This shows that you must be content to go to the judge who is in your days. It also says; Say not, 'How was it that the former days were better than these (Ecclesiastes 7:10).'"

The Talmud tells us not to say the judges of long ago were better than the judges today. We are told even someone who is a questionable character, once appointed a leader of the community is to be accounted like the mightiest of the mighty. We cannot function as a society if we continually second-guess our leaders and compare them unfavorably to ones of days gone by.

I am humbled that I have been accepted as a part of two groups of "radical rabbis," rabbis who are the authentic banner carriers of the rabbis' of old long-standing commitment to the values we learn from Torah even when those values collide with the explicit words of the Torah—Conservative rabbis and Rabbis for Human Rights.

Ribono shel olam, Master of the Universe, please help us all to lead lives guided by the wisdom of Your Torah, both in its details and in its values, and when those values seem to collide with those details, please God, grant us the wisdom to be able to truly discern Your will. When in doubt may we remember to be guided by that important principle in Your Torah, v'ahavta l'ra'acha k'mocha, love your neighbor as yourself.

Amen.

Never Again!

This sermon about the crisis in Darfur was delivered for parshat Tazria, 5766.

In the midst of a whole bunch of stuff about different kinds of ritual impurity, this week's Torah reading has a commandment that stands out like a beacon from amongst all the descriptions of emissions and skin disease: "And in the eighth day the flesh of his foreskin shall be circumcised."

That's all it says on the subject in this section of the Torah. Elsewhere, however, the Torah tells us that circumcision represents a covenant between God and the Jewish people. A covenant going back to the first Jew, all the way back to Abraham.

What is a covenant? It is a reciprocal promise. You do something for me, I do something for you. The covenant between God and Abraham was simple: we circumcise our sons, and God will be our God.

Is that covenant between God and the Jewish people still in force? Last week we observed Yom Hashoah, Holocaust Remembrance Day, a day on which we remember and honor the six million Jews who perished at the hands of the Nazis. In my talk last week, I spoke of the theological challenges of the Shoah. How can we possibly make sense out of the unspeakable? Among those who lived through the Shoah, there are those gave up on God, who said if God didn't protect us in those times there either is no God, or God doesn't care and there is no longer any covenant between God and us.

The Torah says that Jews are a stiff-necked people. Sometimes that's a good thing. Most of us have stubbornly refused to give up on God. We don't see the Holocaust as something God did – we see it as something that people did.

There is a remarkable story told how in one of the concentration camps during the Shoah, the Jews decided to convene a beit din, a rabbinic court, and judge God – to judge whether he had violated the terms of the covenant he made with the Jewish people. After hearing testimony and arguments on both sides, the court found God guilty of violating the covenant.

And what did they do with that judgment? Right after they concluded their judgment, right after finding God guilty of violating the covenant, one of the judges called out "Mincha!!" and they said the afternoon prayers.

Even in the face of overwhelming evidence that God had violated the terms of the covenant, those righteous Jews upheld the covenant. Almost as if they were telling God, "You don't get rid of us that easily, Lord!!" They reaffirmed the covenant. They said even if God has not fully lived up to his part of the deal, and we don't understand why, the deal is still in place.

As important as it is for us to remember the people—Jews and others—who were killed by the Nazis, I believe there is an even more important purpose to observing Yom Hashoah.

The more important purpose to Yom Hashoah is to remind us every year, to reaffirm a NEW COVENANT that Jewish people have made in the wake of the Holocaust.

The new covenant is not a covenant with God. It is, rather, a covenant with future generations.

"Never again!"

The Jewish people's response to the tragedy of the Shoah was to say "Never Again!" Never again should such a horror occur. We promised ourselves, we promised our children, we promised our children's children.

It's one reason that Jews all over the world provide such strong support to the State of Israel. As long as we have Israel to go to, we will never again have a time when Jews are being killed and no one will give them asylum. As long as we have a credible military force, people will think twice before trying to kill Jews.

But "never again" needs to be about more than just the Jewish people.

Never again needs to mean NEVER AGAIN to genocide – regardless of the ethnicity or religious background of the victims. It means we must be diligent in preventing any other people from experiencing what we experienced.

The Torah over and over tells us "be kind to the stranger, for you know what it is like to be a stranger." The experience of slavery in Egypt should inspire us to help create a world in which no one is treated badly. Even though the Torah did not abolish slavery, it DID abolish mistreatment of slaves: knock your slave's tooth out, and he goes free. The Torah tells us that everyone—even slaves—is to be treated with dignity, is not to be abused, and we know that we must treat them this way because we have been there, we have been slaves ourselves.

We must take the same lesson from the Holocaust. We know what it is like to be the victim of senseless hatred for no reason other than religion or ethnic group. We have cried and we still cry and mourn for the innocent people—1.5 million Jewish children among them—who were shot and gassed and burned in the Hell of the Shoah. We know that pain, and we know we must do everything we can to prevent other people from ever having to experience that pain themselves.

Unfortunately, we have not been doing a very good job.

It wasn't just the Jews who said "Never Again!" after the Holocaust. In 1948 the United Nations passed the "Convention on the Prevention and Punishment of the Crime of Genocide." There are 138 signatories to the convention, nations that agreed to be bound by its terms. The Convention confirms "genocide, whether committed in time of peace or in time of war, is a crime under international law," and the Convention bounds signatories to prevent and punish transgressors.

The Convention defines genocide as murder and a variety of other acts of violence intended to destroy in whole or in part a national, ethnical, racial, or religious group.

Even though the US was slow to enter the Second World War, by the end of the war we were among the most passionate supporters of preventing other such tragedies. We took the lead in the Nuremberg trials, bringing many of the perpetrators to justice. When the Convention on Genocide was presented, President Harry Truman called on U.S. Senators to endorse the Convention because America had "long been a symbol of freedom and democratic progress to peoples less favored," and because it was time to outlaw the "world-shocking crime of genocide."

Where were the signatories to the Convention when over 3 million people were killed, mostly victims of genocide, in Cambodia between 1970 and 1980?

Where were the signatories to the Convention when the Hutus in Rwanda murdered 800,000 Tutsis in 1994?

Why did it take so long for the signatories to the Convention to respond the murder of 200,000 Muslims—and the forced relocation of many more—in Bosnia beginning in 1995?

Samantha Power of the Kennedy School of Government at Harvard University describes how much progress has been made in the field of human rights in the last fifty years. There are global conventions outlawing discrimination based on gender and race, which outline rights of refugees and children. There is a planet-wide ban on land mines, and there are international war crimes tribunals that bring mass murderers to justice.

"But," Power wrote, "one ugly, deadly and recurrent reality check persists: genocide. Genocide has occurred so often and so uncontested in the last fifty years that an epithet more apt in describing recent events than the oft-chanted "Never Again" is in fact "Again and Again." The gap between the promise and the practice of the last fifty years is dispiriting indeed. How can this be?"

In the last 50 years the United States has gone to war to stop the spread of Communism in Korea and Vietnam, we went into Panama and forcibly removed Manuel Noriega, we stopped Iraq from invading Kuwait, we attacked Afghanistan and removed the Taliban and we have removed Saddam Hussein from power.

We have been ready to go to war when our own national interests are at stake. We have not been ready to commit troops, money, and American lives to stop genocide in places like Cambodia, Rwanda, or Bosnia.

All recent US presidents have pledged that they would never again allow genocide to occur. Jimmy Carter, Ronald Reagan, George Bush the first, and Bill Clinton all made that pledge. Yet they all did nothing to stop genocide when it was happening during their terms in office.

When current President George W. Bush read a report on the genocide in Rwanda, he is reputed to have marked in the column "Not on my watch!"

The President said "not on my watch," and we, the Jewish people, have said "never again!"

Yet it is happening again, and it is happening on President Bush's watch.

The Arab government and Arab militias in Sudan have murdered 400,000 blacks in Darfur.

We read about what's happening in Sudan and it looks like just a bunch of violence, we think of it as a civil war, it's chaos, it's Iraq, but what's happening in Sudan is far more sinister.

It is genocide.

As the UN Convention defines it, when one ethic group tries to eliminate another ethnic group, it's genocide. Both houses of the United States Congress have declared in official resolutions that what is happening in Sudan is genocide.

Arabs, living on oil-free deserts in the north and east of the country, are taking over the more fertile and oil rich south and west of the country, where blacks live. Blacks in Sudan are being killed by the Arabs for no crime other than being black – just as Jews were killed by the Nazis for no crime other than being Jewish.

Many of the black Sudanese in the south follow ancient tribal traditions, or are Christian. Something that makes what is happening in Darfur, in the west of Sudan, particularly heinous is that the blacks are also Muslim – but the Arabs don't care, for what they see are blacks, not fellow Muslims, and the slaughter and displacement continues. It's as if Ashkenazi Jews were killing Sephardi Jews.

A report from the BBC describes the scene:

> "For months, the Islamic government in Khartoum, together with traditional Arab militia, have been accused of pursuing a scorched earth policy in western Sudan.Everything we saw, everything we heard, suggests that this is true. Strung out along our route, are more deserted, torched villages. In all of them, the signs are of a hasty, panicked departure.

> "Up to one million people - a sixth of the population of western Sudan - is believed to be on the move. The Sudanese of African descent have been "cleansed" from their traditional lands, forced to become refugees in their own homeland."

The BBC reporter also interviewed some of the refugees. The reporter interviewed a 13-year-old girl, named Hawa. "She escaped to Kalma after her village was torched. She identifies the attackers as Arabs on horseback, accompanied by government planes. She and her six sisters managed to run away, but her parents were killed. She takes us to the fragile straw and stick hut where the little girls have set up house. Hawa cradles her three-year-old sister. A battered pot, containing a little porridge, sits outside. During the attack, the family's livestock - cows and horses - were also lost. The family is left destitute."

We cannot allow genocide to happen to anyone. Jews have a long tradition of sticking up for the rights of others—and not just the Jewish activists in the struggles over civil rights. Our tradition of defending the rights of others goes all the way back to Abraham, to when Abraham argued with God to spare the lives of the non-Jewish residents of Sodom and Gomorrah. Years later, the prophet Jonah was reluctant, but he ultimately did the right thing and saved the non-Jewish residents of Nineveh from God's wrath.

Last Monday night, at our Yom Hashoah commemoration, we presented a certificate acknowledging the efforts of Reverend Waitstill Sharp and his wife Martha, who have been honored by Yad Vashem as righteous Gentiles. Reverend and Mrs. Sharp could not sit on the sidelines as genocide unfolded. Leaving their two young children behind, they went to Czechoslovakia and southern France in 1939, saving the lives of hundreds of Jews, smuggling them out of the country, securing false papers, exposing themselves to tremendous personal danger.

We can't all be Jewish Reverend Sharps heading for Sudan. However, we can all be "righteous Jews" working to save people of other nations. We can speak out: in letters to President Bush, letters to Congress, letters to the newspapers. We can stay informed about what's happening, participate in rallies—there's a big one in Washington, DC tomorrow. And as always with a crisis, we can provide financial support. The American Jewish World Service is accepting donations to provide humanitarian aid to help the people of Darfur.

Ribono Shel Olam, Master of the Universe, please God, strengthen the hands of those who would stop the slaughter of your children in Darfur. Bring the survivors under the wings of Your sheltering presence. Help the leaders of the civilized world to remember their promise of "never again," and help them to act on that promise. Help us, Lord Almighty, to bring peace to the land, peace between black and Arab, Muslim and Muslim, Muslim and Jew and Christian and all peoples on this earth, Amen.

On Torturing Prisoners

As a former soldier in the US Army Security Agency, I was especially appalled when I learned the US government condoned abusing prisoners. This response was delivered during parshat Naso 5763.

What's the cure for an overwhelming case of marital jealousy?

This week's Torah portion, Naso, recommends psychological torture and sexual humiliation. The Sotah ritual, the ritual of the bitter waters, is a very abusive procedure.

If a man suspected his wife of having gone astray, and he was caught up in a *ruach kinah,* a jealous spirit, he was to bring his wife to the priest. The woman was told to bring an offering of barley—the lowest category of offering, the most plain, most worthless possible offering. The priest would then take the woman, loosen the hair of her head—the Talmud tells us he would also expose her breasts, in public, for anyone to see—very much against the Jewish value of modesty. He would then take a mixture of water and dust from the floor of the Temple. The priest would tell the woman that if she had gone astray, drinking the bitter water would cause her belly to swell and her thigh to fall, and she would die. She was forced to say "amen" to this curse. The priest would write the name of God on a piece of paper, dissolve it in the water, and make the woman drink the water. She was told if she was guilty of infidelity she would die a gruesome death by the hand of God, after being shamed in public.

Can you imagine the terror a woman would feel being told this drink was going to kill her? The humiliation of being stripped half-naked in front of the entire community?

Let there be no doubt that this treatment amounts to torture. The definition of torture contained in a convention that the United States has signed defines torture as "any act by which severe pain or suffering, whether physical or mental, is intentionally inflicted on a person for such purposes as obtaining from him or a third person information or a confession."

By that definition, it is also quite clear that what has recently happened in Iraq's Abu Ghraib prison is torture. The US military seems to have accepted a notion put forth in a book called "The Arab Mind" that Arabs are especially vulnerable to sexual humiliation. This book was widely discussed in Washington among pro-war Conservatives in the months leading up to the war in Iraq. Whether the Arabs are more sensitive to this than the rest of us is beside the point. I would certainly consider it torture to be tied up naked in a cell, or chained to the bars, or forced to simulate sex with another man. There are pictures of a man with wires on him, standing on a small stool. He was reportedly told if he falls off and disconnects a wire he would be electrocuted. If that's not psychological torture, what is? One of the most disturbing aspects of the pictures are the smiles on the faces of the tormentors. There is one photo of an American female soldier grinning from ear to ear as she points to naked Iraqi men in embarrassing positions.

Perhaps that grin is what led the notorious Conservative radio talk show host Rush Limbaugh say "You know, these people are being fired at every day. I'm talking about people having a good time, these people. You ever heard of emotional release?"

Emotional release? By sexually humiliating prisoners? I've had some hard days at the office. I had some hard days at work when I served in the US military. But somehow I never felt like tormenting other people as a way to release my tensions.

The US government's official reaction to these horrifying events is to claim that Rush Limbaugh is right. It was just a few lower level soldiers getting their jollies. Those soldiers will be punished.

If that was really the case, punishing those few soldiers would hardly be adequate punishment. How come the officer in charge of the prison didn't randomly wander around the prison, unannounced, to see what was going on in her (yes, the general in charge of the prison was a woman) prison? Everyone in the chain of command should have been severely reprimanded and subject to at a minimum an Article 13 (non-judicial punishment) for their actions. IF the problem was simply lack of supervision.

When I was in the US Army, we used to joke that the difference between the Boy Scouts and the Army was that in the Boy Scouts you had adult supervision.

But the problem in Iraq goes much deeper than lack of supervision. This kind of behavior never would have happened if it were not known that there was official condonement of mistreatment of prisoners.

A May 24 article in the New Yorker entitled "The Gray Zone" paints a very disturbing picture of US government policy regarding treatment of prisoners. A report written by Major General Antonio Taguba says that Major General Geoffrey Miller, commander of the detention facility at Guantanamo, authorized the use of sleep deprivation, exposure to extremes of cold and heat, and placing prisoners in "stress positions" for agonizing lengths of time. Bad enough, but US Defense Secretary Donald Rumsfeld and Under-Secretary of Defense Stephen Cambone also authorized treating male prisoners at Abu Ghraib roughly and exposing them to sexual humiliation.

It could be that the people who took the incriminating photos that we have all been disgusted by were not part of the "official" program. However, it could be that some of them saw what was going on, maybe some participated in officially sanctioned torture, and decided to engage in some on their own initiative. Once you tell someone that torturing prisoners is OK, it is hard to tell them that it's only OK when the general says so.

The US government claims that torturing prisoners in this fashion is both legal and necessary. This kind of treatment of prisoners clearly violates the Geneva Convention, the basic rules of war signed by every country in the world. The US gets around this inconvenient fact by arguing that the alleged terrorists are not protected under the Geneva Convention. They also argue they are not protected under US law. The US government seems to be claiming that these prisoners have no rights or legal protections of any form under local, US, or international law.

According to the New Yorker, the war—or rather, the peace—in Iraq was going badly. There were all these attacks against US forces, and no leads on the people behind it. Cambone felt something had to be done, so he authorized a special top-secret interrogation program.

According to a former intelligence official, the US Central Intelligence Agency signed up for a similar program in Afghanistan—one that was targeted at a few "high-value terrorist" targets. Supposedly the CIA quit being supportive when the program was expanded from a few high value targets to include "cabdrivers, brothers-in-law, and people pulled off the streets;"—the sort of people who populate Iraqi jails. CIA's legal people objected, and the agency quit its involvement in the program at Al Ghraib.

Just as the torture of prisoners in Iraq is for a good cause, the Sotah ritual described in this week's parsha was also for a good cause. The Talmud uses this ritual to demonstrate the importance of *shalom bayit*, peace in the home. The ritual allowed the erasing of a name of God, normally strictly forbidden, in order to excise the demon of jealousy from the home. Of course, they do not record how they excised the demon of the woman's anger and shame after having been subjected to this degrading ritual. An innocent woman would not die from drinking the bitter waters—unless she died of embarrassment.

If the Torah allowed psychological torture for shalom bayit, what would the Jewish tradition have to say about applying this kind of pressure in a time of war? Can the actions of the Americans, however repugnant they may seem to us, be justified under Jewish law?

The biggest argument in favor of allowing these kinds of "interrogations" is *pikuach nefesh*. According to the doctrine of *pikuach nefesh*, saving lives is the highest Torah value of all. We are commanded to violate any commandment—except three—to save a life. The three that we do not violate are murder, violating a sexual law like adultery or incest, and public idol worship. One might argue that if torturing prisoners can save lives, halacha would sanction it.

There are a few principles that put limits on *pikuach nefesh*. In the first place, we are all created *b'tzelem Elokim*, in the image of God. Even enemy combatants are created in the Divine image. Even if someone was executed for committing a capital crime the body was to be treated with respect and buried promptly.

The rabbis in the Talmud equate embarrassing someone with killing them, because both cause the face to go white from loss of blood. Humiliating someone is treated as a very serious issue in halacha. The halacha does not record that it is OK to humiliate some people and not OK to humiliate others.

Most significantly, the *pikuach nefesh* argument that trumps the normal rules of behavior only applies in cases where a specific act will save a specific person. For example, Jewish law generally forbids autopsy. The body is supposed to be buried whole. However, organ donation is permitted—because the organ being removed will save the life of a specific person, whom we can identify. An autopsy for research purposes—or donating one's body to science—is forbidden halachically because while the information might be useful, we do not know for sure, or who will benefit. We do not know that any one particular person will be saved by the information. The connection to saving a life is tenuous, not direct, and a tenuous connection is not enough to overrule the normal rules of following the Torah.

Interestingly, invoking this principle, we see that the CIA's position is actually a position that could be justified halachically. If you captured a terrorist that you know is a ringleader and you know he is planning an attack, it very well might count as *pikuach nefesh* to apply unconventional interrogation techniques. But to apply the same techniques to a random population of "cabdrivers and brothers-in-law," trolling for possible information, would be a tenuous connection to *pikuach nefesh*, and hence forbidden under Jewish law.

Even if it could be justified, is this kind of treatment a good idea? What effect does it have not only on the people subject to the torture, but on the people doing the torturing? According to halacha it is forbidden to steal your own stuff back from a thief, because it gives you a taste of being a thief. I am haunted by the image of the woman soldier grinning. I can't believe she was brought up to think this is the right way to treat another human being.

And what about the message it sends to the rest of the world? Kenneth Roth, executive director of Human Rights Watch said, "Some JAGs (military attorneys) hate this and are horrified that the tolerance of mistreatment will come back and haunt us in the next war. We're giving the world a ready-made excuse to ignore the Geneva Conventions. Rumsfeld has lowered the bar."

I am usually proud to be an American. I don't usually make a big deal over this, recognizing I am living and working in Canada. However, America is a great country, and it is built on some great values like respect for the rights of individuals. Right now, I'm ashamed to be an American. I'm ashamed that such torture happened in prisons operated by the military I once proudly served, and I'm even more ashamed that one of the top leaders of my country authorized it. Perhaps if President Bush had instantly fired Rumsfeld and Cambone when he found out about what happened I would feel differently. But the American leadership seems to think what they are doing is OK. They will prosecute a few low level soldiers, while the leadership of the country treats it as a PR problem. When confronted with the situation, President Bush said the pictures were very disturbing. Not the torture was disturbing, rather the pictures. A telling difference.

The Talmud tells us that in the days of the Second Temple, they stopped using the Sotah ritual because licentiousness had become too widespread. Perhaps because of the immoral influence of the Greeks the ritual's power to shock and humiliate was not so great anymore, and it was no longer effective.

Maybe that's why there has not been even more outrage over the prisoner abuse. Maybe we've become so used to seeing violence, murder and sexual exploitation on TV and the internet that we've lost the ability to be shocked. If the Arabs could cut off someone's head in a video, how can we be shocked by piles of naked prisoners?

Then again, maybe the rabbis in the Second Temple period stopped using the Sotah ritual because they realized it was wrong to treat people that way, because even a suspected adulteress is created in the Divine image.

It does not matter that some Arabs cut the heads off innocent people and other Arabs sing and dance when disaster befalls Americans or Jews. It's not our role in life to descend to their level.

It's not America's mission to do what Rumsfeld has done and "lower the bar." America should be raising the bar.

Shabbat Shalom

On Ordaining Gays and Lesbians
This was my Yom Kippur sermon for 5764, in Richmond (Vancouver), Canada.

Later today during our Afternoon Service we're going to take out the Torah scroll and read a verse from the book of Vayikra, Leviticus, which reads "And a man shall not lie with a man as he does with a woman. It is a *toevah*, an abomination."

How do we reconcile this verse with changes going on in our culture? Gays and lesbians no longer need to deny who they are, or who their partners are, in order to be accepted in straight society. Here in Canada same-sex couples can now get married.

Do we have to choose whether to ignore the Torah or to deny what we see around us?

When asked why the Conservative movement refuses to ordain openly gay and lesbian persons as rabbis, Rabbi Ismar Schorsch, the Chancellor of the Jewish Theological Seminary in New York said: "There is no doubt that such a step would fracture the movement, and in a very severe way. If you want to see the end of the Conservative movement, that's the step to take now."

I strongly disagree with the esteemed Chancellor. Rather than seeing the debate as a bad thing that could lead to the destruction of the movement, I see it as a positive sign that the movement is alive and well, and committed to the principles on which it is based.

In fact, the fact that we are debating this issue is one reason why I'm a Conservative Jew and not associated with some other denomination.

People sometimes ask me "why did you choose to become a Conservative rabbi?" It's not the movement I grew up with—when I was a kid the shul we did NOT go to was Orthodox. I could also have chosen one of the three "R's": Reform, Renewal, or Reconstructionist. So why be a Conservative Jew?

It is because the Conservative approach to Judaism is the only one that really makes sense to me, that resonates with my soul. Ever since the destruction of the Temple nearly 2000 years ago, Judaism has had to struggle to reconcile tradition and change. On the one hand, we need to be faithful to our God, to our Torah, and to the traditions of our ancestors. It's what makes us Jews. On the other hand, we are a part of the world around us; we are influenced by both advances in scientific knowledge and changes in that larger society of which we are a part. Adapting to those changes is what has kept Judaism a dynamic, living, vital spiritual practice, and not just a relic, a museum-piece dedicated to showing us the way things once were. It's far more important that Judaism be able to tell us the way things are.

And change is a part of the way things are. In the late 1700s and early 1800s the Haskalah, the Enlightenment, was sweeping through the Jewish world. Jews in Western Europe were being freed from the ghettos; they were given full rights as citizens of the countries they lived in. It was a heady and exciting time. A number of Jews embraced this new freedom wholeheartedly and set out to reform Judaism, to make it more modern, to make it more like the worship followed by our non-Jewish countrymen. There were experiments with the liturgy, with the language of prayer, even with moving the main day of synagogue attendance to Sunday. The Conservative movement traces its origins to 1845, when Rabbi Zecharias Frankel in Germany broke away from his Reform colleagues because they said that Hebrew was not necessary in the prayer service. Frankel felt they had gone too far in the direction of "change." Interestingly, the Orthodox rabbis of the time also did not approve of Frankel, because he said it was OK to change the prayer book—just not that radically!

And that is where Conservative Judaism has been ever since that day in 1845—the philosophically most difficult and nuanced place in the spectrum of religious thought: not blindly wedded to tradition, which is easy to justify because, well, it's the tradition—and not throwing out the tradition in favor of wholesale changes simply because it's a new world.

That effort to balance tradition and change plays itself out in the Conservative approach to halacha, to Jewish law. Halacha is the intersection of belief and action. As it says in Emet Ve-Emunah, the Conservative movement's statement of principles, "Halacha consists of the norms taught by the Jewish tradition, how one is to live as a Jew." The word itself, halacha, comes from the same root as the word "*holach*" which means to walk. Halacha is the Jewish Walk, the Jewish Way. Halacha is what our community understands to be God's will. And that is a crucial point. Conservative Judaism understands halacha to be binding on us all. As my teacher Rabbi Daniel Gordis put it, "mitzvah does not mean suggestion." We call them the Ten Commandments, not the Ten Suggestions. We are obligated to follow the commandments. The sense of being commanded by God is fundamental to the spiritual path that is Judaism. It defines us in a unique kind of relationship with God and the Jewish people.

In that way, we are similar to the Orthodox, who also maintain that we are bound by halacha, and UNlike the Reform, who maintain that the ritual commandments are not binding. Where we differ from the Orthodox is in our approach to halacha: the way in which we decide what is the law, the way in which we determine what we believe to be God's will.

As Rabbi Elliott Dorff says in an article he wrote for a symposium at San Francisco State University, "Unlike the Orthodox, Conservative Jews study the Jewish tradition -- including its laws -- in their historical context. Sometimes the scientific, social, economic, or moral conditions are relevantly different from what they were when a particular law, judicial ruling, or custom became normative, in some cases the rabbis of the current generation find those differences to be sufficient to warrant a different ruling."

That willingness to consider scientific, social, economic and moral conditions when deciding on the law has led to acrimonious debates within the Conservative community. People of integrity and good intentions can strongly disagree about when changes in those external factors merit a change in halacha. Even though everyone in the Conservative movement might agree in principle that we are about balancing tradition and change, we do NOT always agree on how to achieve that balance.

For many issues, the fact that we do not all agree is not a problem. The Conservative movement is a pluralistic movement. For example, most Conservative Jews know that there's a *teshuvah*, a Jewish legal opinion, that says it's OK to drive to the synagogue on Shabbat and holidays. What most Conservative Jews might NOT know is that there is also a teshuvah which says it is NOT permissible to drive anywhere on Shabbat, even to shul. So what do you do if you've got two rules: one says driving to shul is OK, and the other says it isn't? The answer is that each individual rabbi, as the *mara d'atra*, the decision maker, for the community can decide which teshuvah is correct, or which is correct for his or her community.

There are many issues besides the driving issue where we have no agreement in the Conservative community. There are Conservative rabbis who say it is OK to use electricity on Shabbat, and there are those who say it isn't. There are those who say it is OK to eat dairy meals in non-kosher restaurants, and there are those who say it is not. There are those who will allow women to sign as witnesses on *ketubot* (marriage contracts) and *gettin* (divorce documents), and those who will not. While most Conservative shuls are egalitarian, a few back east will not give women an aliyah, allow them to read the Torah or to lead services.

This pluralistic approach to Judaism is the one that I believe is most authentically in keeping with the spirit of Judaism. I love Talmud—I spend at least half an hour every day studying it. And you cannot study a single page of

Talmud without seeing argument, debate, and an acceptance of different approaches to the law. It is possible to draw on traditional sources and come to two radically different solutions to a halachic question, both credibly within the framework of the tradition and within the bounds of halacha. The Talmud is full of debates between the school of Shammai and the school of Hillel. One time when both sides claimed the halacha was with them, a heavenly voice cried out and said "*eilu v'eilu divrei Elokim chayim,*" both these and those are the words of the living God. They are both valid. They both may be right for their community.

When this pluralistic approach becomes difficult to maintain is when it comes to issues that affect the movement as whole. In the 1980s the movement went through a very difficult and divisive debate about ordaining women as rabbis.

There were those who argued that to allow women to serve as rabbis would be to ignore 2000 years of rabbinic understanding of the Torah. One rabbi argued "anyone who will contribute in any way towards enabling women to be admitted to the Rabbinical School will be transgressing the biblical injunction, 'Before one who is blind, do not place a stumbling block.' He will also be violating the rabbinic prohibition to assist transgressors." In other words, he was saying that if you even lobby in favor of ordaining women, you are committing a sin by leading others astray. Foreshadowing Rabbi Schorsch, Rabbi Simon Greenberg wrote, "There are those who predict that the question of the ordination of women at present agitating the Conservative Movement will inevitably result in the dissolution of the Movement." Guess what? It didn't happen.

To be sure, the halachic issues surrounding ordaining gays and lesbians are different from the issues that surround ordaining women. Nevertheless, the overall context of the debate is strikingly similar. The social circumstance in the world around us had changed: how were we going to respond?

Earlier this year, Judy Yudof, the President of United Synagogue, called on the rabbinical leadership in the movement to readdress the status of homosexuals.

There are two major issues surrounding the treatment of gays and lesbians in our community. 1. Should we ordain openly gay clergy? And 2. Should Conservative rabbis conduct same sex marriages or commitment ceremonies?

She made this request because many congregations are not satisfied with the current "official" position on homosexuality, referred to as the "Consensus Document." Approved in 1992, the consensus document says the following:

1. Conservative rabbis should not perform same-sex commitment ceremonies
2. Gays and lesbians who are out of the closet will not be admitted to rabbinical school, cantorial school, or admitted to the RA or CA. Witch hunts will not be conducted regarding people currently enrolled.
3. Whether homosexuals may function as teachers or youth leaders in our congregations and schools will be left to the rabbi authorized to make halakhic decisions for a given institution within the Conservative Movement.
4. Whether or not to give homosexuals synagogue honors or allow them to serve in lay leadership positions in the synagogue is up to the rabbi and lay leadership.
5. In any case, we hereby affirm gays and lesbians are welcome in our congregations, youth groups, camps, and schools.

There are many people in the Conservative movement, myself included, who are very troubled by this consensus document. And I would not call it a "consensus" document anymore, because it certainly does not reflect a current consensus.

To start with, saying that synagogues can choose not to give gays and lesbians honors, or can refuse to allow them to serve in lay leadership positions, seems homophobic. Let us accept for a minute the argument that homosexuality is a sin (which I don't accept, but we'll come to that). There is no logical reason to single out this particular sin for special treatment. Yes, the Torah says that if a man lies with a man as a woman, it is a *toevah*, an abomination. However, the Torah also says that if you eat clam chowder it is an abomination. If we're going to say we'll only give aliyot to Jews who don't break any of the commandments, we're going to have a hard time getting 8 up to the bima on a typical Shabbat. To say that gays and lesbians are "welcome" in our congregations, but that the synagogue leadership can decide not to give them aliyot, or even allow them to open the ark, is disingenuous. How welcome would YOU feel if treated in such a manner?

The current policy regarding gay clergy has been criticized as a "don't ask, don't tell" policy. Only gays who are in the closet can be ordained. If our chazzan—the wonderful, amazing, talented Andrew Lippa—were to decide to quit his day job and become a full time cantor, he would be turned down by the Cantorial School at JTS. And as any of you who have been here over the holidays could testify, this would be a tremendous loss to the Jewish world.

The fact that Beth Tikvah is a community that is welcoming to all Jews regardless of gender, race, or sexual orientation speaks well to the value we place on being inclusive. The fact that we accept gay clergy shows that we are ahead of the official position of the movement on this issue.

The consensus document is advisory in nature: it is not binding on individual rabbis, who are free to make their own decisions. Many Conservative rabbis will perform same-sex commitment ceremonies. My views on this topic are already known from talks I have given in other forums: I do not consider homosexuals in loving committed relationships to be sinners, and I therefore favor ordaining gays and lesbians as clergy. I would be willing to conduct a ceremony celebrating their relationship for a same sex couple.

However, rabbis do not make their decisions in a vacuum. Because something is permitted does not mean it is mandatory, and it is a community decision whether or not to allow same sex commitment ceremonies in the synagogue sanctuary, and how to handle the membership status of gay couples.

Individual synagogues do not need to wait for the movement as whole to take a position before taking a position of their own.

For example, Beth El Congregation, the largest Conservative synagogue in Baltimore, recently voted to allow its rabbis to perform same-sex commitment ceremonies in the sanctuary. Last month, two women became the first couple to take advantage of the new policy. Some Conservative rabbis on the West Coast have been doing commitment ceremonies for at least ten years.

The underlying question in deciding to ordain openly gay clergy or to conduct same-sex commitment ceremonies is the same. Is homosexuality a sin? If it were a sin, as a movement committed to halacha the Conservative movement would no more ordain an openly gay clergy person than it would ordain someone who openly did not keep kosher. If a gay relationship were a sinful relationship, a rabbi would not acknowledge it with a public ceremony. However, if it is not a sin, there are no barriers to ordaining gays and lesbians as clergy, or to conducting commitment ceremonies.

The process though which we make the decision about whether homosexual relationships should be viewed as sinful is at the heart of efforts to balance tradition and change.

The details of the debate go far beyond the scope of what I could cover in a High Holiday sermon. There is just one aspect of the debate I want to touch on, and that is whether in the face of the verse we have in this afternoon's Torah reading, we can make such a change and still call ourselves a movement governed by halacha. The answer is most certainly yes! The Torah itself gives us the power to do so. In Deuteronomy 17:8-9 we are told that if a controversy arises in your gates, you should go to the "judge who shall be in those days and inquire." The Talmud understands this as giving the judge "in those days"—in every generation—a great deal of leeway in determining what is the right answer for the community at that time.

We have many examples of things that are explicitly mentioned in the Torah that have changed over time. Going by the Torah it's OK to own slaves, and it's OK for a man to have more than one wife. All debts are supposed to be forgiven every seven years. A rebellious son is supposed to be put to death. None of those rules is operable today. Most Orthodox halachic authorities hold that it is a matter of Biblical law that women cannot lead services or serve as witnesses. The Conservative movement has obviously come to different conclusions. The Torah prohibits the offspring of forbidden unions from marrying into the congregation; the Torah prohibits Kohenim from marrying divorcees. The Conservative movement has taken positions contrary to what it says in the Torah because we believe changing circumstances compel us to do so.

The real question is not whether we CAN change the law, but whether we should. And that will be a discussion for another time.

Teshuvot, Jewish legal opinions, have been written on both sides of this argument. I will make copies of those teshuvot available in the office for anyone interested in reading them. In the next few months, I plan to hold a teaching session where we will study some of these teshuvot. The other Conservative congregations in Vancouver are also looking at this issue and we plan to have a joint meeting between all three Vancouver-area congregations in December or January so that all three congregations can hear the opinions of all three local Conservative rabbis. It is my hope that out of those discussions will emerge a consensus, which could form the basis for synagogue policy.

Even though I have studied the issue at length and have reached a conclusion, I still feel that the fact that we are grappling with this issue is a very good thing. If we were to say "tradition!" and stop the discussion, it would be wrong, because we would be denying the reality of the world around us. If we were to simply say, "of course we should change, why should there be any prejudice against this group of people?" it would mean we are not giving sufficient consideration to thousands of years of tradition. Halacha should not immediately respond to every change in society. Major changes should be made slowly, carefully, and thoughtfully.

As we consider this issue, I believe we are truly straining to understand the will of God. May God grant us the wisdom, courage, and compassion to find the proper balance between tradition and change.

Amen.

Illegal Immigration

Illegal immigration is always a hot topic in America (Israel too, for that matter!). What guidance does the Torah provide? This was delivered during Passover 5766.

When our ancestors lived in Egypt more than 3,000 years ago, they were the underclass in Egypt. They did the jobs no Egyptians wanted to do. They spent their days in the relentless sun making bricks and helping build cities.

Fast forward a few thousand years and move over a few thousand miles. Today in America, thank God, slavery has been all but abolished (there are a few pockets of sex workers and domestic help that are working in conditions akin to slavery, but they are relatively few). But we do still have an underclass. We have people who do the jobs no one else wants to do.

Those people are variously called "undocumented workers" or "illegal aliens." Estimates vary, but it is estimated that 11 million people are in this country illegally. Many of them labor at the lowest paying jobs with the worst working conditions—some spend their days in the sun picking oranges or lettuce, providing unskilled day labor, some working in restaurants.

There is a big difference between our ancestors in Egypt and today's underclass in America. All our ancestors wanted was to get out of Egypt. All the undocumented workers of today want is to get IN to America. For even though they may be taking jobs that are at the bottom of heap in America, they pay a lot more than higher status jobs in Mexico, China, the Philippines, or elsewhere. Over the years I've had two nannies for my children who held degrees in accounting – one was from India and one was from the Philippines. A nanny in California or Canada makes more money than an accountant in other places. They happened to be in the country legally – but for workers who have no skills, the difference between what they would earn in Mexico and what they would earn in California is easily ten-fold.

Many Americans seem to be afraid of this wave of poor people washing up on our shores. Go to Google and type in "illegal immigrants America" and four of the first five web sites you are directed too are ones screaming in bold print "Illegal Immigration is a Crime!" Well, yes, I suppose that's why it's called "illegal…"

Those who are most upset about illegal immigration claim it causes substantial harm to America. They claim it drains public funds, because illegal immigrants consume more in services than they pay in taxes; they claim illegal immigrants depress the wages of American workers, especially those without high school degrees; and they claim it contributes to population growth, overcrowding, and a strain on natural resources.

I agree that illegal immigration is a problem that needs fixing. The question is, how do we fix it? Do we fix it by putting up big fences, making helping illegal immigrants a felony, and hiring a bunch more Border Patrol people? Or do we fix it in a much easier way – by making this immigration legal instead of illegal?

The House of Representatives passed a bill, HR 4437, which authorizes building 698 miles of fences along the southern, it repeals the "visa lottery," and it adds new penalties for immigration-related crimes.

Last week I was at a lunch with some Christian colleagues, who are appalled by this bill—basically Section 202 of the bill defines "smuggling" so broadly that they would become criminals for offering undocumented workers a meal at their soup kitchen.

A Senate version of the bill is held up in committee as Senators debate provisions such as one that would make being in America illegally a felony – a serious crime. There are also provisions that provide a path to legal citizenship for the 11 million people who are currently here illegally. There are those who think the Senate bill is too strict, because of the felony provision; and there are those who think it is too liberal because the path to citizenship smacks of "amnesty." This provision would not be amnesty, because it holds that illegal immigrants would in essence need to "earn" the right to stay here, among other things by paying any back taxes they owe on income that was earned without withholding.

I am not going to debate the economic aspects and impact of undocumented workers on the American economy. It is a very complicated topic, and in a global economy there are arguments that can be made on both sides. Yes, one could argue that illegal workers willing to work at or below minimum wage hold down wages—if that pool of labor was not available, employers would have to pay the Americans who are here legally more to do undesirable jobs. On the other hand, in a global economy, if no one here is willing to pick lettuce for minimum wage, the alternative may be that the field lies fallow while we import lettuce from Mexico—which would not help workers, and it would penalize farmers. So the real impact of migrant workers is hard to determine.

What I do want to look at this morning is whether there are messages from the Jewish tradition – especially from the Passover story we told at our seders a few nights ago – that can guide us in our thinking about immigration reform.

One of the most fundamental messages of the Passover story is to be kind to strangers. Over and over again in the Torah, we are commanded "do not oppress the stranger, for you know what it is like to be a stranger." The Torah clearly forbids us from having blind prejudice against people who come from different places to dwell among us.

Jews, of all people, should be sympathetic to people coming to America in search of a better life. While some of our ancestors were fleeing anti-Semitism when they came to America, many also came simply seeking a better more comfortable life for their children. To say "we're here, now you can close the door behind us," would be a kind of meanness of spirit characterized by the tradition as *midot S'dom,* the traits of the people of Sodom – those nasty people God wiped out in a storm of hail and brimstone.

In fact, *hachnasat orchim,* hospitality, welcoming visitors, is an important mitzvah. There are several examples given in the Torah, including both Abraham and his nephew Lot who provided warm welcomes to visitors from afar who showed up on their doorsteps without warning.

This does not mean we should take down any fences or border controls and let anyone into the country who wants to come. Jerusalem has been a walled city for thousands of years. Security is certainly a valid concern. The government is not only entitled, it is obligated to check the credentials of people who want to come to this country in order to ascertain that they are not a security threat. If a fence is needed to keep terrorists out, build a fence. However, if we are going to build a fence for security reasons, we need to look at more than a fence along the border between California or Arizona and Mexico—we also need to look to the north. The border between the US and Canada is the largest unprotected border on the planet. A fence on the southern border might stop Mexicans wanting to work here, but it won't stop terrorists, as a terrorist from the Middle East could just as easily smuggle himself into Canada and from there into America as from Mexico.

What would the Jewish tradition suggest we do with people who are already here illegally?

We can look to this week's Torah portion for guidance. We have a special Torah reading for this morning, the Shabbat that falls during Passover. It is from the book of Exodus. Moses asks God *hareini na et k'vodecha,* "please, God, show me Your glory!" God responds with the thirteen attributes of mercy: "And the Lord passed by before him, and proclaimed, The Lord, The Lord God, merciful and gracious, long suffering, and abundant in goodness and truth, Keeping mercy for thousands, forgiving iniquity and transgression and sin, and that will by no means clear the guilty."

The Torah (Deuteronomy 13:5) commands us "You shall walk after the Lord your God." How do we walk after the Lord? The Talmud tells us that the way we walk after the Lord is to imitate his qualities. As God is forgiving of iniquity, transgression, and sin, so we should be forgiving of sin. It is appropriate for us to find a way to forgive those who entered this country illegally—yet at the same time we are also told that God "will by no means clear the guilty."

The application of "will by no means clear the guilty" could come in applying yet another principle from the Torah: *mishpat echad yiyeh lachem kager kaezrach,* you will have one form of law for both the native-born citizen and the stranger. People who came here illegally are required to comply with the laws of the land—they need to pay their taxes, if they drive they have to have car insurance, etc. The proposal in the Senate bill which provides for undocumented workers to normalize their status here by learning English, and paying any back taxes seems quite sensible and in accordance with our values.

Immigration reform is a very hot topic in Congress these days. Senators and Congress-people are nervous about which way to go – they don't want to be seen as soft on security or not concerned about job loss, yet they also don't want to be seen as lacking in compassion and prejudiced against Mexicans – especially at a time of a growing base of Latino voters.

I encourage you to write our Senators, Mike DeWine and George Voinovich and Congresswoman Marcy Kaptur and encourage them to support immigration reform which is both compassionate and sensitive to security considerations. Prejudice masquerading as security has no place in the foreign or domestic policy of a nation built by immigrants.

We sit and eat our matzah in the most comfortable exile the Jewish people have ever known. Jews are now the wealthiest religious denomination in America. This makes it more important than ever that we remember one of the fundamental lessons from the Passover story – we know what it is like to be a stranger. We know what it is like to be oppressed. Even if our children are born with golden spoons in their mouths, we have institutional memory of what it is like to be poor, to be the underclass, to be working the jobs no one else wanted.

May God help us to walk in His ways of compassion, and may He strengthen the efforts of those who work to create a more compassionate and loving community, country, and world,

Amen.

Silence Implies Consent

It is not enough to refrain from evil yourself: you must speak out against evil when you see it. Matot 5765.

Qui tacet consentit is Latin for "silence implies consent." I don't know where the old Romans came up with it, but it's a principle we can derive from this week's Torah portion, Mattot:

> "If a woman vows a vow to the Lord, and binds herself by an oath, being in her father's house in her youth; And her father hears her vow, and her oath with which she has bound her soul, and her father remains silent, then all her vows shall stand, and every oath with which she has bound her soul shall stand. But if her father disallows her in the day that he hears; not one of her vows, or of her oaths with which she has bound her soul, shall stand; and the Lord shall forgive her, because her father disallowed her."

In other words, if a young woman still living in her father's house makes a vow, her father can overrule it, and her vow does not count. On the other hand, if the father does nothing – if he simply remains silent – the vow stands.

The Talmud has an entire tractate, Nedarim, devoted to the rules of vows. In Nedarim it confirms that an unspecified silence means agreement. The medieval commentator Sforno teaches, "When a person has the ability to protest and remains silent, his silence is similar to verbal consent. When you do not say something to disagree, it is as if you agree with what was said or done."

We all know that one of the Ten Commandments is "do not bear false witness against your neighbor." What you might not know is that the rabbis understand this commandment as meaning you can bear false witness by not saying a word—it does not mean the same thing as telling lies. For example, under Jewish law, you need two witnesses to be prosecuted for a crime. If there is one witness, and you stand next to that witness, making it look like you are a witness with him, when you are not, you have borne false witness—you have tried to make someone believe something that is not true with your silence, by just standing there. And you would be considered guilty of violating this commandment.

We have an example in the Torah of someone being punished for remaining silent. At the end of Parshat Baha'alotcha, there is a story about how Miriam and Aaron spoke against Moses because of "the Kushite woman," a reference to his wife. The commentator Ibn Ezra says that Miriam spoke, and Aaron agreed or was silent – and thus he was punished. His keeping quiet while Miriam spoke against Moses was a sufficient transgression to merit his being punished.

Not only in the Torah is silence seen as consent. In civil law, silence does not ALWAYS imply consent, but it can. In cases when the silent person would be bound in good faith to explain himself, silence gives consent, as long as the person knows what he is doing and his silence is voluntary. According to one law dictionary I consulted, "when any person is accused of a crime, or charged with any fact, and he does not deny it, in general, the presumption is very strong that the charge is correct." The same reference indicated, "When an oath is administered to a witness, instead of expressly promising to keep it, he gives his assent by his silence, and kissing the book."

Another well-known example of silence meaning consent is the Presidential veto. When Congress passes a bill, if the President keeps silent, it implies he agrees with the bill and it becomes law. He has to actively protest to stop the bill from becoming law—just like the father in our example from this week's Torah portion.

Think of all the things going on in the world around us that are wrong. They range from the profound and the unjust to things that are much more mundane.

To give a simple example many of us can relate to, many parents are disturbed by the lack of "family programming" on TV. Melissa Caldwell, director of research and publications for the Parents Television Council (PTC), says, "What happens is a lot of the clean shows get branded with being milque-toast or boring. It's so much easier to insert a four-letter word or a sex joke that it almost becomes formulaic."

So what should you do if you wish there were more shows suitable for children on TV? Caldwell says you should speak out. "A lot of people don't like what they see," says Caldwell, "but don't voice their protest. Silence tends to give consent."

Silence tends to give consent. But not only to the relatively banal, like TV programming. Silence tends to give consent for crimes far more heinous than four letter words on TV.

In 1939 the population in Germany was 79 million people. If half of them had taken to the streets in protest, would Hitler have been able to conduct his genocide against the Jews? Isn't it the silence of 78 million plus of those 79 million people that gave Hitler the tacit consent to his wicked plan?

Edmund Burke said "All that is necessary for the triumph of evil is that good men do nothing." That they keep silent.

Now to be fair, the truth is that silence does NOT always mean consent. Silence is actually quite a complicated affair. Nowhere is this better proven than in a brilliant scene from the movie "A Man for All Seasons," which Steven Spielberg and I will act out for you.

"A Man for All Seasons" is the story of Sir Thomas More, who had the temerity to stand up to King Henry VIII when Henry decided to divorce his wife against the wishes of the Catholic Church. He established the Church of England, the Episcopalian or Anglican Church, instead. More had been Lord Chancellor, number two man to the King. He resigned as the schism with the Catholic Church was approaching. A little while later, he refused to take an oath required of all citizens of England repudiating the influence of "foreign powers," meaning the Pope, in English affairs. More maintained that he was not renouncing the king—he was simply maintaining his silence, and silence implies consent, so the King should leave him alone.

The following is the way the movie treats a historical meeting between More (played by Steven Spielberg) and King Henry's chief advisor, Thomas Cromwell (played by myself):

Cromwell: Now, Sir Thomas, you stand on your silence.

Sir Thomas More: I do.

Cromwell: But, gentlemen of the jury, there are many kinds of silence. Consider first the silence of a man who is dead. Let us suppose we go into the room where he is laid out, and we listen: what do we hear? Silence. What does it betoken, this silence? Nothing; this is silence pure and simple. But let us take another case. Suppose I were to take a dagger from my sleeve and make to kill the prisoner with it; and my lordships there, instead of crying out for me to stop, maintained their silence. That would betoken! It would betoken a willingness that I should do it, and under the law, they will be guilty with me. So silence can, according to the circumstances, speak! Let us consider now the circumstances of the prisoner's silence. The oath was put to loyal subjects up and down the country, and they all declared His Grace's title to be just and good. But when it came to the prisoner, he refused! He calls this silence. Yet is there a man in this court - is there a man in this country! - who does not know Sir Thomas More's opinion of this title?

Crowd in court gallery: No!

Cromwell: Yet how can this be? Because this silence betokened, nay, this silence was, not silence at all, but most eloquent denial!

Sir Thomas More: Not so. Not so, Master Secretary. The maxim is "Qui tacet consentiret": the maxim of the law is "Silence gives consent". If therefore you wish to construe what my silence betokened, you must construe that I consented, not that I denied.

Cromwell: Is that in fact what the world construes from it? Do you pretend that is what you wish the world to construe from it?

Sir Thomas More: The world must construe according to its wits; this court must construe according to the law.

If we are silent in the face of great wrongs, how is it to be construed? At its worst, it could be construed as consent. At its best, it could be construed as apathy: a lack of care and concern.

We live in a world where there are many issues that beg for speaking up. Murder on a massive scale in Darfur, Sudan. Terrorism. Torturing prisoners. Slavery. Bias against Israel everywhere you turn, most recently from the Vatican where terrorists in Israel were not condemned while terrorists in London and Madrid were. 45 million people without health care in the United States. 10 million people a year dying from starvation around the world.

We must speak out, on these and other important issues. There is a famous poem, attributed to Martin Niemoller:

> "First they came for the communists, and I did not speak out - because I was not a communist;
>
> Then they came for the socialists, and I did not speak out - because I was not a socialist;
>
> Then they came for the trade unionists, and I did not speak out – because I was not a trade unionist;
>
> Then they came for the Jews, and I did not speak out - because I was not a Jew;
>
> Then they came for me - and there was no one left to speak out for me."

If you want someone to speak out for you, you must speak out on behalf of others. If you are silent, you are making a statement: and Craig Bruce said, "Silence is a statement that is open to gross misinterpretation."

Do not allow your silence to be grossly misinterpreted. I know you are all good people, who do NOT consent to the terrible things going on in the world. Don't let your silence be misconstrued. Speak out. Pick a subject you believe is important and learn about it. Talk to other people about it. Write letters to the editor about it.

Lest someone think that your silence gives consent.

May God bless us all with the strength and determination to speak out about injustice, whether injustice here at home or injustice across the ocean, whether the injustice of Jews or the injustice of Gentiles,

Amen.

Chapter Seven

Business Ethics

"Raba said, When a man is led in for Judgment he is asked, 'Were you honest in your business dealings? Did you fix times for learning? Did you engage in procreation?'"

Babylonian Talmud, Shabbat 31a

Note that the FIRST question one is asked when one dies and is "led in for Judgment" is not whether one studied Torah, or kept kosher. The very first question is whether a person conducted his business affairs with integrity. To be religious does not mean one is simply punctilious about ritual requirements. One must pay equal attention to the moral requirements of the faith.

As a rabbi AND a businessman, business ethics is a topic of particular interest to me.

Aggressive Accounting & Personal Integrity

When is "aggressive accounting" fraud? What guidance does the Torah provide in how to conduct our business affairs? This was my d'var Torah for Yom Kippur on 5763.

Rabbi Yisrael Salanter had a student who was a *shochet*, a kosher butcher. This student once came to him with a problem. He said, "Rabbi, I've been a shochet for many years, and as I grow older I become more concerned about my responsibilities. I'm so worried that I'm going to cause someone to eat non-kosher meat that I want to change careers: I want to give up being a shochet, and instead go into business." Rabbi Salanter asked him if was an expert on the laws of *shechita*, of kosher slaughter. The student replied, "of course, I'm a shochet, I've been studying shechita for years." The rabbi asked, "And are you expert in the laws of business?" To which the student replied, "No, of course not, who bothers to learn Choshen Mishpat (the Jewish laws dealing with business)?" The rabbi said, "Wait a minute, I don't get this. Here you are, you are an expert in the laws of shechita, yet you are ready to give it up because of your fear of sinning. Yet you know nothing about the halacha of business, and you want to go into business? All the more so you should worry about sinning!"

Many Jews are like that shochet. They associate "sin" with doing some ritual thing wrong. You ask them what does it mean to be an observant Jew, and they'll tell you an observant Jew, a religious person, is one who obeys the laws of Shabbat, someone who keeps kosher, who lights candles on Friday nights. Hmmm...I may even have implied that in my sermon from last week! If a person dresses in fashions popular in Poland 200 years ago, people assume he must be REALLY religious.

But is that what being religious is really all about? Who is more religious: a rabbi who's punctilious about kashrut and Shabbat, but fraudulently applies for government grants to support his yeshiva, or an ordinary Jew, who goes to shul sometimes, and keeps kosher sort of, but is very careful in his business dealings to always do the right thing?

Just in case you have any doubt as to how God would answer that question, the Talmud (Shabbat 31a) gives us the answer: When a person dies and is brought before the Heavenly Beit Din for judgment, he is asked: "did you conduct your business dealings with integrity? Did you make time for studying Torah? Did you work at raising a family? And did you wait expectantly for Salvation?"

So when you die, God doesn't first ask whether you kept kosher. God doesn't first ask whether you observed Shabbat. God doesn't even first ask if you studied Torah, although that comes in a close second. The FIRST question is "did you conduct your business dealings with integrity?"

You shouldn't think, *chas v'shalom*, God forbid! that this means ritual is not important. God does get around to asking about whether we studied Torah—and presumably about whether we kept kosher and observed the

Sabbath. The point is we serve God through both the mitzvot that are between ourselves and God—the ritual mitzvot—and through the mitzvot that are between ourselves and other people. Whether we conducted our business affairs with integrity is the "acid test" for how we treated other people.

The world around us seems to have lost sight of the importance of conducting one's business dealings with integrity. The list of corporations caught up in accounting scandals grows longer every day. Enron, WorldCom, and Global Crossing are three of the worst offenders. The crashes of these corrupt companies have put tens of thousands of people out of work and hurt millions of investors. Interestingly, all three shared the same accounting firm, the now virtually non-existent Arthur Andersen, an accounting firm that in 2001 had revenue of over $US 9 billion. Andersen's web site now has practically nothing on it except press releases where they continue to deny any wrong-doing. In a press release dated June 25, Andersen claims, "Our work for WorldCom complied with SEC and professional standards at all times. It is of great concern that important information about line costs was withheld from Andersen auditors by the chief financial officer of WorldCom." Nearly $4 billion dollars improperly accounted for, leading to the biggest corporate bankruptcy on record, the write-off of billions of dollars from investors, vendors, and employees and the audit firm didn't notice anything wrong?

Most of us here in British Columbia probably did not have a lot of money invested in WorldCom—or Enron, or Global Crossing for that matter. You might be wondering, "Why should we care?" Or…"why's the rabbi talking about accounting scandals?"

The reason is that these accounting scandals are symptomatic of a larger problem. They are symptomatic of a culture of greed, a culture that has its values in the wrong things and in the wrong places. A culture that says stealing is OK as long as you can get away with it and don't use a weapon. And we shouldn't think the problems are limited to the US; after all, the former CEO of WorldCom, Bernard Ebbers, is a Canadian.

I know that only a few of the people here today are corporate executives or accountants. Don't worry, it's not only you I'm picking today! We all have "business dealings." We all buy things in stores. Almost all of us have bosses or employees, clients or customers, gardeners or mechanics or babysitters.

So all of us, in order to be good Jews, need to know something of what our tradition teaches about the world of business.

To illustrate some of the principles, let's look at whether "aggressive accounting" practices are forbidden under Jewish law.

Aggressive accountants primarily have two ways to make a company look more profitable than it really is: they can inflate sales by counting transactions that aren't really sales, or they can move expenses off of their books, most commonly by counting them as investments in assets rather than as expenses.

Some forms of "aggressive accounting" clearly amount to fraud; others are in a grey area.

For example, a high-tech company that makes software used in manufacturing computer chips booked $11m in phony transactions to their Japanese distributor, Canon. Canon had never agreed to the transactions—they were completely made up, and thus fraudulent. It's hard to believe that management thought they could get away with something like that.

In this case, the company did more than questionable accounting: they committed fraud. Under Jewish law, there's an important principle called "*dina d'malkhuta dina*," which means "the law of the land is the law." That's a basic minimum. We are obligated under halacha, under Jewish law, to follow the laws of the place where we live. If you speed, you are not only violating Canadian law, you are violating Jewish law. In the example of phony transactions, as they are clearly forbidden by secular law they would also be forbidden by Jewish law.

On the other hand, let's say Canon as a distributor had agreed to buy a certain amount of product. There can be a real honest grey area about whether particular sales are really sales or not, depending on how "final" they are. What if Canon can send the product back if they do not resell it within a certain time frame? Is it really a sale? Maybe, maybe not. Those are the kinds of areas where accountants can have some room to play, some room to be "aggressive," or alternatively they can choose to be more conservative.

Global Crossing and Enron both were playing games with recognizing revenue that wasn't really revenue. Some of what they did involved counting sales from one subsidiary of the company to another—which would be something like taking $5 out of your right pocket, putting it in your left pocket, and claiming you just made $5.

WorldCom, on the other hand, played the other side of the equation: they counted as capital investment almost $4 billion in expenses. It's sort of like what would happen if you took the money you spent on groceries last year, and said you had made an "investment" in food, and claimed your net worth was now that much higher.

What does Jewish law tell us about such situations? What is OK, and what is not OK?

When accounting becomes excessively aggressive is when the accountant—or the management of the firm—can account for a sale one of two ways, and they choose the one that paints a better picture, even if they know that it is not an accurate picture. When they decide that they will take the approach that allows them to recognize a sale—which will boost their profitability—even though they have reason to think the sale won't really stick—they are using aggressive accounting. They are painting a picture of the company for the public that is more favorable than where they think is the reality. Why would they do that? Because if the company looks better, more people will buy the stock, driving the price of the stock up, which of course personally benefits the management of the company since they probably own stock or stock options. They hope that they won't be caught because MAYBE the sale will stick, or by next quarter other business will come in to mask the fact that this piece of business wasn't really good. Sometimes these kinds of shenanigans can get buried and absorbed as "restructuring" costs in a reorganization, which the stock markets usually don't get as excited about as big operating losses. All sorts of rationalizations are available.

In this case, what they did might be legal or at least "arguable" under secular law, but it would be illegal under halacha, Jewish law. It would be forbidden under halacha for the same reason false advertising is forbidden: it's a case of *geneivat da'at*, of creating a false impression (literally "stealing of an opinion"). The Biblical source for the prohibition against creating a false impression is debated by the *poskim*, the Jewish legal experts. R. Jonah b. Abraham Gerondi of 13th century Spain says it comes from the Biblical injunction in Exodus (23:7) to keep far from a false matter. R. Yom Tov Ishbili, also of 13th century Spain, was of the opinion that it came from the Torah's prohibition against theft found in Leviticus 19:11. R. Ishbili wrote that the prohibition *lo tignovu*, don't steal, prohibits both theft of property and "theft of the mind" by way of deception.

Nevertheless, whatever it is based on, everyone agrees that creating a false impression is forbidden.

The executives at Enron, WorldCom, and Global Crossing probably did not think of themselves as crooks. They probably did not think of themselves as thieves. They probably told themselves "we are entitled to be as aggressive as we can as long as we act within the law." They probably even convinced themselves that they were doing their fiduciary duty to their shareholders by doing whatever they could to keep the stock prices up.

Ramban has a name for people like that: they are *called naval b'rshut ha-Torah*, wicked within the boundaries of the law. They may be obeying the letter of the law...but they are scoundrels nonetheless.

If we are going to make the world a better place, we need people who are willing to do more than the legal minimum. We need people who care about doing the right thing.

A focus on doing the right thing is a fundamental characteristic of the Jewish legal system. The Jewish legal system focuses on responsibilities more than on rights. As a member of society, as a member of the community, you are obligated to behave in a certain way. Judaism calls on us to do more than the "legal minimum," it encourages us to do more than what we could get away with—Judaism encourages us to be menschen, not scoundrels.

Harvey Pitt, the chairman of the US Securities and Exchange Commission has said this is exactly what the business world needs. In a recent speech Chairman Pitt said, "It's difficult, and often impossible, for government to discover frauds perpetrated with management collusion in the early stages. This makes the need even stronger for people of integrity in accounting, law and business who detect fraud early, or avert it."

If we are going to create a society of menschen, it's not going happen because we put people like the executives at the Enron's of the world in jail. We have to start earlier than that. We have to start with ourselves, and with the examples we set for our children.

If movie tickets are lot a cheaper for kids aged 2-11, and your child is just barely past her 12th birthday, what do you do? ... Let's raise the ante, how about if it's lift tickets at Whistler, $65 for adults, only $33 for kids?

If the clerk in the grocery store hands you a $20 in change instead of a $10, do you have to give it back? Or do you figure you've been shortchanged enough times it will wash out?

If a contractor gives you a fixed price bid on some work on your house, and they made a major mistake, and gave you a price way too low, do you hold them to it? You might think it's his problem, but halacha tells us otherwise. The principle of *ona'ah*, price fraud, tells us we cannot overcharge when we sell—but interestingly enough, it also tells us we are forbidden to "underpay" when we buy. God wants us to be fair.

If you have a "bank error in your favor" do you give it back, or do you try to keep it? Do not say this never happens—I once had over $10,000 in an investment account that I rolled over from one firm to another via a checking account, and ended up having the same $10,000 in two different places. No one wanted to claim it. It took me months of phone calls to get someone to figure out that they credited me with money that was not mine.

Is it OK to use the color printer at work to print out a page from the internet for your son's book report? Is it OK to browse eBay on company time?

Is it OK to let your kids watch a pirated copy of Harry Potter over the internet? What if you know your kids are bootlegging music?

If you don't have the right change, is it OK to make your babysitter wait a few days to be paid?

If we answer those questions the wrong way, we will find ourselves raising the next generation of "aggressive accountants," who see nothing wrong with what they do as long as they are not TOO blatantly breaking the law. People who are *"naval b'rshut ha Torah."* The rabbis in the Talmud instead encourage us to go *"lifnim meshurat hadin,"* beyond the letter of the law—like Aaron Feuerstein, the CEO and owner of Malden Mills did when his factory was shut down because of a fire. He kept 3,000 employees on the payroll for three months, at a cost of millions of dollars. In an interview Feuerstein said, "I have a responsibility to the worker, both blue-collar and white-collar. I have an equal responsibility to the community. It would have been unconscionable to put 3,000 people on the streets and deliver a death blow to the cities of Lawrence and Mathuen. Maybe on paper our company is worth less to Wall Street, but I can tell you it's worth more. We're doing fine."

Feuerstein went beyond not just the secular law, but he went beyond what the Torah would require. He truly went *lifnim meshurat hadin*, beyond the letter of the law.

As alluded to in the story about the butcher, a businessperson should be just as concerned about learning the halacha of business as a shochet is concerned about learning the laws of kosher slaughter. However, the laws of business, the laws of the marketplace, are relevant not just for business people, but for all of us.

We all need to know how to answer that first question that the Heavenly Beit Din will ask when the appointed time comes: "Did you conduct your business affairs faithfully?"

G'mar Tov

God & Intellectual Property

Both my wife and one of my best friends are intellectual property attorneys, and I am a co-inventor on two patents, so it is no surprise I have some interest in the subject. Terumah 5767

God is a stickler for details.

This week's Torah reading, Terumah, contains all the design details for the Tabernacle, the portable Temple, and its contents.

Look at all the details given in the instructions for building just one of the ritual objects, the menorah:

"And you shall make a menorah (lamp stand or candelabra) of pure gold." The Torah tells us that it is to be hammered out of a single piece of refined gold; we are told it should have six branches from the sides, three on each side, and a lamp in the middle for a total of seven. Design details are given: Three bowls made like almonds, with a bulb and a flower in one branch; and three bowls made like almonds in the other branch, with a bulb and a flower; so for the six branches that come from the menorah. Similar design details are given for the central branch and the base.

After all the design details are given, God tells Moses "And see that you make them after their pattern, which was shown to you in the mount."

The Midrash tells us that after God gave Moses all the construction details, Moses was so confused by the details that he threw up his arms in despair and said "Master of the Universe, am I a god that I should be able to make it exactly to these instructions?" So God sent down a model of the menorah made in fire so Moses could picture it clearly and build one exactly like it.

So this humble menorah – a beautiful and glorified candleholder – was actually a partnership between God and Man. God was the designer. God drew up the plans. God gave the detailed instructions, and according to the Midrash even provided a detailed model. And Man, the artisans of the Jewish people, built the menorah to God's design.

God's involvement – the design, the instructions, the plan – is all what we would call "intellectual property." The design itself is not a physical thing – it's an idea. And the idea for the menorah belongs to God, who shared His idea with the Jewish people.

Besides the construction details of the Tabernacle and its contents, there are other examples of God's intellectual property found in the Torah. God gave Moses a very specific recipe for the incense that was to be burned in the Temple. There is a list of "sweet spices," most of which I have never heard of, and frankincense, all to be mixed together in equal parts. Moreover, God guarded this recipe carefully. Unlike the recipe for Coca-Cola, which is secret, God put the recipe in the Torah; however, God still "reserved the rights" to the incense. He told Moses that the people were NOT to make any incense like that for themselves. It is a special concoction holy to the Lord, only to be used in the Temple rituals.

The rabbis in the Talmud instruct us to protect God's intellectual property – they are clear that we are not to make copies of the menorah. The Talmud tells us one must not make a menorah after the design of the menorah in the Temple. You can make a menorah with five branches or six branches or eight branches, but what you cannot do is make one, like the menorah in the Temple, with seven branches. The rabbis argued whether this applied even if you made the menorah out of different metals or out of completely different substances like wood. Cutting through the fine points of their arguments, they were unanimous that one could not make an exact replica of the menorah in the Temple to use at home.

Just as the rabbis were concerned about protecting God's intellectual property, society is concerned about protecting the intellectual property of inventors, artists, writers and musicians. And that is what I'm going to talk about this morning: protecting intellectual property.

It might seem a little strange to some people that I would choose today, a bar mitzvah, when we have a lot of young adolescents around, as the day to talk about something as abstract as intellectual property. Thirteen year olds, however, are on the front lines of the battle to protect intellectual property. Hence, it is a most appropriate topic for us to talk about this morning.

We all know that kids today are remarkably technologically astute. How many of you parents turn to your kids when you need tech support for your computer system? Kids today even resent it when their parents are clued in technically, as was shown in the comic "Zits" a few days ago. Dad says "I saw this neat video on YouTube" and while the teenage son is sputtering, Dad says, "I think I just single-handedly managed to make YouTube uncool."

Most 13-year-olds today are familiar with many different ways to violate the laws protecting intellectual property. Many 13-year-olds make copies of a friend's CD, or download video or music files, with only a vague sense that they might be doing something inappropriate.

Does it matter? Why should we care about copying music files?

The music industry certainly cares – according to the Recording Industry Association of America, illegal copying costs the music business $4.2 billion / year. Bootleg and pirate videos cost the motion picture industry $6 billion a year, and illegally copied software costs the software industry $30 billion a year. Just those three industries have losses of over $40 billion a year to illegal copying.

Why is intellectual property theft so rampant? It is probably because many people do not even think of it as theft. Many people who would never walk into a store and slip a CD into their pocket and walk out without paying have no problem doing effectively the same thing by making a copy of a friend's CD or downloading music files. Many people who would never sneak into a movie theater to see a movie for free have no problem doing the same thing via a computer.

When a person steals a physical object, like a CD, from a store, he knows there was some cost in producing that object. The theft seems concrete and real. The thief or would-be thief knows that he is taking money out of the pocket of the owner of the store. Not only that, he is confronted with having to sneak around the employees and other people in the store. However, when making an illegal copy, it is done in the privacy of your own home, no one can see you, and the person being robbed doesn't even know it.

This has become more of an issue in recent years because technology has made it incredibly easy to steal people's intellectual property. Before the advent of the printing press, copyright laws were unknown. As soon as the printing press came into existence, laws were created to protect publishers and authors from other people copying their stuff.

We are in the middle of a technological revolution that is on a par with the development of the printing press. Books enjoy a certain amount of built-in protection: while making a photocopy of a book is also intellectual property theft, by the time you pay for the toner and the paper, and spend all the time it takes to turn 200 pages on the copier, you might not save much money. But making a copy of a CD or a video is simple, and downloading files is literally "child's play."

Napster started the whole business with its peer to peer network which setup a piracy partnership: if you let other people copy stuff off of your computer, you can copy stuff off of theirs. The courts said that Napster was facilitating intellectual property theft, and they were shut down. However, it has not made the problem go away. Alternative peer-to-peer solutions such as Morpheus have sprung up. There are legitimate uses for software like Morpheus – there are plenty of files people could choose to share that are perfectly legal. But it's a pretty good bet that a very large percentage of the 51 MILLION people who have downloaded Morpheus are using it to copy material that is protected by copyright.

Many of the people using programs such as Morpheus to trade music files will rationalize what they are doing by telling themselves they are not hurting the music industry because they weren't planning to buy the music anyway. Especially kids whose only income might be a small allowance will say it's not costing anyone money, because they say, "I don't have the money to pay for the songs, so it's not like they are losing a sale."

But just because you wouldn't have bought it is no excuse for stealing it. If you are not willing to pay the price for something, you live without it. It is not right to steal something just because you do not want it badly enough to be willing to pay for it, and it's easy to steal.

The Recording Industry points out how many people are harmed by music piracy: consumers lose out because piracy drives up the cost for people who are honest. Stores lose out because they can't compete with bootleg copies or files swapped for free. Record companies lose – 85% of all recordings don't generate enough revenue to cover their costs as is. And, perhaps most directly, the musicians lose. Musicians, singers, songwriters and producers do not get the royalties and fees they have earned. Virtually all artists depend on these fees to make a living. As recording artist "Tool" put it, "Basically, it's about music -- if you didn't create it, why should you exploit it? True fans don't rip off their artists."

I wrote a teshuvah, a Jewish legal opinion, called "Intellectual Property: Can you steal it if you can't touch it?" which I will be presenting to the Conservative Movement's Committee on Jewish Law and Standards at their meeting next month. Hopefully this teshuvah will be less controversial and divisive than the ones the committee approved in December having to do with ordaining gay and lesbian clergy. Nevertheless, based on my visit to the committee last June, I expect a lively discussion.

Someone asked me why we should need such a paper. Doing things such as swapping music files is against the law. The Recording Industry

Association of America has been finding and suing people who download many songs – parents beware, parents of kids engaged in heavy downloading have been hit with bills enforced by the courts for $3,000 and up. As Jews, we are already religiously obligated to follow the laws of America under the principle of *dina d'malchuta dina,* the law of the land is the law. Why should it matter what Jewish law has to say?

It matters because so many people obviously seem to feel that it's OK to download and trade music files, videos, software, and other forms of intellectual property. So I figured we needed a statement on whether it was ethically and morally proper within a Jewish framework. Perhaps some people who look the other way at the legalities might be influenced by an understanding that the behavior is not only illegal, but it is unethical.

The paper goes on for 17 pages and has 53 footnotes. I'll spare you all the details, but I will share some of the highlights as to why Jewish law says it's wrong to make illicit copies of other people's songs, words, or other creations.

As I pointed out earlier, we see that the Torah itself protected God's intellectual property, as the Torah tells us the mixture for the incense is special, only to be used in the Temple. But maybe we cannot take an example from God. Maybe the incense is protected because God's recipe has extra holiness.

Going back to the early days of the printing press, rabbis added letters called approbations to books that were published. In these approbations, the rabbis would praise the virtues of the book and the author, and they would often add a statement prohibiting the reprinting of the book for a specified period in order to allow the publishers time to print and sell copies of the book to recoup their costs and make a profit. Originally, the approbations were put in place to protect the publisher, not the author. Hundreds of years ago typesetting a book was a very labor-intensive process. The Chatam Sofer points out that if publishers weren't assured of a monopoly in the publication for fixed period of time so they would be able to recoup their costs, they wouldn't want to publish works of Torah—and the community would be spiritually impoverished. Allowing a monopoly on the intellectual property was a benefit to the community, which is similar to the argument used in secular law that society benefits from the protection of intellectual property. The same logic applies not only to works of Torah, but to all forms of intellectual property. Our lives are richer because we're able to enjoy music that musicians can afford to spend their time creating because their efforts are protected and rewarded.

These approbations generally threatened anyone who violated the terms with being banned from the Jewish community. The first example of the protection of Jewish music included not only a threat of a ban, but a curse as well. In 1623, Salamone Rossi published a collection of Jewish sheet music, which included the following statement from a group of rabbis:

"We have agreed to the reasonable and proper request of the worthy and honored Master Salamone Rossi of Mantua . . . who has become by his painstaking labors the first man to print Hebrew music. He has laid out a large disbursement which has not been provided for, and it is not proper that anyone should harm him by reprinting similar copies or purchasing them from a source other than himself. Therefore . . . we the undersigned decree by the authority of the angels and the word of the holy ones, invoking the curse of the serpent's bite, that no Israelite, wherever he may be, may print the music contained in this work in any manner, in whole or in part, without the permission of the above-mentioned author."

In addition to finding that the protection of intellectual property was good for society, the rabbis believed that protecting intellectual property was important to prevent unfair competition, which is a principal found in the Talmud. The Chatam Sofer said that if protection from competition was offered to printers, how "...much more so for one who created a new entity... for example, the consummate scholar, Rabbi Wolf Heidenheim, who spent countless hours in the editing and translating of the piyutim... and why should others profit from his creativity?"

And there is a third reason brought by the rabbis for protecting intellectual property, which is that when someone sells something he is allowed to attach conditions to the sale. An example in the Talmud says that if a person gives money to a poor person to buy a shirt, he cannot use that money to buy a cloak, and vice versa. The Talmud says he who "disregards the owner's desire is called a robber." Similarly, when a book or CD or music file is sold it is only sold for the use of the owner, and the owner is not given the right to make copies to sell or give to other people.

A further reason to condemn casual intellectual property theft such as music or video file swapping is that it contributes to a general weakening of the moral fiber of society. America has been plagued with one financial scandal after another in recent years. We see it in the corporate world with companies like Enron and WorldCom. We see it in the political arena with scandals like the ones surrounding Tom Noe and Jack Abramoff. The Jewish tradition teaches us that there is a slippery slope with regard to ethics. If people see this form of "cheating"—copying music files—as being OK, other forms of cheating are also likely to be taken more lightly. The Talmud forbids us to steal, even from a thief, *batar geneivah ganuv v'tamah ta'im* if you steal from a thief, you get a taste for thievery.

Ted Olson (former US Solicitor General) makes a similar argument in an op-ed piece he authored that appeared in the Wall Street Journal: "These systems [that allow swapping music files] also inflict immeasurable damage to our standards and morals. By enabling millions of persons, especially our children, to take property without paying for it, we are sending a potent message that it is acceptable somehow to steal music if it is done in the home with a computer rather than stuffing CDs from a store into a backpack and walking out. That is why many organizations that represent traditional values have joined in the effort to stop this systematic and widespread theft - unified by the belief in the simple and ancient principle: "Thou Shalt Not Steal"."

The eighth of the Ten Commandments is *lo tignov*, you shall not steal. It is not OK to steal just because it's easy to steal, and it's not OK to steal just because the person being stolen from won't even know he's been ripped off. The Torah teaches us that abstract things like ideas and designs – and by extension, books and music – are valuable. Let's treat them that way.

Shabbat Shalom

Is Snitching a Jewish Value??

Blog entry from January 2008. Nothing gets me more riled up than the hypocrisy of "religious" Jews who are crooks.

Amy Klein (with the help of colleagues in LA) wrote a fascinating article in LA's Jewish Journal about a financial scandal involving money laundering and tax fraud on the part of a Chasidic yeshiva in New York (Spinka).

How, you might be wondering, could a yeshiva get involved in such criminal activity?

The truth is, it is a lot easier than you might think for a non-profit organization to become involved in fraud and tax evasion. Here's how it works. A wealthy individual wants to reduce his taxes. So he gives the yeshiva a $1 million donation – on condition that they return $900,000 in cash to him. Mr. Big Bucks gets a million-dollar tax write-off – easily worth something like $300,000 in real money – and the yeshiva gets to keep $100,000 for their efforts. For most yeshivas, a $100,000 donation is a significant infusion of funds. They did this over and over; authorities identified over $8 million in fraudulent transactions in one year alone.

But it's against the law. How can kippah-wearing criminals justify such behavior?

They make all sorts of excuses to themselves. The government takes too much of our money. It's a mitzvah to keep "yiddishe gelt" away from the secular tax authorities. No one is getting hurt. They don't feel they are doing anything wrong, since they are using the money to support yeshiva bochers learning Torah; they are not using the money to buy yachts.

Notwithstanding any of those excuses, what they are doing is illegal, it is corrupt, and it is wrong. Not only are their clothes stuck in Poland in the 19th century, their attitude toward the authorities is as well.

When a government singled out Jews for "special" treatment, when all taxes were subject to negotiation, when the government may have been conducting pogroms against Jews (or turning a blind eye to those who did), one could justify not paying taxes as a form of "civil protest," as a way to avoid funding institutions that were out to harm you. America in 2008 is not the same as Russia in 1808, when Jews were expelled from the countryside. America has been very good to the Jews indeed – and to try to steal from government using a rationale that applied to a different government hundreds of years ago is a disgrace, and a *chillul Hashem*, a desecration of God's name.

Klein's article talks about the debate among Orthodox rabbis about whether it is permissible to be a "*moser*," someone who hands a Jew over to secular authorities, in this day and age. To me it is scandalous that there are rabbis who say we should be protecting Jews who are violating the laws of a country as democratic, fair, and good to Jews as America. Daniel Treiman in a post on Bintel Blog makes a comparison between this culture and the culture of "stop snitching" put forward by "gangsta rappers."

I also mention the effect of popular culture on our willingness to speak out against corruption in a teshuvah I wrote, which was approved by the Conservative Movement's Committee on Jewish Law and Standards in New York last month. The teshuvah, "Whistleblowing: The Requirement to Report Employer Wrongdoing," was approved by an overwhelming majority of 18 to 1, with a few abstentions. You can read it online at the Rabbinical Assembly web site.

The Conservative movement is sometimes criticized as being a kind of "Orthodox lite." We are criticized for always looking for "*kulot*," for leniencies. I am proud to say that when it comes to moral issues such as this one, we are stricter than many of our Orthodox colleagues.

And this is clearly what God wants of us. The Holy One is more concerned with how we treat each other than with our punctilious observance of ritual commandments. It does not mean, God forbid, that we should not obey the ritual commandments. When the prophet Isaiah railed against the hypocrites of his day, people who punctiliously brought beautiful sacrifices and then cheated their neighbor, when he quoted God saying "is this the fast I desire?!" it didn't mean people shouldn't fast on Yom Kippur. It meant they should not fast if their religious observance is going to be accompanied by immoral behavior. I wonder if the rabbis involved in this scandal felt at all embarrassed when reading that passage from Isaiah in shul on Yom Kippur. I hope they bowed their heads in shame.

To be strict on ritual commandments, and lax on moral command-ments, is completely bass-ackwards. To wear a kippah while cheating your neighbor – or the government – is a classic case of "immersing in a *mikvah* with a *sheretz* in your hand." Whatever good you do is completely wiped out.

And to argue that one should not report a Jew engaged in wrongdoing is to condone such behavior. To stand by and watch someone engage in fraud and to say nothing is to become an accomplice in the fraud.

The Talmud (Shabbat 31a) tells us that when a person passes away and is brought before his Creator in his final judgment, the very first question he is asked – the very first – is "did you conduct your business affairs with integrity?" Only after that is he asked about other mitzvot.

Shabbat Shalom from Ir Hakodesh, Jerusalem

Chapter Eight

Ritual

"And in process of time it came to pass, that Cain brought of the fruit of the ground an offering to the Lord. And Abel also brought of the firstlings of his flock and of the fat of it. And the Lord had respect for Abel and for his offering;"

Genesis 4:3-4

Ritual has been a part of religious expression for as long as there has been religion. The first example of ritual appears in the Torah in the opening chapters of Genesis, when Cain and Abel bring their offerings to God.

Ritual can take many forms. Prayer, Shabbat, kashrut, life cycle events are all different forms of ritual expression. All are designed, in some way, to help increase our "God-consciousness," to help infuse our lives with meaning. This chapter touches on a few of the more important rituals in contemporary Judaism.

The Power of Shabbat

I learned to appreciate the power of being together with community on Shabbat after having to spend a Shabbat without my community. Vayakhel 5763.

"And Moses gathered all the congregation of the people of Israel together, and said to them, These are the words which the Lord has commanded, that you should do them. Six days shall work be done, but on the seventh day there shall be to you a holy day, a Sabbath of rest to the Lord; whoever does work in it shall be put to death."

Exodus 35 1-2.

The commandment to observe Shabbat has already been given a couple of times in the Torah, most notably in parshat Yitro as part of the Ten Commandments. In this week's parsha, why does Moses repeat the commandment, specifically starting out with "*vayakhel*," by gathering the people together? What is there new for us to learn from this version of the commandment that we could not have learned earlier?

The first thing we need to appreciate is the context for this week's Torah reading. Last week we read about how Israel committed the great sin of idol worship, creating a Golden Calf. It's hard to believe, but not long after witnessing the miracles that God performed in Egypt, the people lost confidence because Moses was running a little late coming down the mountain. They "fell off the wagon," and engaged in idol worship.

Rashi explains that the events described in this week's parsha happened on the day after Yom Kippur, the day that Moses came down from the mountain with the Ten Commandments. At the time of this week's parsha, when Moses gathered the people together, it is true that Israel had committed the sin of the Golden Calf, however God had also already been appeased and reconciled with Israel after the intervention of Moses. God wanted to destroy the people and start over with Moses; Moses convinced God to spare the people.

Rashi brings a surprising teaching that the people did the sin of the Golden Calf only to instruct future generations about the power of teshuvah, repentance. To show that even after such a serious sin as idol worship, it is still possible to turn back to God. This week's parsha, starting with the repetition of the commandment to obey the Sabbath, is specifically showing us that observing Shabbat is a powerful part of the process of returning to God. In the Talmud we are told that anyone who keeps the Sabbath according to its laws, even if he did idol worship like the generation of the Flood (even worse than the sin of the Golden Calf), his sins are forgiven him. Observing Shabbat has the power to purify a Jew of his or her sins, regardless of how low he has fallen.

The Slonimer Rebbe points out that this is actually very surprising advice. After all, Shabbat is the high point of the week, the time when you come closest to God, the time for a real cleaving with God; the polar opposite of idol worship. Wouldn't logic suggest that if you were very distanced from God you would need to work your way up to reaching the heights of closeness to God that is the goal of Shabbat? Isn't it too big a jump, like going from a totally dark room into bright sunlight?

What gives Shabbat this remarkable power to bring the greatest sinner back to God is really the power of community.

A few weeks ago I had what for me is an unusual experience: Shabbat without community. I had surgery on a Friday, and Shabbat was spent recovering at home. Most of that Shabbat was spent sleeping. I observed all the traditional observances—we had a Shabbat dinner, I prayed, etc.—but all without the presence of community.

It was a much different experience than a "regular" Shabbat. Yes, it was a very restful day. However, the lack of community—the lack of praying together, studying together, eating together—also made it less spiritually fulfilling and uplifting. A lot of the power of Shabbat to change our lives comes because of the power of community to nurture us.

Which is why this week's parsha starts with Moses gathering the people together. This is the thing that "God commanded to do." God commanded us to *"vayakhel,"* to gather on Shabbat. To be together on Shabbat. The Slonimer Rebbe says that when we come together as one on Shabbat, with one heart, like one person, we can spiritually elevate a Jew in any situation, no matter how distanced she may be from God.

More Jews have been brought back to Judaism by an exciting Shabbat experience than by anything else. I read a story a while back about a young man who was a totally secular Jew who lived near the ultra-religious neighborhood of Mea Shearim in Jerusalem. He went to a protest against the religious people who wanted to close the street on Shabbat. He went out to speak about his right to do what he wanted, to observe or not observe Shabbat in whatever way worked best for him. One of the religious people on the other side challenged the young man to come to spend Shabbat with his family, so he could learn firsthand what they were talking about. Not having a graceful way out, the young man reluctantly accepted…and was amazed by the warmth, love, and joy that filled the Shabbos table. He became a regular visitor to that family's home and eventually became a *ba'al teshuvah*, a returnee to Judaism.

A couple of years ago there was a horrible terrorist attack at the Dolphinarium disco in Tel Aviv. Twenty one young people—kids in their late teens and early twenties, my oldest daughter's age—were killed while standing in line to get in to the popular disco. Mostly young Russian émigrés. A Chasidic rabbi friend of mine was at the Satmar Beit Midrash the following week, and heard an amazing exchange: "What can they expect?" said a stout young Satmarer *avrech* (married student) commenting on the bomb outrage. "They go dancing in a disco on Shabbos night in *Eretz Hakodesh* (the Holy Land)? It's an invitation to the Satan!"

But a bent, white-haired chassid gently raised his hand and said: "They grew up in Russia knowing nothing about Yiddishkeit. They came here and no one taught them a thing about Yiddishkeit. What do they know, except to go out dancing on Friday night? For that the *Ribono Shel Olam* (Master of the Universe) will forgive them. The question is: Will He forgive us for the way WE keep the Shabbos? After all, we claim to know something about Shabbos. If we were to sing, dance and rejoice the way we should on Shabbos, it would be so powerful that nobody would feel the slightest desire to go out to the disco!"

And that, my friends, is the power of "*vayakhel*," of gathering together. And that is the reason we need to continue to work to bring more ruach, more spirit, into our Shabbat.

Shabbat Shalom!

Keeping Kosher – The Letter and The Spirit of The Law

In keeping kosher, it is not enough to follow the letter of the law – we have to pay attention to the spirit of the law as well. From Parshat Re'eh 5766.

Does God care what you eat?

For a Jew, the answer is yes. This week's Torah reading, Re'eh, contains five verses that are the basis for our entire system of kashrut, the dietary laws. Volumes of Talmud and chapters of law codes have been written working out the details given in these few verses.

The discussion of what we can and can't eat starts with a very general statement: *lo tochal kol to'evah*, "do not eat any abominable thing." That's all well and good, but how are we supposed to know what kind of food constitutes an abominable thing? That's sort of in the eye of the beholder, isn't it? Some people love sushi, some think it is gross.

Fortunately, the Torah continues and gives us a few details. Deuteronomy 14:6 tells us that the only animals we can eat are ones that have a split hoof and that chew their cud. In case we are unclear on the concept, the Torah gives us a few examples of animals that might seem border line. Camels are not kosher because even though they chew the cud, they don't have a split hoof. Pigs are not kosher because even though they have a split hoof they do not chew their cud.

Verse 9 tells us that anything that lives in the water has to have fins and scales. Tuna is OK; catfish, Shrimp Scampi, and Lobster Newberg are out.

Verse 11 tells us *kol tzipor tahorah tochalu* "of all *tahor*, ritually pure, birds you shall eat." When it comes to birds, the Torah doesn't give us the definition of what makes a bird *tahor*. Instead, the Torah simply gives us a list of birds we cannot eat: eagles, hawks, owls, vultures, ravens among them. Not mentioned—and therefore kosher—are birds like chickens, ducks, geese, and so on. The rabbis in the Talmud were able to figure out the common denominator of the birds on the forbidden list – basically, they are raptors, "flesh eating" birds –

which was very helpful when the Jewish people encountered a new species not mentioned in the Torah: turkeys.

In addition, verse 21 of the same chapter contains one verse which includes the final two basic rules of keeping kosher, the requirement for kosher slaughter and the requirement to separate meat and dairy. The verse reads, "You shall not eat of anything that dies of itself; you shall give it to the stranger that is in your gates, that he may eat it; or you may sell it to a foreigner; for you are a holy people to the Lord your God. You shall not boil a kid in its mother's milk."

The Torah tells us the reason we are to follow these rules about what to eat is because we are an *am kadosh*, a people set aside for God. Rashi explains that "for you a holy nation to me" means that we sanctify ourselves with what is permitted to us. The Hebrew word *kadosh*, usually translated as "holy" in the Hebrew has more of a connotation of "set apart." Keeping these rules is part of what sets us apart as a people, part of what gives us our group identity – part of what unites us with our fellow Jews wherever they may live. The verse tells us we are allowed give or sell non-kosher meat to non-Jews; they are not prohibited from eating it, and we are not prohibited from having a financial gain from non-kosher meat.

But there are also some universal values embedded in the many rules of keeping kosher, and it is one of those that I want to explore this morning. But before we can get to the universal value, we need to understand some of the details.

As I mentioned earlier, Deuteronomy 14:21 tells us *lo tochlu kol neveilah*, do not eat a "*neveilah*." The simple meaning of "*neveilah*" is an animal that died of natural causes. One might think of a *neveilah* as just being a land animal—the commentator Ibn Ezra points out, no, it includes both birds and animals (but not fish).

This verse is understood to prohibit more than animals that died of natural causes. It is understood as prohibiting animals that are *treifah*, literally "torn," which includes both animals that were killed by other animals and animals that were killed by people not using the proper procedure for kosher slaughter. Sifrei, a halachic midrash, says when we read the verse do not eat a "*neveilah*" we might think it means only animals that died of natural causes; how do we know it includes the more expansive category of *treifah*? The verse says *kol neveilah*, all the *neveilah*, which includes any animal not slaughtered in a kosher way. So while deer may be kosher, we cannot eat deer killed through hunting – we can only eat deer that were raised on a farm and subjected to kosher slaughter. And no eating road kill.

When I started keeping kosher, it took me about a year to go from eating ham and cheese sandwiches to having two sets of dishes. I started out by giving up what I called the "high treif," the foods specifically prohibited by the Torah—pork, shellfish, and so on. The next step was not mixing meat and dairy, and phase three was buying and eating only kosher beef. But for a while I did keep eating chicken in non-kosher restaurants, until I discussed it with my rabbi who said, no, you really need to give up the chicken too because chicken also has to be slaughtered properly. So, slightly reluctantly, I gave up the Kung Pao Chicken at non-kosher restaurants.

The rules of kosher slaughter for animals are very stringent. Eating meat is seen as a compromise—we are taking an animal's life to benefit ourselves. It would be better not to do that, but since we have a strong appetite for meat, God allows us to eat it, but there are restrictions. A blessing is said before the slaughter. The animal must be killed with a very sharp knife, without even a single nick. A very clean cut must be made across the majority of the trachea and/or esophagus. If the knife drags a little in the cut, the meat is not kosher. All the blood must be removed. Additionally, the animal must be inspected to make sure it was not diseased.

Most of these rules – the requirements for a sharp knife and a clean cut in particular – clearly seem to be based on preventing unnecessary suffering for the animal. Sefer Hachinuch, a 13th century commentary on the commandments is explicit about this: "The reason that slaughter must be done at the throat with a knife that is thoroughly inspected is , *k'dai sh'lo netza'ar ba'alei hachayim yotar midai*, in order that there will not be unnecessary suffering to animals, for the Torah permits people to sustain and nourish themselves and take care of their needs, but NOT to cause gratuitous pain. The sages spoke at great length about the prohibition against *tz'ar ba'alei chayim*, causing pain to animals in the Talmud, and these things are prohibited by the Torah."

For most of Jewish history, the practice of kosher slaughter was clearly in line with both the details of the law of and the intent of the law. But when we come to 20th century America, a problem arose. In 1906, the passage of the U.S. Pure Food and Drug Act required that animals not fall on the floor or come into contact with the blood of other animals. The way this rule was typically implemented—at both kosher and non-kosher slaughterhouses—for a long time was with what is called the "hoist and shackle" method, in which chains are placed around the rear legs of the animal and it is hoisted up in the air by its rear legs. This technique is patently cruel—it not infrequently breaks the leg of the animal, and clearly causes a great deal of pain, fear, and discomfort. After hoisting the animal in the air, sometimes nose tongs would be used to pull the head back to expose the throat, which could then be slit with the carefully prepared knife without a nick in it. In 1958, the US government banned hoisting conscious animals because of the cruelty involved – yet, ironically, kosher slaughter was exempted, because there was no other way to meet both the halachic requirement that the animal be conscious when slaughtered, and the sanitary requirements of the Federal government.

Talk about a great irony! Kosher slaughter—whose rules were designed to minimize suffering to animals—was exempted from a rule of the US government, and was conducted in a way that was crueler than secular slaughter. By 1963, alternative methods of kosher slaughter were developed which could keep the animal upright and calm during slaughter – but many kosher slaughterhouses failed to implement them because they were more expensive than using the hoist and shackle technique.

To use a very sharp knife to kill an animal that is hanging upside down and thrashing in distress is clearly a case of following the letter of the law, but not the spirit!

Agriprocessors of Postville, Iowa – a plant run by rabbis affiliated with Chabad Lubavitch – was in the news a few months ago for alleged ongoing mistreatment of animals. A few years ago the situation at Agriprocessors—one of the country's largest kosher slaughterhouses, which includes the Aaron's and Rubashkin's brands—was truly horrible. They did use the "hoist and shackle" method, and there were videos of workers ripping out slaughtered animals' tracheas while the animals were clearly still alive and suffering. Is meat like that kosher? Just what are the requirements for meat to be kosher?

A few months ago I got into an email discussion with someone who presented the following case: if someone who keeps a kosher home lives in a rural area and only has access to kosher meat that was processed at a plant using inhumane technique for slaughter, would it be better for them to eat local meat and poultry that is slaughtered on farms by local farmers who demonstrate compassion and consideration for their animals?

The question is asking "what's more important?—to follow the letter of the law, or the spirit of the law?"

Clearly, there are Orthodox rabbis who say that the letter of the law is what is important – they continue to certify as kosher meat that is slaughtered in cruel ways.

Just as clearly, many Reform and Reconstructionist Jews would go with eating the "eco-kosher" meat of the local farmers.

The Conservative movement has addressed the issue in a teshuvah, a legal opinion, written by two of the "*gedolim*," the leading lights of the Conservative movement, Rabbis Elliot Dorff and Joel Roth, who ruled "Now that kosher, humane slaughter using upright pens is both possible and widespread, we find shackling and hoisting to be a violation of Jewish laws forbidding cruelty to animals and requiring that we avoid unnecessary dangers to human life. As the CJLS (Committee for Jewish Law and Standards), then, we rule that shackling and hoisting should be stopped."

Personally, I do not believe that the CJLS went quite far enough. They said shackling and hoisting violates the laws forbidding cruelty to animals – but they did NOT say it renders the meat not kosher.

My own view is that the meat is literally rendered not kosher. You might as well eat a hamburger from McDonald's as meat that has been slaughtered using the hoist and shackle method. So here is an instance where I am more stringent than many Orthodox rabbis – meat they would consider glatt kosher, I would consider treif.

At the same time, I would not say that it is OK to eat "compassionately raised and killed" meat from a local farmer that was not done in accordance with the rules of kashrut. It is not enough to follow only the spirit of the law, no more than it is enough to follow only the letter of the law. The intent behind the law is part of the law.

Look at speed limits for example. Why do we have speed limits? We have speed limits to keep people safe – excessive speed is dangerous. If you are driving a new Porsche on a long straight stretch of the interstate where there are no other cars in sight, and it's a nice clear day, you could drive 90 miles an hour and certainly still be safe—well within the spirit of the law. But I don't recommend you try it—the Highway Patrol will still give you a ticket. The letter of the law says the speed limit is 65 miles an hour, not 90.

Similarly, you could be driving 60 miles an hour in that 65 mile an hour zone, and get a speeding ticket. How? If it is a very foggy day and visibility is seriously reduced, 60 miles an hour is a very dangerous speed. And the spirit of the law is the law as well. Ohio statute 4511.21 provides the details on speed limits, including 65 on highways that are part of the interstate system. However, it also says in section (A): No person shall operate a motor vehicle, trackless trolley, or streetcar at a speed greater or less than is reasonable or proper, having due regard to the traffic, surface, and width of the street or highway and any other conditions.

I maintain the same principle applies in Jewish law. It is not enough to follow only the spirit or only the letter of the law. What God wants of us is both. One of the reasons we have the laws is to refine our characters. Nachmanides (Ramban) has an interesting comment on the other part of the verse that we have been considering, the part that deals with separating meat and dairy – "you shall not boil a kid in its mother's milk." Ramban says that we are given this rule in order that we will be holy – that we will not be cruel, so lacking in compassion that we could milk the mother and cook the child in the same milk.

If the laws were given to us in order that we should be kind and considerate to animals, that we should not be cruel, it is totally ludicrous to think it is OK to follow the technicalities while violating the essence.

So what should the people trying to keep kosher in a rural area do? I offered three options:

1) Go vegetarian, or just stock up on meat on those occasions then they visit the big city.
2) Order kosher meat over the internet. You can get kosher meat delivered anywhere these days.
3) Learn how to supervise the shechita of the local farmers to make it kosher, or import a rabbi to supervise.

All spirit and no ritual lacks connection to community and tradition; all ritual and no spirit is deadening and does nothing to deepen faith. But if we combine spirit and ritual the result is spiritual. We can elevate our souls and draw ourselves closer to God through the most mundane of activities – such as paying attention to what we eat.

Shabbat Shalom

PS. Agriprocessors has stopped using the hoist and shackle method and they claim to have changed their processes. Several rabbis from the Conservative movement visited the Agriprocessors plant last week. When they report on their findings, I will share them. The meat I most wholeheartedly recommend is the Chai Chicken, which can be found at Hiller's in Ann Arbor, which is both free range and kosher.

Honor Your Parents

The rabbis teach that honoring your parents is the hardest commandment in the entire Torah to obey. Yitro 5763.

"Honor your father and your mother; that your days may be long upon the land which the Lord your God gives you."

Exodus 20:12

To honor your parents is no simple thing. The rabbis taught that this is the most difficult commandment of all to obey...so much so, that one rabbi in the Talmud said it is better to be born an orphan. I have a colleague who refuses to teach this commandment, on the grounds that he has a terrible relationship with his father, and feels it would be hypocritical for him to teach it, since he feels he is not doing a very good job with following this mitzvah. I disagree with that approach; even though I have issues in my relationship with my father, I am not going to let that deter me from teaching about this important subject.

Why are parents singled out for such special treatment in the Ten Commandments? The Talmud in tractate Kiddushin teaches us that there are three partners in the creation of a person, the Holy One, blessed be He, the father, and the mother. When people honor their parents, God says "I ascribe [merit] to them as though I had dwelt among them and they had honored Me."

Bringing a new life into the world is surely one of the most mysterious and "God-like" activities we can engage in. The connection with God is pretty clear: ask any infertile couple whether the decision to have children is entirely in human hands. And even for those of us blessed with fertility, we have little control over the specific nature of any individual child. Anyone who has more than one child has surely marveled at how different kids can be who come from the same genetic stock and grow up in a very similar environment. As I said a few weeks ago in my talk about cloning, one of the problems I have with cloning is that it seems to want to take God out of the equation. Cloning is an attempt to create a child without that pesky genetic variation that God likes to introduce into the creation of a child.

If we can understand the special role that parents have as partners in creation with God, we can appreciate why the commandment to honor them is important. But what does it mean to honor your parents? If you ask a child, nine times out of 10 they will tell you we honor our parents by obeying them. Not to discourage obedient children, but the truth is that is not what the commandment says—and advisedly so. The reason is simple: what if your parent tells you to do something wrong? If your parent tells you to do something against the Torah, you should not do it. But at all times, even if the parent gives you bad instructions, you are still commanded to honor them. So how do we go about this task? How far are we supposed to go in honoring our parents?

The Talmud in tractate Kiddushin brings an interesting story: "Rab Judah said in Samuel's name: R. Eliezer was asked: How far does the honor of parents [extend]? — he said, Go and see what a certain heathen, Dama son of Nethinah by name, did in Ashkelon. The Sages sought jewels for the ephod (the high priest's breastplate), at a profit of six-hundred-thousand [gold denarii], but as the key was lying under his father's pillow, he did not trouble him. The following year the Holy One, blessed be He, gave him his reward. A red heifer was born to him in his herd (a 100% pure red heifer—without even one white hair—is VERY rare, and is essential to a critical ritual in the Temple). When the Sages of Israel went to him [to buy it], he said to them, 'I know that [even] if I asked you for all the money in the world you would pay me. But I ask of you only the money which I lost through my father's honor.' Now, R. Hanina observed, If one who is not commanded [to honor his parents], yet does so, is thus [rewarded], how much more so one who is commanded and does so! For R. Hanina said: He who is commanded and fulfils [the command], is greater than he who fulfils it though not commanded."

Of course, in my family, I imagine Dad would be pretty upset if I let a 600,000 gold denarii profit disappear in favor of a nap, but maybe they really did not need the money. However, the message from the Talmud is clear: honoring parents is more important than money.

The hero of that story also respected his mother. The Talmud continues, Dama son of Nethinah was once wearing a gold embroidered silken cloak and sitting among Roman nobles, when his mother came, tore it off from him, hit him on the head, and spit in his face, yet he did not shame her. How many of us would be able to put up with such treatment in public, and not at least speak harsh words? By now, you are probably getting the idea why the rabbis say this is such a difficult commandment to obey.

Have you ever seen a bumper sticker on a big RV that says, "We're spending our children's inheritance?" The rabbis tell us the kids certainly have no grounds to complain. "R. Eliezer was asked: How far does the honor of parents [extend]? — He said : That if the father should take a purse full of money and throw it into the sea in his son's presence, the son should not shame him." The Talmud raises the question, if it's the father's purse, why does it matter to the son? The response: "Say it refers to a potential heir. "

These stories from the Talmud show how difficult it is to honor your parents. However, as if honoring our parents was not enough, there is another closely related commandment. In Leviticus 19:3 it is written: "A person shall revere (fear) his mother and father, and keep my Sabbaths, I am the Lord your God." This command is a little different than the one we read in this week's parsha: *yirah*, or fear, instead of *kavod*, honor. Additionally, the sequence of who to honor is different. The verse we have in this week's parsha says to honor your father and mother. The verse in Leviticus tells us to fear our mother and father. Why the change in sequence?

"Rabbi said: It is revealed and known to Him Who decreed, and the world came into existence, that a son honors his mother more than his father, because she sways him by words; therefore the Holy One, blessed be He, placed the honor of the father before that of the mother. It is revealed and known to Him Who decreed, and the world came into existence, that a son is more in awe of his father than his mother, because he teaches him Torah, therefore the Holy One, blessed be He, put the fear [reverence] of the mother before that of the father."

I find it fascinating that 1,500 years after those words were written, human nature remains the same...most people would agree with the Talmud, that we tend to honor our mother more and fear our father more.

But as a practical matter, what's the difference between fear/awe, and honor? The rabbis of the Talmud said, "'Fear' means that [the son] must neither stand in his [father's] place nor sit in his place, nor contradict his words, nor tip the scales against him. 'Honor" means that he must give him food and drink, clothe and cover him, lead him in and out."

So if we are commanded to feed, clothe, and house our parents, the next obvious question to ask is at whose expense? Do you provide the service, but spend the parents' own money, or do you foot the bill yourself? This is a very real question for those of us who have parents who are in need of assisted living type arrangements, who cannot care for themselves, and who need help in arranging where and how to live.

As is often the case, the rabbis had an argument, this time over who should pay. The side that said the son should pay based their view on a verse which says to "honor the Lord with your substance (wealth)." Since the rabbis made a connection between honoring parents and honoring God, one view is that just as we honor God with our money, we should do the same for our parents. The side that said at the son's expense, argued with the others, saying that if you say it is at the father's expense, what kind of honor is that? How does that affect the son? The response was through loss of time. And that is not an insignificant thing. I've talked to many people who spend a lot of their spare time taking care of aging parents, helping with shopping, housecleaning, driving to medical appointments, etc. Even using the parent's money, it is still truly doing the mitzvah of honoring your parents to take care of them in this way during their old age.

It is also well worth remembering that "what goes around comes around." Our children will learn how to treat us from how they see us treat our parents. There is a story told of a family that had an elderly grandfather living with them. Grandpa was getting pretty feeble, and when he ate he kept making a big mess and breaking the dishes. The parents got tired of the continual struggle, so they gave Grandpa a wooden bowl, which he could not break, and fed him in the kitchen so he wouldn't make a big mess at the table. One day the parents came home and found little Timmy sitting and carving a piece of wood. Dad asked, "What are you doing?" Timmy said, "I'm carving a bowl for you for when you get old." That evening Grandpa was back at the regular table with real dishes...

Shabbat Shalom!

Why I Fast on Tisha B'Av

Tisha b'Av, the ninth of the Jewish month of Av, is the saddest holiday on the Jewish calendar. It is the only holiday other than Yom Kippur when we fast for a full 24 hours.

Tisha b'Av is not a widely observed holidays in the "progressive" movements of Judaism. Many modern Jews don't connect with the disasters the holiday commemorates—the destruction of the First and Second Temples, the fall of Betar (signifying the end of the Bar Kochba rebellion in 135CE), the expulsion from Spain in 1492. The centerpiece of Tisha b'Av observance is certainly mourning for the loss of the Temple. Which can make it a difficult commemoration since many of us feel at least ambivalence, if not outright opposition, to the idea of the restoration of the Temple if it also means the restoration of animal sacrifice.

The annual cycle of Jewish holidays covers the full range of human emotions—joyous, sad, reflective, commemorative, and so on. Tisha b'Av is the time for mourning. However, I believe that for Tisha b'Av to accomplish its purpose, it needs to be more than a time for commemorating disasters that have befallen our people. It needs to be a time to inspire us to do something to prevent more disasters from occurring.

Kabbalah, Jewish mysticism, teaches that the Messiah will not come until we have done "*tikkun olam*," healing or repair of the world. There is a teaching that says the Messiah will not come until three days after he is no longer needed. According to this view of the Messianic age, the Messiah doesn't come to make everything perfect—instead, the Messiah's arrival is sort of a "graduation ceremony," an acknowledgement that we created the kind of world into which the Messiah could come. It is taught that when the Messiah comes, Tisha b'Av will be turned from a day of fasting to a day of feasting.

If we are fasting on Tisha b'Av, it means we have failed. It means that once more, we have not done the work to create the kind of world into which the Messiah could come. The Temple has not been rebuilt. There is still strife and senseless hatred in the world. I fast on Tisha b'Av not so much in mourning for the destruction of 2,000 years ago, but to remind myself that we have not accomplished our work of making the world a better place. Given the realities of the "neighborhood" Israel lives in, the Temple will not be rebuilt until our Arab cousins decide to invite us to do so—and today we seem further away than ever from such an eventuality.

PART III: THE MEANING OF LIFE

"For the meaning of life differs from man to man, from day to day and from hour to hour. What matters, therefore, is not the meaning of life in general but rather the specific meaning of a person's life at a given moment."

Viktor Frankl

There are many different ways we find meaning in life, and at different times different things will be in the foreground. In addition to exploring the question of the meaning of life directly, this section discusses a variety of topics that are "near and dear" to my heart, that contribute to the meaning I find in life: such as Israel, the Conservative approach to Judaism, interfaith relations, and remembering those who have come before us.

Chapter Nine

The Meaning of Life

"Rabbi Tarfon used to say: you are not obligated to complete the work (of fixing the world), but neither are you exempt from contributing."

Mishnah, Avot 1:16

"What is the meaning of life?" is probably the second oldest question that humans have ever asked (I would assume "what's for dinner?" is the oldest). From the most idealistic person to the most pragmatic, everyone has pondered this question at some point in their lives. Some give up, and settle for bumper stickers like one I saw which read "he who dies with the most toys wins." Personally, I think the answer is as Rabbi Tarfon put it: you are here to help make the world a better place. But that's a proposition that not necessarily everyone will readily accept. And even if you accept it, how do you accomplish it?

I have been interested in this question since I was a teenager. I studied psychology and philosophy looking for insights. I turned to Eastern religions and martial arts. I tried ignoring the question. Eventually I found the answers in Judaism.

What is Your Mission in Life?
There is something unique that we can each contribute to the world. There is a special reason each of us is here. This Yom Kippur sermon provides some suggestions for figuring out why you are here.

"Your mission, Jim, should you choose to accept it..."

When I was a kid, I would hear those words coming from the TV, and then sit on the edge of my seat waiting to hear what kind of difficult, no, impossible, mission was going to unfold over the next hour.

Real life is not so simple. We don't wake up one morning when we turn 21...or 31, or 41, or 51...and receive a tape from God that begins, "Your mission, Barry, should you choose to accept it..." Instead, one of life's biggest challenges is to figure out just what the heck our mission is.

And I believe that discovering one's mission in life is one of the most important spiritual tasks a person can undertake. It is an active response to the question of what is the purpose of life.

So what does Judaism say about the purpose of life?

We find the answer by starting at the beginning: the creation of the world. The Torah opens with: In beginning, God created the heaven and the earth. And the earth was without form, and void; and darkness was upon the face of the deep. But that's not the whole story: the Jewish mystical tradition, Kabbalah, elaborates on our Creation myth in a way that has profoundly influenced the way Jews view the meaning of life. Keep in mind that we do not look at these stories as in any way competing with the scientific view of what happened—they work in a different realm, a beautiful tale designed to enlighten us on how God chooses to interact with the world.

Before the beginning, God filled the Universe. The first step in creation was a contraction: God had to withdraw, concealing God's self, so that there would be room for the physical world. God then began to emanate into the world, pouring His divine energy into vessels called sefirot, which represent different ways God has of interacting with the world—a bridge between the finite and the infinite. The vessels were not able to contain God's light—it was too powerful—and the vessels shattered. The remnants of those shattered vessels are the physical world we live in. Yet those shattered shards contain remnants of Divine energy, just as a broken honey jar would still have honey stuck on the pieces of glass. The world, in a sense, was created in a cosmic work accident. Our communal mission is to put God back together again, to restore those slivers of the Divine that have been cast down with the physical.

And the way we do that, the way we fix the world, is through doing mitzvot. To the mystics, any mitzvot we do—whether feeding the hungry and clothing the naked, or lighting Shabbat candles and keeping kosher—contributes to "*tikkun olam*," the repair of the world, the bringing of the holy sparks back to God.

Yesod HaAvodah, the first Chasidic rebbe of Slonim, wrote that each of us has a unique *tikkun*, a particular healing of the world that we are uniquely qualified to do. It is for the purpose of fulfilling this unique mission that our souls began the long journey downward into our bodies, into the physical world. The mystics tell us that no one else can accomplish our missions: by dint of our uniqueness, those special characteristics that come with our soul being put in our bodies and the things we have experienced in our lives, there is some special thing that each one of us can accomplish that no one else can.

But how do we find that mission? As Po Bronson puts it in his book "What Should I do with My Life," "Wouldn't it be much easier if you got a letter in the mail when you were seventeen, signed by someone who had a direct pipeline to Ultimate Meaning, telling you exactly who you are and what your true destiny is? Then you could carry this letter around in your pocket, and when you got confused or distracted and suddenly melted down, you'd reach for your wallet and grab the letter and read it again and go, "Oh, right.""

One of the people Bronson interviewed for his book actually got such a letter. Choeaor Dondup, who grew up in a refugee camp in southern India, was a 17 year old who had not yet figured out what to do with his life when he got a letter from the Dalai Lama telling him he wasn't actually Choeaor Dondup, but rather he was the reincarnation of a warrior who along with his five brothers ruled a poor and remote region of Eastern Tibet six lifetimes ago. In that earlier lifetime he founded thirteen monasteries and became the great spiritual leader of the region. It was now Choeaor's turn to train for this position.

I would not suggest that you go home and wait for a letter. In the Jewish world, we don't have the equivalent of the Dalai Lama, and I don't think the Dalai Lama has found any reincarnations of Tibetan warriors among the Jews. Besides, having the answer dropped in your lap would NOT be the Jewish way to address the question of what to do with one's life. Jews focus much more on questions than on answers.

In figuring out what we should do with our lives, asking the right question is of critical importance. We ask our kids "what do you want to be when you grow up?" And we smile when we hear the usual answers – ballet dancer, astronaut, fireman, actor, rock star. I am particularly tickled when one of my kids says "rabbi." But we get so used to hearing the question framed that way when we are kids, it is still that same question we ask ourselves when we get to college: "What do I want to be when I grow up?" And this is the wrong question to be asking.

What do I want? The answer will almost always be a job that is "fun." A job that is "exciting." A job that is NOT boring, not ever. And this becomes the impossible dream and can lead to bouncing from job to job as the excitement of each new experience wears off.

We live in an exciting, fast moving world. Email is not fast enough anymore: we have to have cell phones and Blackberries and Treos and Instant Messaging so we can be in constant contact. We don't play chess, we play video games. Instead of thinking about a move for minutes, we react in a fraction of a second. The impact of all of this modern technology is to make us stimulation junkies, easily bored if things don't move fast enough. And we expect the same kind of stimulation in our work.

The truth, however, is that stimulation is not enough. Stimulation is not enduring. Our mission in life is not to spend the next forty years or so being stimulated. Being stimulated is not the same as being fulfilled. Being stimulated is not the same as making a meaningful contribution to the repair of the world.

In his book, Po Bronson suggests that a better question is "What should I do with my life?" Many of us have a sort of phobia of the word "should." We do not want to be told what we "should" do. A good friend of mine told me he always avoided even using the word "should." "Should," he said, "was a 'religious term,'" and as he was not religious, it was something to be avoided like the plague.

Since I'm in the religion business, I have a license to use the word "should." But even this question, "what should I do with my life," doesn't go far enough in the spiritual dimension. It is still focused on "I," on the "me." In Po Bronson's book he gives an example of a young man who enjoyed helping people, and he was good at golf—he realized his perfect job was to help people play better golf! And it launched him on a career working for a golf equipment manufacturer designing things that help people improve their golf game. This young man may have found a worthwhile career—he may even be what the psychologist Abraham Maslow would call "self-actualized," doing what he has the potential to do—but could that really be his unique mission in the world, his contribution to the healing of the world? He might be happy and feel fulfilled at work, but is that all there is?

Judaism does not teach that God's greatest concern is our personal happiness and feeling of fulfillment. God is not here to serve us; we are here to serve God. There is a goal for each of us to accomplish. A story is told of Rabbi Shneur Zalman, the founder of the Chabad branch of Chasidic Judaism. One time Reb Zalman was in jail on a trumped-up charge. The rav looked quiet and majestic as he sat meditating and praying awaiting his trial. The jailer figured he looked like a thoughtful person, and wondered what kind of man he was. They began to talk, and the jailer brought up a number of questions from scripture that had been bothering him. In the story of Adam and Eve, right after they eat from the tree of knowledge, they get embarrassed, try to cover up with a fig leaf and hide. God calls out "where are you?" So the jailer asked: "How are we to understand that God, the all-knowing, said to Adam, 'where are you?'" "Do you believe," answered the rav, "that the Scriptures are eternal and that every era, every generation, and every man is included in them?" "I believe this," said the jailer. "Well then," said the rav, "in every era, God calls to every man: 'Where are you in your world? So many years and days of those allotted to you have passed, and how far have you gotten in your world?' God says something like this: 'You have lived forty-six years. How far along are you?'" When the jailer heard his age mentioned, he pulled himself together, laid his hand on the rav's shoulder, and cried: "Bravo!" But his heart trembled.

And why did his heart tremble? Forty-six years have gone by, and had he gotten very far in his world, in his mission in the world?

My mentor (or as he sometimes describes himself, "mentor and tor-mentor") from my business career, Dr. Abe Zarem, shared with me a great question that his mother used to ask him: "Why were you put in my womb?" Can you imagine your mother asking you this? I suppose it could feel very different depending on the mood she was in when she asked!

This is a much better way to phrase the question. Having a child is a blessing from God. When God put us in our mothers' womb, God had some reason for choosing to do that. There was some purpose, some mission that God had in mind for us to accomplish. Our challenge then, is to figure out what that purpose is, and to go do it.

For Abe, his answer is "to identify talented people and push them to accomplish more than they otherwise would." This is a mission that can be accomplished in any number of jobs and any number of settings—and Abe has done just that in a variety ways from mentoring young entrepreneurs he invested in—I met Abe almost 20 years ago—to being generous with his time and advice to young (and not so young) people who are struggling with the question of what to do with themselves. Abe has a unique way of contributing to the improvement of the world.

I have grappled with this question myself, and I believe for me the answer is to bring Jews closer to Torah and mitzvot—which will also bring them closer to God. Clearly, I hope I am doing this as a pulpit rabbi. However, I am also aware that there are other paths, other avenues by which I could accomplish this task.

Identifying the crucial question: "why was I put in my mother's womb?" is important. But how do we find the answer to the question?

Some would dismiss a question like this as a sign of upper middle class Western angst. Poor people do not get to choose. They are happy to have whatever job they can find to put food on the table and a roof above them. Why worry about ultimate meaning? Why not just go out and get a job and make a living, and be done with it?

Our tradition says EVERYONE—rich, poor, with great gifts or modest gifts—has a contribution to make to tikkun olam. We each have a role to play in making the world a better place. In the book of Deuteronomy it is written, *"re'eh, anokhi notan lifneikhem hayom bracha u'klala,"* "see, I set before you today blessings and curses." The Slonimer rebbe taught that figuring out your mission in life, your unique tikkun, and accomplishing it, is the greatest blessing a person can have. It is its own reward. Toiling for 70 years and not accomplishing your mission, or not even figuring out what it is, is the greatest curse. It is to waste your life.

Viktor Frankl, analyst and Holocaust survivor said the same thing in more contemporary language: "Everyone has his own specific vocation or mission in life; everyone must carry out a concrete assignment that demands fulfillment. Therein he cannot be replaced, nor can his life be repeated, thus, everyone's task is unique as his specific opportunity to implement it."

Your life mission—your unique task—does not necessarily have to be working at a job that is overtly altruistic. The world needs people who do the most mundane of jobs. My first Talmud teacher was a Chabad rabbi. When I announced to him that I was thinking of giving up high tech to become a rabbi, he sort of discouraged me; he said not everyone needs to be a Torah scholar. Some people have the role of making money, which they can give to tzedakah to SUPPORT Torah scholars. This is a model, by the way, described in the Midrash, where it says the tribe of Zebulun was full of merchants who worked to support the men from the tribe of Issachar, who were scholars. And of course, secular Israelis support the haredim in the Yeshivas today, but we'll leave that for another sermon. I do not think that Chabad rabbi was really trying to raise money from me -- he was just stating a simple fact: we can't all have the same mission, we are not all destined to be rabbis!

But when doing a mundane job, the person who is accomplishing a mission will bring meaning to the task. The story is told of three bricklayers who were asked why they were doing what they were doing. One said for a paycheck. The second said to support his family. The third said, "I'm building a cathedral."

Sometimes we have to try a few different jobs or courses of study before we find the one that resonates, the one that we recognize as the right one. Disaster and failure can often provide the stimulus that one needs to move in a new direction. Many people find their life's calling in working for organizations like the Cancer Society, or Mothers Against Drunk Driving, after they have been struck with personal disasters. While not all of us encounter such life-changing issues, most of us have had failures on a smaller scale: jobs that were not quite right, that were not working out the way we had hoped. It can be scary when it happens, but it can also be the time of opportunity.

Six and a half years ago, I was working as VP Marketing for a smallish ($100 million) computer chip company. I had left a very large company six months earlier for a position that in many ways had less responsibility, but I thought I'd be happier in a smaller company. The company had hired me based on my expertise in the cell phone business—they wanted to move into this business because it was much higher growth and much sexier than the mundane timing chips they were making. It turned out the company did not have the products, the technology, or the capability for investment needed to succeed in this new business; in other words, there was nothing I could do for them. It was a bad fit. When it became clear that I should move on to something else, the easiest thing, certainly the easiest thing financially, would have been to take a comparable job in a company that DID have the right technical capabilities. Instead, I took a deep breath, and with three kids and a wife due to deliver another in a few days, I quit my job, put the house on the market, and went to rabbinical school.

Which points to one of the biggest potential barriers to accomplishing our life's mission: success at the wrong job. There is nothing harder than to leave a job where we are basically content and successful, but unfulfilled— where we know we are not living up to our potential, but are comfortable. When we encounter adversity, we really need to make the most of it because it is so difficult to change when things are going well! It is of critical importance to take advantage of the opportunity when a little adversity comes your way.

Some people have an idealistic vision of something they want to do when they are young. They figure they'll get a "real" job for just a few years to put some money away, and then they'll quit and pursue the dream. A lot of people go to law school because they want to change the world. They want to protect the rights of the oppressed as a public defender. They want to save the environment. Then they get to law school, rack up tens of thousands of dollars in student loans and take a job with a big law firm, telling themselves it's just until they pay off the loans. But somehow those student loans turn into car loans and mortgages, and somehow the original dream gets lost. Do you know anyone who had a dream, put it on hold a few years to make money, and went back to it? I only know one such person. It happens, but it is very rare. The message is don't put your dreams off—as the great rabbi Hillel said, "if not now, when?"

Your life's mission is not necessarily what you do at a regular full time job. Today's Torah reading was about Aaron, the Kohen Gadol, the High Priest, and the details of what he did on Yom Kippur. We can't all be the High Priest, and not every day is Yom Kippur. Some of the most important characters in the Biblical narrative were relatively ordinary people: for example, last week we read the story of Sarah becoming pregnant and giving birth to Isaac— the story of one of the ancestral mothers of the Jewish people. Her mission was to be a mother, and a role model. It could well be that you fulfill your most important work as a volunteer, or on a part time basis. I have known successful people who do not derive great satisfaction from their careers, but rather from their outside activities. Rashi, perhaps the greatest Torah scholar who ever lived, whose light still shines for anyone who studies Torah or Talmud, did his life's major work as a "part time" task—his income came from his work as a wine merchant. Or more likely, his Torah work was his full time work, and his part time work as a wine merchant paid the bills. But the point is the same. Don't confuse your main purpose in life with your job title.

Today is Yom Kippur. The Day of Atonement. As we reflect on our year and the things we are asking God to forgive us for, we shouldn't be content with recounting the sins we have committed and what we have done or will do to correct them. We also should consider the curse of not living up to our full potential. When Rebbe Zusya was dying, his students found him crying. They asked him what was the matter. Rebbe Zusya said, "When I die and am brought before the heavenly Beit Din, I'm not worried that they will ask me 'why weren't you more like Moses?' I'm worried they will ask me 'why weren't you more like Zusya?'"

Are You a Net Asset to the Planet?

This was my Rosh Hashanah sermon in Toledo for 5766. It really does summarize what I believe is the meaning of life: the planet should be a better place because you were here.

Today is the great Day of Judgment. Our prayers today reflect a teaching from the Talmud that tells us that God has two books open today, the Book of Life and the Book of Death. The totally righteous—those who have all assets and no debts, all mitzvot and no sins—go straight into the Book of Life. Those who are totally wicked—all debts and no assets, all sins and no mitzvot—go straight into the Book of Death. Everyone else has their judgment suspended for ten days until Yom Kippur. It's not that God needs more time to do the accounting—rather God is giving us more time to get our affairs in order.

But we can't just rely on God to do the accounting—we are each charged with doing that for ourselves. The Hebrew verb to pray is *l'hitpalel*, which could be translated as "to judge yourself." Today we stand in the light of God, and that light shines into our souls, giving us an opportunity to look into corners of our soul we rarely see.

How do we judge ourselves? How do we know if we are successful with our lives? Many people define success in material or professional terms: making partner in a law firm, being promoted to Vice-President, being awarded tenure. But is that what makes for a successful life? I think not. Here's a different definition of what it takes to be a success:

"To laugh often and much; to win the respect of intelligent people and affection of children; to earn the appreciation of honest critics and endure the betrayal of false friends; to appreciate beauty, to find the best in others; to leave the world a bit better, whether by a healthy child, a garden patch or a redeemed social condition; to know even one life has breathed easier because you have lived. This is to have succeeded."

My wife Lauri found this lovely quote in the newspaper a while back, and clipped it for me. What a pleasant sounding sentiment. "To know even one life has breathed easier because you have lived. This is to have succeeded." OK, we're all successes, sermon's over, turn to page 266 for Musaf.

This aphorism, attributed to Ralph Waldo Emerson, but more likely by a woman named Bessie Smith, sets the bar far too low. Don't get me wrong: it's a good thing that one life should breathe easier because you lived. But does that make you a success?

How about the lives that have MORE trouble breathing because you lived? How much air pollution have you generated driving your car and using electricity? How much water pollution have you created with the thousands of showers you've taken, thousands and thousands of dirty dishes you've created? How much room is taken up in landfills because of the garbage and junk you've thrown away? How many people have hurt feelings because of something unkind you did or said?

Has the amount of good you've done for the world offset the amount of harm you've caused?

Often we don't intend to cause harm. Thomas Austin released 24 rabbits on his farm in Australia in 1859. He thought it would be fun to have rabbits to shoot at, like back home in England. At first he was considered quite successful by the sporting crowd—rabbit hunting became all the rage, and there were plenty of them. By the time it became possible to shoot 1200 rabbits in one three and a half hour long session, however, it was apparent that something was amiss. Instead of being considered a great success, the introduction of rabbits came to be seen as having created a blight on the landscape, a "grey carpet" which destroyed all the crops in its path because of a lack of natural predators. Thomas Austin had failed to see the consequences of his decision to bring rabbits to Australia. The initial success was soon seen to be a dismal failure—one that Australia continues to struggle with today. The amount of good the hunters enjoyed has been entirely overshadowed by the amount of harm borne by the farmers, ranchers, and the ecology.

The 16th century Japanese swordsman, Miyamoto Musashi, in his classic book of martial arts strategy, "Book of Five Rings," advises "learn to distinguish between gain and loss in worldly matters." This is one of those simple ideas that can be difficult to implement. The rabbits turned out to be a loss, not a gain.

Let's take an example. If you have two people, both making a salary of $50,000 a year, one owns a home worth $150,000 free and clear, and the other has a home worth $200,000 with a $225,000 mortgage, which is the one in better financial shape?

The one with the $200,000 house has more assets. But he has nothing of value. His net worth is negative—he's $25,000 in the hole. The one with the house only worth $150,000 has a lot more money in the bank.

This simple piece of accounting explains why you can have a millionaire go bankrupt: someone can live in a million dollar house, but if he has two million dollars in debt, he's bankrupt. It explains why airlines go bankrupt all the time, despite having billions of dollars in assets—they have billions more in debt. Donald Trump, with his name all over casinos, hotels, and expensive apartment buildings managed to go bankrupt—as much as he owned, he OWED more.

It's important to understand the math, because the Jewish tradition tells us that God is right now, at this very moment, making the exact same sort of accounting with us. But that image—God as judge, we as the judged—is far too passive. It implies all we have to do is sit like prisoners in the dock while God does His job.

The truth is, we are all judged all the time. Our bosses judge our work performance. Our spouses judge our contributions to running the household. The bank judges whether we're worthy of being given a new loan. The person sitting next to you may be judging your new hairstyle even as we speak. And I'm sure by the time I'm done many of you will be judging the rabbi's sermon.

But how often do we judge ourselves? We each have a spark of God within us—so when we judge ourselves, God is judging us too. If today is going to be a day that changes our lives—and it absolutely has that potential—it won't happen if WE don't participate.

The imagery of the holidays is not meant to be taken literally. Rather the images are there to spur us to make a greater effort at self-scrutiny. At this time of year we're presented with the picture of scales, hanging in the balance; you can even see them behind me, carved around the doors to the ark.

In trying to understand how those scales are balanced, the Talmud tells us we should view ourselves as though we are half guilty and half righteous. If we only do one more mitzvah, we tilt the scales in our favor. If, God forbid, we do one more sin, we tilt the scales down toward the Book of Death. As it says in the Bible, "one sinner destroys much good," which the rabbis understand as meaning on account of a single sin much good is lost to a person. R. Eleazar in the Talmud takes this teaching even further: he says because the world is judged by its majority, and an individual is judged by his majority, it could be that entire judgment of the world revolves around whether you do a single sin—or a single mitzvah.

What I would like to do this morning is to explore how to do our personal accounting. How to figure out our life's balance sheet.

Accountants use the language of assets and liabilities. If you add all the stuff you own—your assets—and take away all you owe—your liabilities— and you still have something left over, you have a positive net worth. If you have more debts than assets, you have a negative net worth—you're either bankrupt or heading there.

If our personal spiritual balance comes out with a positive net worth— if the good things we've done outweighs the harm we've caused—the whole world is a better place because we are here. We get written into the Book of Life. If the harm we've caused outweighs the good we've done, we're harmed everyone else, and our names are written in the Book of Death—which I'm interpreting not as the book of those who will die immediately, but those who are causing death, causing the diminution of the Godly in the world.

We all start out with a zero balance in our account. The good things we do add to our assets; the bad things we do add to our liabilities.

Traditionally we say there are 613 commandments. 365 "lo ta'aseh's," "do not do's," the negative commandments—one for every day of the year. And 248 "ta'aseh's," "do's," positive commandments—one for every bone in our bodies.

The Maharal of Prague says that there are 365 lo ta'aseh's, negative commandments, because 365, the days of the solar year, represents the order of creation. We have 365 things that if we do them, can disrupt the order of creation. We have 248 positive commandments because our bodies are a vehicle for bringing holiness into the world. These do's and don'ts combine to tell us what we are supposed to do with our lives: don't cause damage, and DO bring in holiness.

When we violate a negative commandment, we bring harm to the world. Doing harm is worse than doing nothing—as Hippocrates said with respect to the practice of medicine, "first do no harm." The Jewish tradition acknowledges this as well. According to the Torah, if you fail to fulfill a positive commandment—for example, you fail to honor your parents—there was no explicit punishment. But if you violate a negative commandment—for example, "do not curse your parents"—there was a punishment, such as lashes or even death.

When we violate a negative commandment, the harm can have a "ripple effect" and an impact beyond the immediate. If you steal from someone, obviously you cause the harm of taking someone's property—but the harm, the damage, goes beyond that. Anyone who has been the victim of a burglary, as I have been, knows that there is psychological damage as well. You feel violated, you feel your space has been invaded, you feel less trusting of the world around you. The personal accounting for a crime like theft has to include the psychological harm done to others as well as the physical harm.

I'm sure none of you sitting here today is a burglar or murderer. But just because we are here and not in jail does not mean we're perfect.

We've all heard that there are 613 commandments in the Torah. Maimonides put together a convenient numbered listing of the commandments 900 years ago.

Negative commandment number 301 on Rambam's list is "do not gossip." This is probably the most widely violated commandment of all. I've read articles in secular psychology magazines suggesting that gossip was a good thing because it facilitated group cohesion. Maybe. But I'm sure all of us have had our feelings hurt by gossip. People sometimes get mad at other people over things that are not true. Or over a second hand story that is incomplete. When we gossip about someone we throw a stone in a pond that has a ripple effect—or in the Maharal's terms, we create a disruption in the order of creation.

Number 305 on the list of negative commandments is "do not bear a grudge." Think of all the negative energy we have that is wrapped up in grudges. Do you have a friend or family member you haven't spoken to in years because of some slight? A colleague you're mad at, and he doesn't even know what he did to offend you? Bearing grudges goes on our list of debits.

Have you done anything to embarrass someone in the last year? If so, you have violated negative commandment number 303…and accumulated more debits in your account.

There are some commandments that require a little bit of study. Number 57 on Rambam's list of negative commandments is a big one, but one that those of us living in the modern world might overlook: "Do not destroy fruit trees in time of siege."

At first, you might feel a sense of relief. Gee, I haven't besieged any cities lately, there's at least one of the 613 I don't have to worry about! But Maimonides explains that this mitzvah is not just referring to trees—in the Mishneh Torah he wrote "And not just trees, but any destruction of utensils, tearing clothes, destroying buildings, stopping up wells, destroying food in a wanton fashion, transgresses "do not destroy," and the transgressor is lashed for violating a rabbinic ordinance."

If we do any kind of wanton destruction—BING—we get demerits in our scorecards, add liabilities to our accounts. Sefer haChinukh explains this mitzvah further:

> "The purpose of this mitzvah (known as *bal tashchit*, do not destroy) is to teach us to love that which is good and worthwhile and to cling to it, so that good becomes a part of us and we will avoid all that is evil and destructive. This is the way of the righteous and those who improve society, who love peace and rejoice in the good in people and bring them close to Torah: that nothing, not even a grain of mustard, should be lost to the world, that they should regret any loss or destruction that they see, and if possible they will prevent any destruction that they can. Not so are the wicked, who are like demons, who rejoice in destruction of the world, and they are destroying themselves."

Good people regret any needless destruction or waste. They strive to prevent unnecessary losses. Sefer haChinukh informs us that when we tell our children not to leave every light in the house burning because it wastes electricity and light bulbs, and therefore money, we are not only saving ourselves a few dollars, but are leading them onto a path of righteousness. Put into modern language "do not destroy fruit trees in time of siege" becomes "do not harm the environment."

For every person in the United States we consume 433 gallons of gasoline every year. For a family of four, that's over 1,700 gallons of gas every year. Between gasoline, heating oil, coal, etc.—all of the fuel we consume to live our energy-intensive lifestyles—we as a nation spew an amazing 21 tons of greenhouse gases into the atmosphere for each and every one of us. Those gases contribute to air pollution, allergies, cancer, and global warming.

We not only do a lot of harm to the air, we generate an awful lot of garbage. Each and every person in the United States generates, on average, 7 pounds of garbage a day. 2,500 pounds a year. A family of four generates 10,000 pounds of garbage a year, much of it toxic and/or non-biodegradable—stuff that will be around in the environment for a very long time. Try to imagine for a moment how big a pile is made by 10,000 pounds of garbage.

When we add up the liabilities in our account—the ways in which we've brought harm to the world—we can see that someone who lives in America generally has a bigger load of debts to overcome than someone living in India. We are able to live in a way that many others cannot. We are "haves" and when we create 21 tons of greenhouse gases it hurts not only us, but it also hurts the "have nots." In the Talmud, Rabbi Shimon bar Yochai tells a story about someone who was traveling on a wooden boat who pulls out a drill and starts drilling a hole under his seat. The horrified fellow passengers cry out and say "what do you think you're doing?" The guy with the drill says "what concern is it of yours? I'm only drilling under my own seat!"

Here in America we have a lot of choices. Someone who lives in a single family home in the suburbs and commutes to work in an SUV creates a lot more pollution than someone who lives in an apartment in the city who takes public transportation. When we create pollution we are "drilling under our own seats." The greenhouse gases we generate here contribute to a shrinking polar ice cap and more powerful hurricanes elsewhere.

We can see that someone who lives in America starts out his accounting with a lot more debts, more negative things, weighing down his scale in a bad way than someone living in a hut in Africa.

In our efforts to make the scales come out on the side of merit, there are two things we can do: reduce or nullify the bad we do, or increase the good.

We don't have to be such a disaster for the environment. In Sweden, they only generate 5 tons of greenhouse gases per person per year—which still sounds like a lot, but it's a lot better than 21 tons. And the Swedes don't seem to be suffering in terms of living standard; they haven't all given up their Saabs and Volvos.

Taiwan is a small country—they found themselves running out of places to put all their garbage, and went on a big campaign to reduce waste. They cut the amount of garbage created per capita per day down to 1.6 pounds—about one fourth the amount of garbage created per person in the United States. Instead of 10,000 pounds of garbage per family of four they only create 2,300 pounds.

We can also try and find other ways to offset the damage we do. British Airways has acknowledged that greenhouse gases caused by traveling in a jet plane contribute to global warming. They have come up with a fascinating plan—they allow you to make an optional donation when you book your ticket to nullify the effect of emissions made by your trip. If you fly roundtrip from London to Madrid, they ask for a voluntary donation of about $9 which goes to an organization called Climate Care which works to reduce energy consumption and greenhouse gases. You do $9 worth of harm to the environment with your trip to Madrid, make a donation of $9 to an organization that tries to fix things up. If only it were that easy to do all of our spiritual accounting! Unfortunately, it's not.

Even if we do what we can to try and reduce our impact on the environment—buy more fuel-efficient cars, prefer products that don't have a lot of excess packaging which goes in the garbage, and we do what we can to avoid the other debts we acquire by gossiping, holding grudges, and so on, we're still going to have some "liabilities." We have to offset those with positive things.

According to the Kabbahlists, the Jewish mystics, any mitzvah you do—whether it's giving to charity, lighting Shabbos candles, or honoring your parents—contributes to the healing or repair of the world. By doing these positive things we draw down holiness, we draw God's presence into the world—and we thereby offset some of the damage we've done.

There are several mitzvot associated with observing Shabbat. Negative commandment 320 is not to work on the Sabbath, positive commandment 154 is to rest on the Sabbath and number 155 is to sanctify the Sabbath. Shabbat brings healing to the world in all sorts of ways: for one thing, if you're not driving all over town on Shabbat, you're not creating air pollution. If you spend quality time with your family it will help heal and repair and strengthen those relationships.

Rambam's positive commandment number 19 is to say the grace after meals. While it is meritorious to recite the full *Birkat Hamazon*, if you don't remember it you can fulfill the commandment by saying "Thanks God for the good food you provide us with." How does it improve the world and offset damage? You are bringing a moment of "God consciousness" into the world, you are making God's presence be felt more strongly in the world—which the Jewish tradition says is a good thing.

A few weeks ago, in the wake of Hurricane Katrina, I talked about how there is a commandment to put a parapet on the roofs of our homes (number 184), which is understood as meaning we have a responsibility to create a safe society. Anything you do to help make a safer society—whether it's installing smoke alarms in your home or lobbying Marcy Kaptur to get her to work to have the government fund building stronger levees in Louisiana—it all helps fix the world. Giving charity of course is a great way to add "assets to your account"--there are several mitzvot concerned with giving charity.

You've heard the saying from school that "attendance counts." It also counts with God. Let's say you walked in the door today and you were completely balanced between *aveirot* and *mitzvot*, between assets and liabilities, you were right on the borderline. By being here instead of at work, you are fulfilling a mitzvah not to work on Rosh Hashanah. It is also a mitzvah to hear the shofar being blown. So just by showing up, you get credit for a couple of mitzvot, which, who knows, might be all you need to push you over the top and win you a place in the Book of Life!

I recommend taking the idea of a spiritual accounting literally. Something you do with a piece of paper, or as I do it, at my computer. Not necessarily today—we don't write on Rosh Hashanah. But after Rosh Hashanah is over—and before Yom Kippur—take a piece of paper, make two columns on it. On one side list your spiritual assets—the good things you've done in the last year, the charity you've given, the people you've cheered up, the people you've helped, the Shabbat candles that you've lit. On the other side list your spiritual liabilities—the bad things you did in the last year, the hurt feelings you may have caused, the time you may have wasted, the pollution you created.

What you'll find is that it's a difficult accounting. How do you trade off the air pollution created vs. the good you do by driving your parents to shul in a Hummer? It's hard work not to make excuses for the liabilities in our accounts, or to try and write them off as not important.

An important point in the accounting is that sins do not erase merits—or vice versa. If you do a mitzvah, you always get credit for that mitzvah. Gossiping does not somehow "erase" the charity you gave. That money you gave to charity is always there giving you credit. The tradition gives you a path to erase liabilities from your account: it's called *teshuvah*, or repentance. By doing teshuvah you repair any damage that you did—you remove the liability from your account completely. If you keep your assets and get rid of your liabilities you can go from bankrupt to prosperous.

Spiritual accounting helps you clarify what last month's scholar in residence, Dr. Alan Morinis, called your "spiritual curriculum." If your spiritual balance sheet looks like Donald Trump's business—lots of assets but even more liabilities—you might find that what you need to work on is reducing your liabilities, minimizing the harm you do to the world, doing teshuvah. On the other hand, if your spiritual balance sheet is very modest and you don't have much in the way of either assets or liabilities, maybe you should focus on doing more good things to benefit the world and those around you.

Either way, the goal, ultimately, is the same. As the Bratzlaver Rebbe put it, "Always say, The world was created for my sake. Never say, what does all this have to do with me? And do your share to add some improvement, to supply something that is missing, and leave the world a little better for your sojourn in it."

Leave the world a little better for your sojourn in it. That's the real measure of a successful life. When you do your accounting of your sins, your consumption, and your good deeds, can you say for sure that you are a net asset to the planet? Is the world better off because you are here?

Passing on the Tradition

The future of the Jewish People depends on each individual. This was the talk I gave on the occasion of the dedication of Congregation B'nai Israel's new building in Sylvania, Ohio, parshat Bamidbar 5767.

If the Jewish people seem obsessed with demographics, continually counting ourselves and mulling over the implications of the numbers, at least we come by it honestly.

God Himself seems obsessed with counting the Jewish people. Today we read from the beginning of the book Bamidbar, whose English name, Numbers, reflects this obsession.

Our parsha begins with God commanding Moses "count the heads of all of the congregation of the people of Israel, by families, by the house of their fathers, according to the number of names, every male by their polls." In other words, it was time for the National Jewish Population Survey!

According to Rashi, the census in this week's parsha is the fifth time God took a headcount of the people of Israel: the first was when they were leaving Egypt, the second after the sin of the Golden Calf (in order to know how many were left!), the third when God came to place His divine presence on them, the fourth on the first of Nisan when the tabernacle was set up, and this counting, which took place on the first of Iyar.

Why all the counting? Rashi says, "because of their preciousness to Him, He counts them all the time." At first I thought this made God sound like a miser counting his gold; I prefer the imagery the Hazzan shared with me, that of a shepherd counting his sheep.

Not only does God count his flock all the time, he counts them into different categories. The total number of Jewish men of an age to go out to war was 603,550 (the total excludes the Levites who did not serve in the army). This total is broken down into camps – agglomerations of three tribes. For example, *machane Yehuda*, the camp of Judah, numbered 186,400. Each camp was further broken down into tribes; for example, the tribe of Zevulon consisted of 57,400 men of fighting age. When the Levites were counted, they were further broken down into families – the Gershonite family included 7500 men and male children.

Just as the Torah's count of the Jewish people is broken down into four different categories – nation, camp, tribe, and family – our modern counting of the Jewish people also commonly happens at four different levels. We pour over the statistics for the number of Jews in the world, and each nation, in the city or community, and in the congregation. Our Torah portion gives us the statistics of the Jewish population over 3000 years ago. This morning I'm going to review Jewish statistics of today.

Starting at the top level, there are around 13 or 14 million Jews in the world. We are a tiny fraction of the 6 billion people alive on planet Earth. We are about .2% of the world population – meaning out of every 1000 people on the planet, only two of them are Jewish. By comparison, 330 out of every thousand are Christian and 210 out of every thousand are Muslim. There are more people who practice a religion most of you probably never heard of— "Spiritism" a hybrid of Christianity and paganism indigenous to Brazil—than there are Jews. Yet Jewish influence on the world stage has far out stripped our meager numbers. More than one out of every five Nobel Prize winners has been Jewish. Many of the technological innovations that define life in the modern world were invented or co-invented by Jews, including the transistor, the printed circuit board, cell phones, camera phones, the first video game console, supersonic flight, lasers, nuclear power and drive-through banking. Many incredible advances in medicine came from the minds of Jews: the vaccines for polio, plague, and hepatitis; the birth control pill, cataract surgery and the pacemaker. Many more mundane inventions that we encounter every day were invented by Jews, including the Barbie doll, the shopping cart, and blue jeans. Would our importance on the world stage be greater if there were a million or two more Jews? Would it be less if there were a million or two fewer Jews? Hard to say. Many of our accomplishments came after a time when the population of Jews in the world was reduced by a third because of the Holocaust.

At the next level of detail, the national level, we find an interesting statistical comparison: Israel and America have roughly the same Jewish population, a little over 5 million in each country. Given that the Jewish population in Israel is increasing, and the Jewish population in America is decreasing, it is quite certain that if it has not happened yet, it will very soon be the case, for the first time in almost 2000 years, that there are more Jews living in Israel than in any other country in the world.

And that number – the number of Jews in Israel – is vitally important not only to Israel, but to Jews all over the world. Just over 59 years ago – on May 14, 1948, David Ben-Gurion presented the Declaration of the Establishment of the State of Israel, in which he said "[WE] HEREBY DECLARE THE ESTABLISHMENT OF A JEWISH STATE IN ERETZ-ISRAEL, TO BE KNOWN AS THE STATE OF ISRAEL." Ben-Gurion also said "THE STATE OF ISRAEL will be open for Jewish immigration and for the Ingathering of the Exiles; it will foster the development of the country for the benefit of all its inhabitants; it will be based on freedom, justice and peace as envisaged by the prophets of Israel; it will ensure complete equality of social and political rights to all its inhabitants irrespective of religion, race or sex; it will guarantee freedom of religion, conscience, language, education and culture...."

In other words, Israel was to be both a Jewish and a democratic state. The existence of a Jewish state is important for all Jews, not just Israelis. It is important because of the cultural revitalization that a connection to Israel provides for all Jews, and it is also important as the ultimate insurance policy. I recently had the honor of welcoming a new Jew to our midst as Av Beit Din for a conversion. As part of the interview, one of the members of the beit din asked the conversion candidate about the issue of anti-Semitism. "Obviously you read the papers and know there are lots of people who hate the Jews. Why would you want to sign up for exposure to that?" She replied "I believe the religious depth and satisfaction I will find in Judaism outweighs any negatives that might come from Anti-Semitism. Besides, if things get really bad, I could always go to Israel."

"If things get really bad I could always go to Israel." But for Israel to remain a Jewish state, for Israel to remain a home of last resort if not first choice, we have to pay very close attention to demographics. Pretty soon there will be more Muslims than Jews living between the Jordan and the Mediterranean if you include the West Bank and Gaza. The Jewish population of Israel may be increasing, but the Muslim population in the region is increasing even faster.

Former Prime Minister Ariel Sharon was very aware of this, as he declared in a speech to Israel's National Security College: "we must not ignore the demographics. It is impossible to maintain a Jewish and democratic country here, over the years, while ruling over millions of Palestinians in Judea, Samaria, and Gaza."

This is a case where demographics are compelling Israel do the right thing, even if it's for the wrong reasons. If Israel is to remain both Jewish and democratic, there is no viable long term alternative to the Palestinians having a state of their own.

The next level of detail, the city or community, is also very important. The two cities most on my mind these days are my current home – Toledo – and the city which, God willing, will become my home 51 days from today: Jerusalem.

Once upon a time there were more than 10,000 Jews in Toledo. Today, that number is less than 4000. Does it matter?

You bet it does. It takes a certain number of Jews for a community to have critical mass. To be able to support Jewish institutions like synagogues, Jewish Family Services, and a Jewish Day school. Some of you here today come from families that have roots in Toledo going back five generations. For those roots to endure to a sixth generation, a seventh generation, the community needs to maintain a minimum number of Jews to have that critical mass. Already our day school struggles with declining enrollment and has recently closed its middle school.

The other city much on my mind these days – Jerusalem – also has serious demographic challenges.

This past Wednesday we celebrated Yom Yerushalayim. 40 years ago this week (on the Jewish calendar), in the heat of the Six-Day War, the Israeli army captured the old city of Jerusalem and the eastern suburbs from Jordan. It was an incredibly emotional moment. From the founding of the state of Israel until that June morning in 1967, Jews were unable to pray at the holiest site in Judaism, *kotel hama'aravi*, the Western Wall. On Wednesday I watched the story of news coverage from that day 40 years ago, and tears came to my eyes when I heard the announcer call out *har habayit shelanu! Har habayit shelanu!* The Temple Mount is ours! The Temple Mount is ours! And the pictures of the Israeli soldiers touching the Wall with tears rolling down their battle-hardened faces…. What an amazing moment.

But the joy of Yom Yerushalayim for me is tempered slightly by some of the baggage that comes with it. With the joy of reuniting Jerusalem, no one was able to foresee that a demographic train wreck was only forty years away. In 1967, right after the war, the population of Jerusalem was 74 percent Jewish and 26 percent Arab. Today, the city is 66 percent Jewish and 34 percent Arab, and the gap is narrowing by about one percentage point a year.

The Arab population of Jerusalem has been increasing rapidly; at the same time, the Jewish population has been increasing very slowly, despite a very high birthrate among the city's Haredi Jews. The slow Jewish growth rate is because more Jews are leaving Jerusalem than are moving to the holy city. Jews moving out of Jerusalem have outnumbered Jews moving to Jerusalem for 27 of the last 29 years. Secular Jews are finding Jerusalem less and less attractive; the NY Times reports "When it comes to job opportunities, affordable housing and a varied cultural life, Jerusalem is less appealing to secular Israelis than Tel Aviv or other cities." Not only that, many secular Israelis are turned off by increasing religious and political intolerance. One woman in the NY Times report told a story of how she was dressed casually but modestly and was accosted by an ultra-Orthodox Jewish woman who began yelling at her that she was not properly clothed. The women said "I just felt less and less welcome."

While my family and I are doing what we can to help Jerusalem's demographic problem, many Americans are actually making it worse. Real estate prices in many major American cities such as New York are so sky-high that Jerusalem looks like a bargain. Absentee Americans (and Frenchmen and British) who buy apartments in Jerusalem and live in them for two or three weeks a year are driving up the price of real estate for those of us who would like to live there year round. Certain parts of Jerusalem are virtually ghost towns except during the holidays.

The situation is so critical that last Sunday Jerusalem Mayor Uri Lupolianski said that if current trends continue control of Jerusalem could fall into the hands of Hamas in 12 years; the Arab population could reach 50% by 2035. Of course, Lupolianski is a politician, and he was probably trying to scare people into supporting his preferred solution to the problem – annex more Jewish towns further and further away from Jerusalem into the "municipality."

I'm reminded of the Chinese proverb, be careful what you wish for, for you may get it. Israel succeeded in reuniting the holy city of Jerusalem – but now what are we going to do with it?

There are no easy solutions to Jerusalem's demographic problem, but the simplest and most obvious is to redivide the city into two. For all practical purposes, the city already is divided. You don't see many Jews wandering around Arab Abu Dis, and you don't see too many Arabs wandering around Emek Refaim, the main drag in the heavily English speaking German Colony.

As on the national level, demographics may drive the Israeli government to do the right thing – to provide the Arab citizens of East Jerusalem with a city of their own – even if it is motivated by less than noble reasons.

At the next and lowest level of detail in this morning's demographic survey – the congregation – we also have demographic issues. Forty years ago B'nai Israel had a thousand families; now we are fewer than five hundred. But here numbers certainly fail to tell the whole story. Even though it was mostly the changing demographics that led to the congregation's decision to move to a smaller building, one look around at this beautiful facility and inspiring sanctuary shows that we are alive and well. For a community declining in numbers to be able to build such a wonderful home, without having to burden future generations with a long term mortgage, is a powerful testimony to the strength and depth of commitment in the Toledo Jewish community. It's a statement of commitment to the future of Jewish Toledo.

And that commitment is made not by a statistic, not by a number, but by a real-life person. And that is a lesson we might have trouble learning from reciting statistics – each and every one of you is important. Each and every one of you counts.

The Slonimer rebbe taught that every letter in the Torah corresponds to a soul in Israel. In this week's Torah portion we are told there were 600,000 standing at Mt. Sinai, and there are 600,000 letters in the Torah. For each and every soul at Mt. Sinai there is letter in the Torah, and each and every one of us is a descendant, physically or spiritually, of one of those 600,000 souls. Each of the four letters in God's name corresponds to one of the four "camps," groups of three tribes, encircling the Tabernacle. The Slonimer teaches that every soul illuminates its letter in the Torah, and joins it to the camp, joining it to God's name. The expression of God, God's name, is only complete when we are all joined together.

And that coming together makes it appropriate that we read this parsha this week, the week before Shavuot, the holiday that commemorates receiving the Torah. We need to be joined together as a community, a complete community, no one left out. We need to be a community that is whole to receive a Torah that is whole.

Pirkei Avot, the Teachings of our Fathers, begins with a recitation of the transmission of the Torah: MOSES RECEIVED THE TORAH AT SINAI AND TRANSMITTED IT TO JOSHUA, JOSHUA TO THE ELDERS, AND THE ELDERS TO THE PROPHETS, AND THE PROPHETS TO THE MEN OF THE GREAT ASSEMBLY.

That line of transmission continued through various rabbis, including Hillel and Shammai, on to the rabbis of the Talmud, the Rishonim, the Acharonim, down to the rabbis of today. And today, here at B'nai Israel, we are very fortunate indeed to have several generations of the congregation's rabbis, past, present, and future, here celebrating this dedication weekend with us...and Rabbi Ungar to Rabbi Kamens, and Rabbi Kamens to Rabbi Leff, and Rabbi Leff to Rabbi Saks.

But the transmission of Torah is not just a job for rabbis. There's a great story that illustrates this which I found in a story from the New Yorker magazine about a lawyer named Harley Lewin who chases people who make counterfeit watches and handbags. Harley talked about going kayaking with a paddle based on a thousand year old Eskimo design and he said "There are some things that are spiritual in nature. There are things that you put in your hands that other people have made and when you feel those things you feel...well, let me give you an example. When my first son was bar-mitzvahed,

I gave him my tallit to wear, the one I was bar mitzvahed in, and I wore the one my father gave to me that he was bar-mitzvahed in and that his father had been bar-mitzvahed in. It has the names of six people who wore it on a little piece of paper that's kept with it in a bag, so it's at least six or seven generations old. It's shredding. I told the Rabbi afterwards, I said, "Rabbi, you put it on and it's like being wrapped by dreams."

And that, for the Jewish people, is our dream. That our tradition keeps getting passed down to the next generation, onward and onward. That our generation won't be the one to break a chain going back over 3000 years. And that's why we obsess about our numbers, always have and probably always will.

The Mei Shloach, a Chasidic commentator, brings a beautiful picture of the Jewish people as a mosaic image. He says, "the meaning of counting the number of the children of Israel is that everyone is absolutely necessary. The greatness of the Blessed God is seen in the entire community of Israel as a whole, and if just one member of that community is missing then the mixture will be deficient. It is as if the image of the King were made up of a mosaic of many small parts, and if just one of the parts were missing, then the picture of the King would be lacking. So at the time when each member of Israel is counted, then He is the greatness in all of Israel, for each one of Israel is a portion of the Blessed God."

Our new building is amazing, but if any one of us missing, the king's image is deficient. If someone is missing from the congregation, the mosaic is missing a piece. What the building needs to complete it is our souls filling it with *"kol sasson v'kol simchah, kol chatan v'kol chalah,"* the voice of mirth, and the voice of gladness, the voice of the bridegroom, and the voice of the bride.

The future of the Jewish people depends on you.

We Are All Jews by Choice

Earlier generations assumed that their children would be Jewish, even if they didn't do anything particularly Jewish. We can no longer make that assumption: we are all "Jews by choice." From Rosh Hashanah 5763.

We take it for granted that life presents us with a series of choices -- whom to marry, where to live, what career to pursue. Sometimes the number of choices seems overwhelming—so many brand names fighting for our attention, so many TV channels to surf, so many billions of internet sites....

And it all started on Rosh Hashanah, for today is the anniversary of the creation of free will—the birthday of the freedom to choose.

You might have thought that Rosh Hashanah celebrates the first day of creation; however, that milestone would have occurred Monday, which was the 25th of Elul. Rather, today commemorates the creation of human beings, which came much later, on the sixth day.

But what makes people so special? Why shouldn't Rosh Hashanah commemorate the beginning of creation, the first day, "In the beginning...?" Why the sixth day? Or why not the first Shabbat, when Creation was complete?

Rebbe Nachman of Breslov teaches us that before the creation of Man, there was, in essence, nothing but God. There was no free will. Plants and animals are not free to make choices in the way that people are and therefore, by definition, must be doing the exact will of God. They cannot choose to do otherwise. If there is nothing around capable of going against the will of God, in a sense everything is still part of God. Without free will, the world is "all God." It is not until the creation of the human being, whom Rebbe Nachman calls "*bal habechira*," the master of choice, that the world as separate from God came into existence.

When the Torah says that we are created *b'tzelem Elohim*, in the image of God, you shouldn't think, God forbid, that it means that God has hands, feet, a nose, and all those other body parts. What makes us God-like is our free will—our ability to choose.

It is taught that people are HIGHER than the angels because we have free will—and they don't. Angels are too close to God's presence—they know with 100% certainty what God's will is, and what the rewards and punishments are for following or disobeying God's will. Thus, it's impossible for them to do anything other than what God wants. They are so close to God that God's presence overwhelms whatever sense of self they might have or free will they might have. It's as if God is a powerful magnet—people are far enough away that we can turn in any direction we want. Angels are so close they have no choice but to align themselves with that powerful field.

God had to hide God's self, had to do what the kabbahlists call *tzim-tzum*, a contraction, a hiding, in order for us to have free will. We may complain about God's seeming hiddeness, yet without that hiddeness we would not truly be human—we would be as overwhelmed and powerless as the angels.

Which makes it appropriate that the Day of Judgment, Rosh Hasha-nah, comes on the day in which judging was first brought into being. There can be no real "judgment" without free will, which is the essence of the insanity plea in the secular court system. You cannot hold a mentally ill person responsible for his actions because he does not truly have free will. He is incapable of choosing between good and bad, because he doesn't understand the difference.

We exercise our free will in a variety of ways. We choose our spouses, we choose our work, we choose where we want to live. Some of the choices we make are choices about how we express our Jewishness.

Not so many generations ago, for most Jews there was no real "choice" about being Jewish. Jews were forced by secular authorities to live in ghettos and shtetls, where anyone rejecting the norms of the community would be ostracized from that community, cut off from friends and family, and would not have had a lot of choices about where to go or how to live.

That's not the case anymore. Most Jews live like we do in Richmond, among Christians and Buddhists, Moslems and Sikhs. No one's going to be peeking in our windows, making sure we came to shul today. No one's going to ostracize anyone for going to the mall instead of the synagogue. We are all here because we choose to be here.

I want to commend all of you for making that choice, for deciding to be here today, to affirm your Judaism by celebrating our holy days. I've been told that the Jewish population of Richmond numbers four or five thousand. Since Beth Tikvah is by far the largest synagogue in Richmond, it's obvious that a lot of our fellow Jews are "at the mall," so to speak. Probably fewer than half the Jews in Richmond will be in synagogue over the holidays.

According to one survey, there are 1.8 million people in the United States who were born Jewish who no longer even identify themselves as Jewish. According to a study from the Jewish Federations, as many as 1 million Jews might assimilate out of Judaism in North America in the next 20 years. Rabbi Adin Steinsaltz defines a Jew NOT as someone whose grandparents are Jewish; rather, says Rabbi Steinsaltz, a Jew is someone who is concerned about whether their grand*children* will be Jewish.

Rabbi Mordecai Kaplan wrote that before the beginning of the nineteenth century, all Jews regarded Judaism as a privilege; since then most Jews have come to regard it as a burden. You may have heard your parents or grandparents say *"es shvair tzu zein a Yid,"* "it's hard to be a Jew." In earlier generations, *"es shvair tzu zein a Yid,"* was a rallying cry of sorts…it's tough, but it's who we are, and we're proud of it, and we'll do the difficult things it takes to be a Jew. However, later generations have heard their parents say that and have agreed that it's difficult, and simply said, "No thanks!"

The truth is, it has never been easier to be a Jew. At least in North America, the social impediments that once went with being Jewish have been all but obliterated. Jews serve in high public office, run major corporations, serve in leadership positions of all sorts. Our governments protect us against discrimination, and prosecute the perpetrators of anti-Semitic hate crimes. In the US, Jews have recently passed Episcopalians as the wealthiest religious denomination in terms of per capita income. Very few non-Jewish parents would object if their child wanted to marry a Jew.

The challenges of practicing Judaism have also largely been eliminated. We have pluralism in Jewish expression, which I think is a good thing: if the Orthodoxy that your ancestors brought from the "old country" doesn't speak to your soul, you can be a serious, committed Reform or Conservative Jew. A hundred years ago our observant ancestors who immigrated to North America would lose their jobs if they insisted on taking Shabbat off. Today, while taking Shabbat off may be difficult for some people, for most of us it is not impossible. It has never been easier to keep kosher, no matter where you live; many products in every supermarket have heckshers, and kosher food can be ordered over the internet. Here in Richmond, it's even easier, with the Garden City kosher bakery, the kosher deli in Vancouver, and plenty of great vegetarian restaurants.

Yet, even though it's getting easier and easier to be a Jew, large numbers of born Jews are saying "No thanks!"—giving up their Jewish identity, assimilating, blending into the melting pot. Given a choice, they are choosing to opt out.

To those of us concerned about whether our grandchildren will be Jewish, it is a frightening situation.

The reasons for this crisis are many and complex. The temptations of the secular world around us are many. In the post-Enlightenment world, we are no longer compelled to be Jewish or to do Jewish things. Some see Judaism as just another activity—as something that competes with soccer, skiing, going out to a movie, going to a hockey game. For some the money it takes to support

Jewish institutions is money that competes with other uses that are more fun or seem more rewarding.

How did this state of affairs come about? How did Judaism come to be viewed as just another leisure time activity, and one that does NOT compare favorably with other leisure activities?

A few generations ago, many Jews in North America were immigrants themselves, or were the children of immigrants. Parents who escaped the pale and the pogrom, who survived the ghettos and the death camps, very aware of *"es shvair zu zein a Yid,"* wanted to make sure their kids would "fit in." Yet they still lived in Jewish neighborhoods, socialized with other Jews, and strongly identified themselves as Jewish. That, for the most part, is the story of my parent's generation. Often excluded from the benefits of WASP society, they started their own summer camps, their own country clubs, and their own law firms. Being Jewish wasn't so much a religion as an ethnic and cultural heritage—something taken for granted.

However, when the next generation left home, they also left the Jewish environment. They moved out into the secular world. And THIER children grew up surrounded by non-Jews. When my family moved to Denver, Colorado in 1967 I was the first Jew some of my 7th grade classmates had ever met. I'm sure that Jewish kids who go to public schools here in Richmond are often the only Jewish kids in their classes, since we only make up 2-3% of the local population.

Some parents see Hebrew school as a way to give their children a Jewish identity. Hebrew school is great—but I can tell you from my own experience, it's not enough. I went to Hebrew School, I had a bar mitzvah—and then I went 25 years barely setting foot in a synagogue, 25 years without celebrating Shabbat or keeping kosher, 25 years without opening a siddur, 25 years without enjoying the riches of Judaism that now enrich my life every day.

For those of us who do not live in Israel, if we want our grandchildren to be Jewish, we have to have a Jewish home. Being Jewish has to be something more than an ethic memory and a predilection for bagels and matzah ball soup. If your children love Judaism, live Judaism every week, have Judaism ingrained as a part of their persona, it becomes pretty unlikely that they would consider a spouse who couldn't share that important part of their life with them.

A Jewish home is more than a house occupied by Jews; a Jewish home is a home where Judaism is a real presence. A home where the rhythms of the Jewish calendar affect the rhythms of our lives. Creating a Jewish home may not be so easy for those of us who didn't grow up observant. It can feel silly, awkward, even embarrassing, to integrate new rituals, new practices, into our lives. I remember the first few dozen times I sang the grace after meals, I always stumbled over the tune at the same place. I remember how uncomfortable I felt when I told my boss that I wouldn't be attending an important offsite meeting if it was scheduled for a Saturday. I remember the discussions my wife and I had about my discomfort with stopping at garage sales on the way home from shul on Shabbat. I remember my rabbi nudging my kashrut practices along with suggestions about what it is appropriate to eat in non-kosher restaurants.

It may not be easy, but, trust me, it's worth it. I love it when we're gathered at the table for Shabbat, and after my wife and I bless the children, they bless US in return—an idea they came up with by themselves. I love it when my daughter Lizzy rushes to be the first to wash her hands and say the blessing, and then hugs the challah to her chest during the *motzi*. I love it when Katherine has insights about the parsha that I've never thought of, and knows more about kashrut at 6 than I knew at 36. I love it when Devorah, our baby, bounces up and down during the grace after meals. I love it when the whole family does the "Eliyahu dance" for Havdalah. I love our interactive Passover plagues—which include a talking frog, rubber locusts, and ping-pong ball hail. I love knowing that however crazy and fast-paced the week has been, Shabbat with its 25 hour respite from the craziness of modern life will come.

Children yearn to have an identity, yearn to know where they fit in the universe. A Jewish home gives a child that identity, tells the child, "You are important. You are part of a tradition that stretches back five thousand, seven hundred, and sixty-three years. You are a child of Abraham and Sarah, of Isaac and Jacob, of Rachel, Rebecca, and Leah. These are the customs of your people and these are their laws, these are their stories and these are their songs."

But we can't give this gift to our children unless we ourselves KNOW the customs and the laws, the stories and the songs. Fortunately, there are many opportunities to learn. We have over 30 adult education events planned for the next 4 months here at Beth Tikvah. If you want to learn some new Jewish songs, be here on Monday, September 23 at 8 p.m. If you never had a bar or bat mitzvah, whether you're 23 or 83—it's not too late—I'm going to be starting an adult bar and bat mitzvah class after the holidays. You can be up here reading Torah in 6 months and your kids can give YOU a party. If you'd rather do your learning in private, there's a list of recommended books available on the new Beth Tikvah web site (www.btikvah.ca). Book markers with information on the Jewish Theological Seminary's on line learning program are available on the table outside the sanctuary.

But it all starts with making a choice—to grow in learning and observance, to enrich your children's lives...and to have Jewish grandchildren.

On this Rosh Hashanah day, I invite you to celebrate the anniversary of free will by making that choice.

Shanah Tovah

Lesson on Intermarriage from Abraham

This is an article that appeared in the United Synagogue Review magazine, adapted from a sermon I gave on parshat Chaye Sarah in 5766. I hope my daughter who intermarried forgives the statement below where I wrote I would be mortified if one of my children intermarried. My Gentile son-in-law is a wonderful guy, and I am happy for them personally, even if intermarriage is a problem for the Jewish people. Any children they have, would, of course, be halachically Jewish since my daughter is Jewish. What they do with that, will of course be up to them.

Every Jew who is dedicated to his heritage is concerned about who his children will marry. The first Jew to worry about who his son was going to marry was the first Jew: Abraham.

In parsha Chaye Sarah, Abraham gives his servant Eliezer explicit instructions. He tells him to swear he "will not take a wife for my son from the daughters of the Canaanites, among whom I live," and further instructs him to "go to my country, and to my family, and take a wife for my son Isaac."

Eliezer retorts, "Maybe the woman won't want to come with me; should I bring your son back to the land you came from?"

Abraham, aghast, says "Take care that you do NOT bring my son there again."

And of course the result is that Abraham's son Isaac intermarries. Rebecca may be "kin," but she's not Jewish – at least not when Eliezer first finds her. In Biblical times, it appears that getting married to a Jewish man was the way that the women became Jewish themselves—they simply joined into the tribe.

There's a lot we can learn about how to deal with intermarriage from studying this passage in the Torah. But before we try to tease out those lessons, I want to put intermarriage today into perspective.

It's a topic that Jews are acutely aware of, yet a lot of rabbis avoid talking about it from the pulpit. After seven years of preaching and teaching, having given hundreds of talks and sermons, I never gave a sermon specifically about intermarriage until quite recently. And I don't think I'm unique—I think for a lot of rabbis intermarriage is the elephant in the living room, impossible to ignore, but not openly discussed. I had to ask myself, why don't people talk about it?

Well, it's a topic that makes people uncomfortable. But anyone who has heard me speak more than once knows that I don't shy away from making people uncomfortable. I think the reason is a little more basic. The topic makes ME uncomfortable!

Why does the topic make people uneasy? It's divisive; it seems somehow "unwelcoming." To speak of the benefits and rationale for endogamy (in-marriage, marrying other Jews) seems somehow exclusivist, elitist, and against American ideals of everyone being created equal. A recent survey found that 50% of American Jews – of the JEWS – felt opposition to intermarriage was racist. Our discomfort may also come from tensions in our families because of intermarriage, and as parents we might be worried about whether our kids will intermarry.

And I've got another reason for feeling personally uncomfortable with the topic. My family motto could be "intermarriage is us." My father intermarried—my brother, my sister, and I were converted as children and raised as Jews. I intermarried, my brother intermarried, and my sister intermarried. I have aunts, uncles, cousins, and two-half sisters who are Jewish and married Jews, but the non-Jews in my family circle significantly outnumber the Jews.

Despite all that intermarriage in my family—despite the fact that I my-self intermarried, more than once—I am now adamantly opposed to intermarriage, and would be mortified if one of my kids married a Gentile. So how can I speak out on this topic without sounding like a hypocrite?

I hope that rather than making me a hypocrite, my personal and family experience qualifies me to address the topic with authority.

Intermarriage is a huge issue for the Jewish community. As someone said, "the problem Jews have today isn't that Christians want to kill us: it's that they want to marry us!"

Rabbi Ephraim Buchwald, founder of the National Jewish Outreach Program said "Our grandparents prayed for a melting pot. What they got instead was a meltdown!" 60% of all Jews live in households that are not identified as Jewish. 54% of all American Jewish kids are raised either with no religion or a religion other than Judaism. Alan Dershowitz in his book "The Vanishing American Jew" predicts that in a few generations the only Jews left in America will be the ultra-Orthodox. He predicts liberal Judaism will intermarry itself out of existence.

We're all familiar with the statistic that 52% of Jews intermarry. There are things that make that statistic not as bad as it sounds, and things that make it worse. On the one hand, the intermarriage rate is much higher for second and third marriages than it is for first marriages. The later marriages are less likely to have children, so this ameliorates the impact of the intermarriage statistic to a degree.

On the other hand, to put it in a scarier context, a 50% intermarriage rate means that two out of every three weddings involving a Jew are intermarriages. Out of four Jews, two (50%) marry each other, and the other two each marry a non-Jew. No wonder our demographic decline is forecast to be so precipitous.

And demographics are really what the intermarriage issue is all about. That was the issue for Abraham—he wanted to increase the number of Jews— and it's the issue for us. In parshat Lech Lecha God promises to make Abraham's descendants as numerous as the grains of sand on the earth. That's not going to happen if we can't keep our descendants Jewish.

Judaism is not a proselytizing religion. We don't go from door to door handing out leaflets encouraging people to convert. It's not because we don't want people to join us—it's because we don't have the same theological motivation that many Christians have. Christians believe if they convert you, they are saving your soul from eternal damnation. Jews believe that if we convert you, we are raising the bar for you, making your life tougher—it's actually harder in some ways for a Jew to get into heaven than a non-Jew. All a non-Jew has to do is follow the seven Noachide laws, which means basically to be an ethical monotheist. A Jew, on the other hand, has 613 mitzvot to obey—a much greater level of responsibility.

We believe it's worthwhile to be Jewish, that it enriches our lives and the world around us, but we don't have the same drive to try and convert the whole world. So the number of "fresh adherents," people joining from the outside, has always been rather small. Therefore, when it comes to growing the Jewish population, we have historically done it by marrying other Jews and having lots of kids.

So given the low rate of conversion, we can see that, at least outside of Israel, intermarriage is a real threat to Jewish survival.

OK, fine, intermarriage is a threat to Jewish survival. But we have to ask ourselves "why does it matter?"

If Jews are just a tribe, a collection of people with a common heritage, it really does NOT matter. Lots of tribes have disappeared. All the ancient civilizations other than Judaism are basically gone, at least as far as continuity with their culture goes. There are still people called Egyptians, but they don't build pyramids, worship Isis, or make mummies. For a totally secular Jew— someone who does not believe Judaism has an important message for the world, who does not practice Judaism at home—to be concerned about intermarriage frankly would smack of racism.

But if you believe Judaism has an important message to share with the world, if you believe God made a covenant with Abraham so that the Jews would be a blessing to the world, or as Isaiah put it, to be a light to the nations—then it is vitally important that Judaism continue and that the Jews continue to exist as a people.

And that is why, despite my personal experience with intermarriage, I am now opposed to it. I realize that I am something of a fluke: it's pretty rare that someone intermarries, and the end result is he ends up becoming a rabbi. I thank God that I somehow married someone with a Jewish neshamah whose journey to Judaism inspired me to really explore my own Jewish heritage for the first time as an adult. But I know we can't count on such fortuitous circumstances every time.

A couple of years ago, I got a call from an Israeli couple living in North America. They were very upset because their teenage son was dating a non-Jew. They wanted to know if I had any ideas on what they should do.

I asked them if they did anything Jewish at home. They told me no, they were secular.

My reaction was they were coming to talk to me way too late. Being a secular Jew is a long-term option in Israel. In a place where everyone is Jewish, you can be totally secular, and still be reasonably sure your grandchildren will be Jewish. But if you live in the Diaspora, that is no longer true. If your kid is the only Jew in his classes in high school, and Judaism is not important to him—if he doesn't do something to observe Shabbat and holidays for example, does not participate in Jewish youth groups like USY—of course he will marry a non-Jew. There's no reason not to.

So what do we do about intermarriage? How do we prevent it, and how do we deal with it when it happens?

We can get some advice from the story of Abraham. First of all, Abraham is concerned that his son marries the right person. Do we communicate to our kids that we care who they marry? If you don't express an opinion about whom your kids date, it's tough to express an opinion about whom they marry.

Secondly, why was Abraham so adamant about Eliezer finding a bride for Isaac from far away—not from the local Canaanite girls? Why does he further insist that Isaac NOT go to live in Babylonia among his own family? The Kli Yakar, a 16th century rabbi, explains it this way: "Abraham said to himself; If my son marries a girl from Canaan, since we live amongst them, my son will frequent their homes and will learn from their (idolatrous) ways. Furthermore if my son marries of the daughters of Laban and Betuel (Abraham's relatives) and will go to live with them, there is also a probability that he will be influenced by their actions. By marrying a woman from abroad who will come to live here, there is no worry at all." So basically, he was worried about his son's future in-laws.

Abraham was afraid if Isaac married a local girl, he would be absorbed into her culture—the dominant local culture—and he would lose his identity as a Jew. If he lived among the idol worshipers in either place, there was a good chance he would assimilate. He needed a strong Jewish identity, he needed to establish a Jewish home.

We need to implant a strong Jewish identity in our children. How do we do that? What we do at home is much more important than sending kids to a Jewish Day School or Hebrew School. If we light candles every Shabbat and make every Friday night dinner an occasion to look forward to with a special meal, with friends and family, with words of Torah, we make Shabbat something our children won't want to give up—it will be something they will want to have as part of their lives, something to share with their spouses. If we send our kids to Day School, but hardly ever do anything Jewish at home, what's the message we send our kids? They learn about keeping kosher and how important Shabbat is, but if they don't do it at home, they get the message it's not really important – it's just school work, not real life.

But no matter how strong a Jewish identity we implant in our young people, intermarriage will still happen. Jews are only about 2% of the population in America. Even committed Jews meet and fall in love with Gentiles. What then?

Trying to stop them with a guilt trip is a non-starter. Love is very powerful -- more powerful than guilt. Telling them "it's giving Hitler a posthumous victory" or "you're breaking a 3,000 year old chain of your ancestors going back to Mt. Sinai" is simply not going to carry much weight in the face of love. Reminding them that it is a commandment in the Torah not to intermarry is probably not going to help much either. We have to do something different.

In the story of the search for Isaac's wife, after Eliezer brings Rebecca back to the land of Israel, the Torah tells us "And Isaac brought her to his mother Sarah's tent, and took Rebecca, and she became his wife; and he loved her; and Isaac was comforted after his mother's death."

The first step was Isaac took Rebecca into his mother's tent—he brought her into HIS home, into HIS culture. Only after that did he marry her. If our kids fall in love with a Gentile, we should encourage the Gentile to convert to Judaism. This can be a very positive thing for the Jewish people.

The story is told of a young Jewish man who fell in love with a Gentile. His father was very upset, and told him "don't marry a shiksa, you'll regret it!" The young woman saw how important Judaism was to her fiancé's family, she started learning about Judaism and liked what she saw, so she studied with the rabbi and converted. The first week after the couple returns from the honeymoon, the son is back at work in the family business. Friday afternoon Dad tells the son, "see you tomorrow morning, we'll go over the books," and the son replies, "Sorry Dad, can't come, tomorrow is Shabbat, so we'll be at shul" Dad says, "I told you not to marry a shiksa!"

We may laugh, but it's true that very often converts become some of the most knowledgeable and dedicated members of our congregations. They not only enrich us spiritually, they help strengthen our gene pool — too much in-breeding leads to a concentration of genetic diseases like Tay-Sachs.

Of course Jews have brought in converts everywhere we have lived. Polish Jews look like Poles and Iranian Jews look like Iranians. Welcoming others into our tent is nothing new. Moses married a non-Jew, Tzipora, the daughter of a Midianite priest. King David is descended from Ruth, a convert, whose story we read every year on Shavuot.

But not every Gentile who marries a Jew will want to convert. Some are committed to their own religions, and if someone believes Jesus is the only path to salvation they are not really a candidate for conversion to Judaism. But even then, we can encourage the family to raise their children as Jews. Non-Jews are often sympathetic to the demographic plight that the Jewish people face, and if the Jewish partner says it's important to him or her they will often agree to raise the children as Jews.

But for that to happen, it is incumbent upon us as a Jewish community to be as welcoming to intermarried couples as we can. Rejecting intermarried couples because we don't approve of intermarriage is the surest way to see the next generation grow up Christian or nothing.

If Judaism is to remain vibrant in America, it will only happen if we are successful in encouraging non-Jews to embrace Judaism. So we must remember the commandment *v'ahavta l'ra'echa k'mocha*, love your neighbor as yourself. If we welcome these non-Jews and prospective Jews in our midst with love we will draw them close. We can't afford to turn our backs on them. The future of the Jewish people depends on it.

Chapter Ten

Israel

"And the Lord had said to Abram, Go out from your country, and from your family, and from your father's house, to a land that I will show you;"

Genesis 12:1

"Lech Lecha," "Go out [from your country]" – those are the opening words of my bar mitzvah parsha. Israel has a powerful place in the things that bring meaning to my life. I first visited Israel in 1978, a secular tourist on vacation from an assignment in Tehran. If you had told me that 30 years later I'd be a rabbi living in Israel I would have accused you of smoking something stronger than tobacco!

Israel is the most important thing to happen to the Jewish people in the last 2,000 years. The next few essays describe why it is important to me personally as well. It is also includes some observations on challenges facing Israel in the early 21st century.

A visit to Israel

This was written in February, 2004…it was a visit that helped convince me Israel is where my family belongs and we should move there. It is a report on my experiences when I was in Jerusalem for a Rabbinical Assembly Convention.

Tuesday morning as I was walking to the Kotel (the Western Wall) for morning prayers I was at the top of Yemin Moshe just as the sun was coming up over the hills of Jordan in the distance. The sky was red, the Old City of Jerusalem was right in front of me, it was a truly beautiful site—I was moved to recite the blessing for seeing a beautiful sight, which is basically, "Thanks God, you do good work!" From the top of Yemin Moshe I walked down the steps, down to the upper end of GeiHinnom, the Valley of Hinnom. GeiHinnom, the

Hebrew word for Hell, the place where Canaanites offered child-sacrifices, is now a park. I couldn't help contrasting this spot with Iraq. There was an article in the New Yorker a while back, about how in Iraq there is tree in a courtyard which the locals claim is where the Garden of Eden was, and it's supposed to be the tree that Adam and Eve ate from. Now it's all paved over around it, and run down and decrepit looking, and the tree is fading and dying. When I read the article I thought of the old 60s song with the line "they paved Paradise and put up a parking lot."

By contrast, Israel turned Hell into a Garden. As I left Hell, I walked the short distance to God's address on the planet Earth—the site where the Temple once stood. For a Jew to move to Israel is called making "aliyah," going up. To get to the site of the Temple, you have to go up, you ascend in a physical as well as a spiritual sense. Just like I tell my friends when I take them flying in a small plane—I'll get you closer to God one way or the other!

When I arrived at the Wall, I have to admit I felt uncomfortable about the way our people make a big deal about this place. The Wall itself, of course, is not even a wall of the Temple, but rather the retaining wall that Herod built. But my concern was this—does the big deal we make about praying at this physical place border on *avodah zarah*, on idol worship? Are we making the physical manifestation more important the spiritual? More important than God?

But as soon as I started praying with my 300 colleagues, the magic of the place took over. We were praying at the "Conservative section" of the wall, by Robinson's Arch, south of the section that the tourists visit, which is run as an Orthodox synagogue. We have a section of the wall where we can pray with men and women together. When I got to the spot in the prayers when we say "*Baruch k'vod Adonay mimkomo*," praised is God's glory from His place, I stopped short. I was standing there, at the spot that for 3000 years the Jewish tradition has said is God's place on Earth. I felt a powerful connection with God, with the Jews around me, and with the Jews who prayed there before. I realized the power of coming to the place is not because of anything that relates to idol worship. It's not that God is more present at the Wall—after all, the prophet also said *m'lo kol ha'aretz k'vodo*, "the whole world is full of His Glory"—but rather we are more open to feeling God's presence in that place because of the historical connection.

Despite being a rabbi, I'm not the kind of person who goes around spouting Scripture all the time, but Jerusalem is a place that brings Scripture to mind all the time. As I was on my morning run yesterday, as I approached the walls of the Old City, a line from Psalm 51 came to mind, *tivneh chomot Yerushalayim*, "build the walls of Jerusalem." And as we continue when we bring the Torah out from the ark, "For in You alone do we trust." As I rounded the corner and began my climb to the church which sits at the Zion Gate (which isn't REALLY Mt. Zion, but no matter) the words from Isaiah chapter 2 came to mind *ki miTzion tatzei Torah*, "for from Zion shall go forth Torah, and the word of the Lord from Jerusalem." And I prayed that the word of the Lord would again be going forth from a Jerusalem at peace.

One of the things I love about being in Jerusalem is the feeling of being in a place that is important, a place where news is made. Our convention has drawn a fair amount of press. After our prayers Tuesday morning, we went up to the Western Wall Plaza to check out what's going on there. The Orthodox rabbis who run that section of the Wall engaged in a "land grab" to expand the amount of the plaza taken up by the separate men's and women's sections— reducing the amount of space available behind the separate sections which is often used by groups of visiting Conservative and Reform Jews for minyans. The paper reported that we conducted a vigil and one of our members was detained by the police. It wasn't quite as exciting as it sounds. We went up there and took a look around, and one rabbi who disagreed about moving on when the police told him to move on was briefly taken inside the police station for a talking to.

We were also in the paper thanks to a speech Tomy Lapid gave to us on Tuesday night. Tuesday night both Shimon Peres and Tomy Lapid spoke to us. Peres was very thoughtful and statesman-like, but nothing he said was picked up by the papers. Lapid (head of the very secular Shinui party, and Justice Minister) on the other hand, got covered by the papers because he had some very outspoken things to say.

Lapid gave what would have been a great campaign speech, if we were eligible to vote for him. He told us, a group of Conservative rabbis, "Israel is the only country in the world where Conservative and Reform rabbis are Class B citizens, and I don't understand why you are willing to live with it." He said he doesn't understand why we tolerate this insult. He also said he felt that this discrimination poses an existential threat to the State of Israel: if Reform and Conservative Jews from America feel discriminated against, they will not be such strong supporters of Israel, and Israel absolutely needs American support. He told us we should be more aggressive in standing up for our rights. He said Judaism has a bad name amongst the secular Jews in Israel because they associate Judaism with people like Rabbi Ovadiah Yosef and Arieh Deri of Shas, and they want nothing to do with such a Judaism. R. Yosef is very radical in some of his pronouncements, and Deri, the former head of Shas, did jail time on charges of bribery.

As if there wasn't enough going here, there was an earthquake Wednesday, when I was on a trip to the Negev. The Israelis immediately started joking—Hamas has claimed responsibility for the earthquake, while Yasser Arafat denies having anything to do with it.

Yet another connection to the news--Wednesday night the mayor of the town of Omer was supposed to meet with us, but his son who is a pilot in the IAF had to bail out of his plane (!) earlier in the day; the plane, an A4

Skyhawk was destroyed by the crash of course. His son was OK, but was taken to the hospital in Tel Aviv for observation. The mayor didn't get back in time to meet with us. We understood; Israel really feels like small place sometimes.

One of the messages that came through from several people we met with—from Lapid, from Avishay Braverman, the president of Ben Gurion University in Beersheva, and from a formerly secular Israeli who is now a congregant in the Conservative congregation in Omer, is that Conservative Judaism very well may have a critical role to play in the future of Israel.

Braverman told us he was very concerned about the moral and ethical fiber of the Israeli people. Israel is NOT living up to the standards of the Jewish tradition with our behavior toward the Palestinians, with our behavior toward each other in politics, with the culture of greed that is flourishing here. Israel desperately needs to have Jewish values be part of what drives Israeli society forward. Yet many of the 80% of Jews in Israel who are secular have been totally turned off to religion because of the shenanigans, close-mindedness, and seemingly immoral statements and acts that frequently emanate from the ultra-Orthodox community. They think that's what Judaism is and want no part of it. Yet when they learn about Conservative/Masorti Judaism, they see that Judaism CAN have a "kinder and gentler" face. When they meet rabbis who also have solid secular educations, they learn that not all rabbis are racist fanatics. And they are willing to learn from us, and are willing to let us teach their children. The values of Judaism we share can deepen their connection and dedication to Israel—and perhaps help to reduce the "brain drain" Israel faces, the problem that many of Israel's best and brightest often decide to leave for America.

One way Conservative/Masorti Judaism is helping is through the Tali School program. Thanks to the Tali program, thousands of kids in *mamlachti* schools (secular curriculum) are getting at least a few hours a week of Jewish education, which may play a crucial role in bringing Jewish values to the next generation of Jews in the Holy Land.

Nowhere were the values of Conservative Judaism shown in greater force than in a bar mitzvah ceremony for "special needs" kids I attended today. The Orthodox position has traditionally been that someone who is severely retarded is NOT eligible for an aliyah to the Torah. Reuven Hammer, an Israeli rabbi who is head of the world-wide Rabbinical Assembly, wrote a teshuvah, a Jewish legal opinion, which says that as long as the person can "direct their attention to God" they can have an aliyah. Some of the kids study for six months to be able to just recite the blessings. Some kids can't even do that…they are trained how to use a machine which can recite the blessing for them. They all study, and work at it for six months—and they do whatever it is they can do at that point. One child had someone signing the blessings for him to recite.

It was incredibly moving. I found myself thinking that this was a real testimony to the Jewish concept that the value of life is infinite. And if the value of life is infinite, someone with handicaps is certainly the "equal" of someone without handicaps, and deserves to be treated with the same respect and honor, because they too are created "*b'tzelem Elohim*," in God's image.

More Jewish values were shown in the relationship between the Bedouin community in Tel Beersheva and the Masorti synagogue in Omer. It was wonderful to hear of Jews and Muslims celebrating holidays together, not just tolerating each other, but enjoying each other's company. It was delightful to see religion being a bridge between Jews and Muslims, instead of a barrier, or worse.

As if I haven't been on the run enough in the three days I've been here so far, this morning I participated in the annual "Rabbi's Run" sponsored by Behrman House. I didn't know this when I started out, but they make it a real race—at breakfast I was handed a trophy, for coming in third! When I noticed that the trophy said "second place," I told a colleague I was concerned about violating the Biblical precept to stay far from a false matter. So I pointed the error out to the organizer, and he said that the trophy store gave him two first places and two second places. My colleague told me not to worry about the "false matter" issue, I'll always be third place in his mind… ☺

Amongst all this fun was a reminder that times in Israel are still difficult. Due to Israel killing 15 Palestinian militants and terrorists in an operation in Gaza Strip, the country is on a high alert because Hamas has vowed revenge, and the Israelis are bracing for an ugly terror attack.

May the children of Isaac and the children of Ishmael reconcile their differences and live together as brothers in the land God promised to their father Abraham.

Amen.

Why We Made Aliyah

This was the last Kol Nidre sermon I gave in Toledo—given 9 months before we actually left on aliyah in July, 2007. This is the only sermon I ever gave where a congregant actually wrote me a letter to complain! America has been very good to the Jews, he wrote… "you have some nerve trying to make us feel guilty!"

God willing, this time next year, Lauri and I, and our three youngest children will be living in Israel. We won't just be tourists or there on sabbatical, we'll be citizens of the world's only Jewish state. The fact that we can do that – that we can go live in a Jewish country – is truly miraculous.

For most of the past 2,000 years, Jewish history was the story of one disaster after another. In the year 70 Romans destroyed the Temple, Jerusalem was laid waste. In 132 the Bar Kochba revolt was brutally crushed, and with it died the dream of an independent Israel. During the Middle Ages, Jews were massacred by the Crusaders on their way to "liberate" the holy land. When Christian Europe was flourishing during the Renaissance, Jews were packed into ghettos. In 1492, when "Columbus sailed the ocean blue," Ferdinand and Isabel ordered the Jews of Spain to convert, flee, or die. When the Enlightenment, and citizenship, came for the Jews of Western Europe, those in the East were being killed in pogroms, a foreshadowing of the horrors that would come later during the Shoah, when a third of the Jews then alive were slaughtered by the Nazis.

We were overdue for some good news.

The good news came in 1948. In 1948, a miracle happened. A miracle every bit as great as the parting of the Red Sea. A miracle which shows us that God truly has not forgotten His promises to the Jewish people. In May of 1948, for the first time in 2,011 years, the land of Israel was free. An independent Jewish state was reborn on the soil of ancient Judea. More miracles followed. Tiny Israel turned back the armies of Egypt, Lebanon, Syria, Iraq, and Jordan, and won the War of Independence. Tiny Israel ended the war with substantially more territory than had been originally granted by the UN. And again our tiny country defeated vastly larger Arab forces in 1967, and yet again in 1973.

The modern state of Israel is the most wonderful, exciting thing to happen to the Jewish people in the past two millennia. For 70 generations, our ancestors prayed for this day. And the day has finally come!

And yet here we are, still sitting in Exile! What an anti-climax!

Tonight I'm going to ask each of you to consider making aliyah—to "go up" to the land of Israel.

To become a citizen of Israel is the right of every Jew, and it does not matter whether you were born Jewish or converted—and for purposes of making aliyah Reform and Conservative conversions are just as valid as Orthodox ones. Your Jewishness is your visa. And you become a full citizen the day you arrive.

I want all of you to think about it, at least for a few minutes. It doesn't matter whether you come to shul every Shabbat, or only once a year on Kol Nidre. It doesn't matter where you are in your life, whether you're just starting a career or retiring. It doesn't matter whether you are married, single, with or without kids. Whether or not to make aliyah is a question every Jew needs to consider. If the answer is no—if you make the conscious decision to continue to live in Exile from our ancestral homeland—clearly the choice is yours, but you should be clear about WHY you are making that decision. Because whichever way you decide—to return to Israel, or to stay in Galut—it has profound implications for the nature of your relationship to Judaism, it has profound implications for your family, and I believe it has profound implications for Israel and the Jewish people.

Literally millions of Jews HAVE made the decision to pack up and move to Israel. The early pioneers a hundred years ago were fleeing pogroms in Eastern Europe. They were followed by Jews displaced by World War II and the Shoah. Then in the 1950s came the Jews fleeing Arab persecution, and later, when Jews were finally allowed to leave the Soviet Union a million more came. In more recent times Jews fleeing discriminations and poverty in Ethiopia have come to Israel, along with Jews leaving the economic collapse of Argentina. Forty percent of Israelis were born outside of Israel!

But through it all, there have also been Jews from the Western world. 80,000 Israelis were born in the US or Canada, another 20,000 were born in the United Kingdom, and many thousands more came from France and elsewhere in Europe long after the war ended.

It's easy to understand why a Jew suffering from persecution, or living in a terribly impoverished country would want to make aliyah.

But why would a Jew from a safe and prosperous country like America make aliyah? Why is our family doing moving to Israel?

An economist would probably think I'm an idiot. I left a high-paying job in Silicon Valley and racked up student loans for four years – loans I should get paid off right before I get my first Social Security check – in order to become a rabbi and earn a lot less money. Now I'm going to leave my job as a rabbi – a job I really love – and will probably go back into work in high tech, except this time in Israel, for less money than I make as a rabbi in America. And I'll be paying higher taxes, too.

Am I meshugenah?!

Our children are excelling in school, they're getting a good Jewish education, they have lots of friends here. Yet we plan to uproot them from all that. We're going to send them to school in a place where they not only have no friends, they barely speak the language.

What kind of parents are we?!

We giving up our wonderful six bedroom, three and-a-half bath, three-car garage, Tudor-style Old Orchard house—which will be for sale in a few months, by the way—to move to an apartment that's maybe one third the size.

Are we masochists?!

We're leaving a city where the only signs of anti-Semitism are events like last year's march by out-of-town neo-Nazis, so unusual that it makes the national news, and going to a place where anti-Semitism is expressed with rockets and bombs.

Are we suicidal?!

It's not surprising that people ask me "why are you doing this?" The short answer is two-fold: 1) the modern state of Israel is the most exciting thing to happen to the Jewish people in 2,000 years, and we want to be a part of it; and 2) Israel is our home.

For two thousand years our ancestors dreamed of the day we would once again be able to live in a Jewish state. Our generation has the wonderful merit of living at a time when we can fulfill that dream. For too many generations our ancestors mostly sat passively on the sidelines while history was made all around them. We had supporting roles on the world stage – usually cast as the victims. Now, once again, Jews are in charge of their own destiny. That's pretty exciting stuff!

Israel is not only the most exciting thing to happen to the Jewish people in 2,000 years, it's the most important thing. And as the Chancellor-elect of the Jewish Theological Seminary said in 2003 article, Israel is a great and terrible blessing, a blessing granted to us, but not our grandparents. Arnold Eisen wrote "What does one do, as a Jew, in the face of such a blessing? At the very least, if Jewishness is at the center of one's life, one takes it with ultimate personal seriousness. One asks -more than once, at more than one stage of life - whether one should not be living there. Not out of guilt (though this guilt would not be unhealthy), nor out of obligation (though I feel a certain obligation), nor because aliyah is necessary to become a better Jew (it is not). One goes, if one so decides, because one physically cannot sit by and let other people blow it."

"One cannot sit by and let other people blow it." Boy, that sounds arrogant, but as Eisen puts it, such arrogance is necessary when we engage in the work of tikkun olam, our collective drive to make the world a better place. If Israel becomes a place we are not proud of, if Israel fails to live up to our ideals, the dream will die, and one of the pillars of Judaism will have been destroyed. The Jews living in the Diaspora need an Israel we can be proud of, an Israel that is a light to the nations.

Israel desperately needs more Jews like us. As Americans, we're part of a society that's made huge strides toward solving some of the problems that Israel's still struggling with.

For example, Bedouins and Druze, loyal citizens of Israel who vote, pay taxes, and serve in the Israeli army, have neither equal rights nor equal opportunities. The disparity between the Jewish and Arab education systems makes America's so-called "separate but equal" schools look good by comparison. Jews were in the forefront of the American civil rights movement. We marched in Selma and fought in the courts, and some of us even gave our lives, not for our own rights, but for the rights of others. Now we need to lead the way in Israel.

The environment in Israel is so polluted that when four athletes fell from a poorly-built bridge during the Maccabiah games in 1997, they weren't killed by the fall but from being poisoned when they accidentally swallowed some of the water.

Jews from North America know what it means to live in a dynamic functioning democracy that affords protection for minorities and for the environment. Israel needs more citizens who will lobby hard to fix the things that are wrong with Israeli society.

All Jews from North America could make important contributions to Israel, but there are some additional reasons why Israel needs more Conservative and Reform Jews. We had a young Israeli woman staying with us last summer. We brought her to shul and gave her her first aliyah; she enjoyed the fact that men and women could sit together and participate equally in the services, that both men and women could sing (which is not true in most Orthodox shuls). If shul was like that in Israel, she said, she'd go all the time. Our brand of Judaism can reach out to otherwise secular Jews, bridging the religious divide in Israeli society.

But let's face it. Not very many people are going to move to Israel because it's good for Israel. Most people ask "What's in it for me?"

If you're religious, then it's a mitzvah to live in Israel. And I don't mean mitzveh, as in the Yiddish phrase your Bubba used to mean "good deed," but I mean mitzvah, the Hebrew word which means commandment.

You probably know there are 613 commandments. What you might not know is there is no agreement on exactly what those mitzvot are. Ramban, Nachmanides, includes *yeshivat Eretz Yisrael*, settling the land of Israel, making aliyah, as one of them. Rambam, Maimonides, does not include this in his list, but as Rabbi Garsek shared with me, that may be because it's so obvious it doesn't need to be listed – there's no commandment to breathe either. Rambam does include other commandments which cannot be performed unless you are living in Israel.

I'm in the camp that says making aliyah is a mitzvah. The Torah seems pretty clear: in Numbers 33:53 we read: "And you shall inherit the land and settle in it."

In the Talmud in tractate Ketubot it says "A person should always live in Eretz Yisrael, even in a city of mostly gentiles, instead of outside of Israel, even in a city of mostly Jews, for someone who lives in Eretz Yisrael is like someone who has a God, and someone who lives *chutz la'aretz* (outside Israel) is like someone who doesn't have a God." In other words, better to live in secular Tel Aviv than in Orthodox Boro Park.

In the weekday Amidah we say a prayer which includes the words *v'kabtzanu yachad ma'arba kanfot ha'aretz,* and "gather us together from the four corners of the earth." We pray for God to gather us together in Israel. An observant Jew says this prayer three times a day. How many times do you have to say something before you get the message?

Israel is the easiest place in the world to be a Jew. Here in Toledo, if you want to keep kosher, it means going to Bakery Unlimited to buy bread, Giant Eagle to buy meat, and not forgetting to bring your reading glasses when you go to grocery store, because you have to read labels very carefully. If you want kosher marshmallows, you have to shlep to Ann Arbor. In Israel, almost every bakery is a kosher bakery, you have to go out of your way to find treif meat, and in most grocery stores you can buy anything on the shelves. Kosher restaurants offer every kind of cuisine from Moroccan to Chinese to Italian. And of course there's the best falafel in the world.

Here in Toledo, it's a struggle to balance family life with Jewish observance. The kids' soccer games, hockey matches, dance recitals, and track meets get scheduled for Shabbat. Once the kids are out of the day school, their classmates' birthday parties get scheduled for Shabbat and Jewish holidays. In Israel it's not a conflict. The soccer tournaments and high school plays won't be scheduled on Shabbat and holidays. Period.

Here in Toledo if you want your children to have a Jewish education, it's an expensive proposition. Day school tuition runs as high as $7000 a year per child. And that's a bargain – in other parts of the country you can spend $15,000 a year per child on day school tuition. In Israel you can choose to send your children to either secular or religious public schools—in essence, day school is free.

If you are under the age of 27 when you make aliyah, you can get a Bachelor's degree at an Israeli university for free. If you're under 30 and have a Bachelor's degree, you can get a Master's for free, the Ministry of Absorption picks up the tab. If you're a parent and concerned about tuition, resident tuition at Israel's world-class universities is a fraction of the cost in the US – just a few thousand dollars a year.

And you can get your degree in English if you want.

. An inexpensive education in Israel is nice, but it's daily life that's really special. Shabbat in Israel is an amazing experience, especially in Jerusalem or other religious areas. In Jerusalem, you can tell when Shabbat is coming. There is less traffic on the streets. The stores close early Friday afternoon. A peaceful atmosphere descends on the city.

During the holidays you can especially appreciate what it is to be part of the majority culture for a change.

On Yom Kippur there are no cars on the streets of Jerusalem. It's eerie. But there are hundreds of bicycles and skateboards—everyone lets their kids take advantage of the lack of traffic.

You walk the streets of Jerusalem during Sukkot, and it seems every house, every apartment has a sukkah. If an apartment has a "sukkah balcony" it's always mentioned in the real estate listings. You walk down the street and you hear singing, laughing, and enjoyment coming from every roof top, every scrap of a garden. And in Israel, the weather is almost always very pleasant around Sukkot.

On Passover every grocery store in Israel goes "kosher l'pesach." In some neighborhoods they will have big cauldrons of water bubbling on the streets to simplify kashering your pots and pans.

Shavuot, a holiday little noticed here, is a night when the entire city of Jerusalem stays up all night learning Torah. Walk around the streets at 2 a.m. and every few blocks you'll pass a synagogue with people learning. World-class scholars offer lessons open to the public at 3 a m. And about 4 a.m. there is an amazing sight: streams of people join together, all walking towards the Western Wall to converge and pray at dawn.

And even if you're totally NOT religious there are plenty of other good reasons to make aliyah. For many Jews in Israel, simply living in Israel is the expression of their Zionism. I had one Israeli tell me, "we don't need religion, that's for you Jews who live in Galut."

And in one way he was right. Even if you're not religious, you may care about Jewish culture, Jewish continuity. You may care whether your kids and grandkids are Jewish.

Here in Toledo, your child is likely to be the only Jew in a public middle or high school class. The chances are pretty high your kids will marry someone who isn't Jewish. After all, who are they going to meet? And only about a third of the children of intermarriage are raised Jewish. The intermarriage rate in Israel, on the other hand, is minuscule.

It's a fantastic feeling to be someplace where you are part of an "us," not part of a "them." Your kids will never come home from school singing "Rudolph the Red-Nosed Reindeer" or announcing they got the part of the Easter Bunny in the school play. December 25 is just another day at the office. You're not going to be bombarded with Christmas carols from Thanksgiving to New Year's Day.

Israel is a beautiful place. In a space of a few hundred miles you go from the forests and mountains in the north to fertile agricultural plains, to the Mediterranean beaches, to the olive groves on the hills of Judea, to the Caribbean-style resorts of Eilat. In January you can drive a couple of hours in one direction and go spa hopping at the Dead Sea, and a few hours in the other direction and go skiing on Mt. Hermon. No wonder so many people fought over this little scrap of prime real estate.

A lot of people move away from Toledo because of the weather, especially when they retire. Some of you will be heading south right after the holidays. The weather in Israel is perfect. Mild winters, with clear blue skies, and beautiful summers. Year round outdoor café weather. And unlike Florida, there aren't any hurricanes!

And Israel is very safe. You may laugh, but even in the worst years of the latest Intifada, the homicide rate, including terrorist attacks, in Jerusalem was LOWER than in any American city of a comparable size. If you wouldn't be afraid to live in Denver, you shouldn't be afraid to move to Israel. And as we learned on September 11 five years ago, "safe" is a relative term, even here in America.

When we lived in Jerusalem, we felt perfectly comfortable having our then-13 year old daughter and niece walk home from a friend's house, half an hour away, at 10 at night. And this is in the heart of Jerusalem, a city of 600,000, not in some secluded suburb. Would you do that in any neighborhood in Toledo? Our neighbors sent their five year old kid to the grocery store to buy rolls in the morning. Could you do that here? Women can walk throughout the city at any time of night and feel safe. The only drunks on the streets are American college kids on Birthright trips, and they're pretty harmless.

We've heard that some people are afraid to go into downtown Toledo at night.

As I said, "safe" is a relative term.

Being an Anglo, an English speaker in Israel, you're part of a community within a community, one that will embrace you from the first moment you begin to explore the possibility of aliyah. There are tens of thousands of "landsmen," people from the home country. We even had someone else from Toledo, Jay Traugott, make aliyah within the last year. There are English language newspapers, English language theaters, English radio and TV shows. All the Israeli kids learn English starting in elementary school. And all the waiters speak English. I strongly recommend learning Hebrew, but I have met people who made aliyah 20 years ago who still don't speak much Hebrew. It's easy to get by.

Before we moved to Israel for the year in 2000, Katherine, who was then four, said, very seriously, "when we live in Israel we'll be VERY Jewish." I thought it was cute, and it's true, you do feel "very Jewish" just being there. But more than feeling Jewish, when I'm in Israel I feel alive. I feel like I'm part of history in the making. I feel like I'm part of something larger and grander than myself just by being physically present.

And a survey has shown that living in that intense environment is very satisfying. A survey was taken of how happy Israelis are. 83% reported being "satisfied" or "very satisfied" with their lives. The author, Hillel Halkin concluded "Knowing what you are living for makes up for a lot of other things. This is as true of countries as it is of individuals. And 83% of us appear to realize that."

If you have kids, however, I think the most compelling reason to make aliyah is so that your children will be Israelis. A few years ago I was studying in Jerusalem at the Hartman Institute. One evening three young ladies, soldiers in the IDF, came to speak to us. Each of them was 20 years old, and each came from a religious background. Two of them are on a hesder program, where they combine religious studies with military service for a few years. I was blown away by the maturity, wisdom, and solid moral values of these three young ladies. They work in a program teaching soldiers who came from disadvantaged backgrounds high school equivalency studies. Which by itself also says something about the nature of Israeli society—their students were at the END of their service, not the beginning. The IDF was sending these kids to school for six months to benefit society, not to benefit the IDF. We are so obsessed with the security situation in Israel, I was really taken aback when one of them said "Security is not the most important issue facing Israel today. There are so many issues regarding integration of newcomers, education, housing, etc., that people who decide who to vote for strictly on the security issue are not doing the right thing." The young lady who brought this up was clearly influenced in her thinking by having real contact with the disadvantaged segments of Israeli society that she had never really interacted with before...e.g., Druze who didn't speak Hebrew, and didn't have much of an education. She had no idea there were people like that in Israel, and felt something really needed to be done. I listened to them, and said to myself "I want my daughters to be like that!"

Once upon a time, making aliyah required a much greater level of commitment. The people who made aliyah in the 1940s and before were pioneers. Israel was a backwards, barren, impoverished country. People lived hand to mouth, in tents and shacks, clearing the swamps and planting seedlings in the wilderness. They didn't even have a TV station until 1968! Today Israel has a modern, developed economy, with high speed wireless internet in the cafes, and the largest concentration of technology businesses in the world outside of Silicon Valley.

One of the most powerful reasons for making aliyah is the feeling you get in Israel that we're all family. Our youngest child, Devorah, was born in Israel during the year we spent there. Lauri took her for a checkup at a clinic one block from our apartment. On the way, a guy jumped off a garbage truck—which in itself is pretty cool, living in a place where even the garbage-man is Jewish—he jumped off the truck and pointed at Devorah, and starting lecturing Lauri in Hebrew. She finally figured that the guy wanted her to cover up Devorah's elbow, so she wouldn't get sunburned. That episode for me so captured the Israeli "sabra" character: a little gruff perhaps, but sweet under-neath. You really get to feel like we're all family.

And our family wants us to come home: it's never been easier to make aliyah. An organization called Nefesh b'Nefesh provides financial help to Jews from North America who want to make aliyah. Grants can be as high as $25,000 US for a family, and can be used to cover moving costs, pay off student loans, purchase new appliances, etc.

The Ministry of Absorption and the Jewish Agency will cover your expenses for five months while you go to ulpan to learn Hebrew and look for work. You'll get breaks on your mortgage and your taxes. You'll get subsidized help with re-training if you need it.

If you've been to Israel, you know what I'm talking about, and there's a pretty good chance you have at least momentarily thought about what it would be like to live there. If you have not yet visited Israel, you owe it to yourself to spend some time there.

There are many ways to visit Israel—on a mission, part of a group, by yourself. The Toledo UJC is planning a community mission in October of 2007. If enough B'nai Israel people want to go, I'll be happy to lead a congregational trip. And if you're fortunate enough to be between the ages of 18 and 26 you can go for free on a Birthright trip. How can you turn down a deal like that?

The Talmud promises that anyone who walks four cubits in the land of Israel is assured a place in Olam Haba, in the World to Come. That's a pretty cheap insurance policy for the afterlife!

There's a rabbi in New York who took **50** families with him to Israel this summer. A large part of the Bukharan community in Queens made aliyah *en masse*. I'm not quite that ambitious, but Lauri and I would be delighted to have some other people from Toledo join us on our Nefesh b'Nefesh charter flight to Israel next summer. And of course, the plane ticket to Israel is also free.

A handout with information about making aliyah can be found on the table in the hallway. I would of course be delighted to talk with any of you individually if you have any questions about making aliyah.

And whether you make aliyah or not, I hope that in the future I will be able to welcome many of you in Israel. It's been an honor and a privilege to be your rabbi for these last few years, and I would love to maintain a connection even after I'm living in Israel.

This year in Toledo, *b'shana ha'ba'ah birushalayim*, next year in Jerusalem.

G'mar chatimah tovah, may you be sealed for a good year,

Amen.

For purity of arms

The next several pieces could have gone with either human rights or Israel, as they concern human rights IN Israel. I put them with Israel because they involve more than human rights – they also involve Israeli politics, and the nature of Israel as a Jewish state.

This article about Israel's vaunted military moral code, *taharat neshek,* was originally published as an op-ed in the Jerusalem Post, September 4, 2006.

On August 21, The Jerusalem Post reported that the Rabbinical Council of America (RCA), an association of Orthodox rabbis, had called on Israel to reevaluate its military rules of war in light of Hizbullah's "unconscionable use of civilians, hospitals, ambulances, mosques and the like as human shields, cannon fodder and weapons of asymmetric warfare."

Rabbi Basil Herring, executive vice-president of the RCA, was quoted as saying, "Our traditional sensibilities tell us that it is not right to risk the lives of our soldiers to minimize civilian deaths on the other side."

We beg to differ. Surely Rabbi Herring is not suggesting that we should have carpet-bombed southern Lebanon and killed tens of thousands of Lebanese civilians to avoid the Israeli casualties that go with sending troops in on the ground?

There are some who would counter with the opposite position. They ask whether the damage inflicted on Lebanon was excessive - and whether the IDF sufficiently followed its code of ethics.

All Jews should be proud of those Israeli rules - even those sitting in the Diaspora. The basic principle of "purity of arms" says: "The IDF servicemen and women will use their weapons and force only for the purpose of their mission, only to the necessary extent, and will maintain their humanity even during combat. IDF soldiers will not use their weapons and force to harm human beings who are not combatants or prisoners of war, and will do all in their power to avoid causing harm to their lives, bodies, dignity and property."

The Post also quoted Rabbi Shmuel Eliyahu of Safed as saying: "Our corrupt military morality, which tells us that our soldiers must endanger their lives to protect enemy civilians, is the reason we lost the war."

Another Orthodox rabbi from the North, Rabbi Tzefania Drori of Kiryat Shmona, said, "Anti-Semites demand that we use Christian morality while our enemies act like barbarians."

As if this gratuitous reference to "Christian morality" isn't bad enough, he went on and said we should follow "Jewish morality," which dictates that "he who gets up to kill you, get up yourself and kill him first."

YES, JEWISH morality does allow for a preemptive strike. But preventing civilian deaths is not "Christian morality" - or if it is, they got it from the Jews! The Talmud (Sanhedrin 57a and 74a) commands us not to use excessive force. The Talmud says that if you kill someone who is coming after you when you could have stopped him with lesser force, like maiming a limb, you have committed a capital offense.

Maimonides codified as law that Jews must avoid civilian deaths by leaving an "escape route" for anyone who wants to flee. We are told we cannot besiege a city on all four sides; we must only encircle it on three sides, leaving non-combatants a way to escape. The IDF's dropping of leaflets before bombing was an attempt to fulfill this mitzva, even if it meant some of our enemies were also given a warning to leave.

Not only are we to allow people to escape, but the Torah commands us not to engage in gratuitous destruction. Deuteronomy 20:19 forbids Jews to destroy fruit trees to make siege engines in a time of war - a passage which later authorities (like Maimonides) extended to the principle of *bal taschit*, forbidding any kind of unnecessary destruction of property, whether in times of war or peace, whether it's your property or someone else's property.

YES, IT is painful when more of our soldiers die because we try to minimize civilian deaths by sending in ground troops rather than dropping bombs.

But this also comes from the wisdom of our tradition. The Talmud (Sanhedrin 74a) tells us that you cannot kill an innocent person to save your own life. Raba said, "Let him rather slay you than that you should commit murder; who knows that your blood is redder? Perhaps his blood is redder."

There will be times when innocent people will perish in a war. There will be times when an enemy is hiding behind a human shield, and those will be excruciating moments for our soldiers. We must both defend ourselves, and we must avoid unnecessary loss of innocent life. The real decisions, shoot or don't shoot, are not easy.

But we must make those difficult decisions. The Prophet Isaiah charges us with being a "light to the nations." We are supposed to show the world how God wants all human beings to behave.

Just because there are Islamists who cut the heads off innocent people they kidnap does not mean we should emulate them.

War is ugly. The other side doesn't always fight fair. That's no reason to throw *our* values, morals and Torah principles out the window. When our enemies act badly is exactly the time we need a code of ethics to remind us not to allow ourselves to become as debased as those we fight. We Jews are here on Earth to raise the bar, not to lower it.

Instead of calling on the IDF to rethink its code of war we commend them for remaining committed to it, and we urge everyone in the military establishment, from the generals to the foot soldiers, to always keep it in mind.

Responses to Purity of Arms

The vitriol that gets posted on "talkbacks" can be shocking. This piece quotes some of the nasty – and some of the nice – things people wrote in response to the above Jerusalem Post op ed. Parshat Ki Tavo, 5766.

Getting cursed is no fun.

This week's Torah reading, Ki Tavo, contains a section called the *tochecha*, the rebuke. The rebuke starts out with the penalty for failing to follow God's laws – "Cursed shall you be in the city, and cursed shall you be in the field." There are a few particularly harsh words of rebuke: "The Lord shall send upon you cursing, confusion, and failure, in all that you set your hand to do, until you are destroyed, and until you perish quickly; because of the wickedness of your doings, by which you have forsaken me. The Lord shall make the pestilence cleave to you, until he has consumed you from off the land, which you are entering to possess. The Lord shall strike you with a consumption, and with a fever, and with an inflammation, and with an extreme burning, and with the sword, and with blasting, and with mildew; and they shall pursue you until you perish."

This section is so ugly that traditionally the Torah reader recites them in a low voice, and no one wants to have that aliyah.

I was thinking of that rebuke in this week's Torah reading a few days ago when I found myself being cursed in a very public forum – on the web site of the Jerusalem Post! And what I find particularly astounding is I wasn't being cursed for criticizing Israel – quite to the contrary, a bunch of very right wing people were cursing me for praising Israel and the IDF. Go figure.

It all started with an op-ed piece I wrote that appeared in the Jerusalem Post on September 4th.

The article was a response to a statement by the Rabbinical Council of America, the largest group of Orthodox rabbis in the United States, which said that Israel should revise the Code of Ethics under which the Israeli Defense

Forces fight. In particular I disagreed with a statement by their Executive Director, Rabbi Basil Herring, who said "Our traditional sensibilities tell us that it is not right to risk the lives of our soldiers to minimize civilian deaths on the other side." I brought in several sources from our tradition which say we are obligated to minimize civilian deaths on the other side, even if it does carry some risk to our soldiers.

Any sense of morality tells you that one Israeli soldier's life is not worth the lives of some very large number, say 10,000 innocent civilians. And at the same time no one is saying you should sacrifice 10,000 Jewish soldiers to save one innocent civilian. So the truth is, it really comes down to an argument over how much risk is acceptable to save how many lives.

In my article I did not say Israel did anything wrong; to the contrary, I praised Israel and the IDF for following the Code of Ethics, and I said that nothing needed to be changed. The article I was responding to said Israel was being forced to adopt a "Christian morality." In my article I drew heavily on sources from the Torah and the Talmud to justify why the Code of Ethics is solidly Jewish morality.

The Jerusalem Post, like many newspapers these days, has a "talkback" feature to their online edition. The talkback feature allows readers to write in comments on articles published online. It's not edited like "letters to the editor." Since they don't have to pay for the space, they let anyone say more or less anything they want unless it's threatening or obscene. After my article was published, the talkback for it seemed to become a magnet for the incoherent.

Reading what some of these individuals wrote was a painful and un-pleasant experience for me. So you may think I'm crazy, because I'm going to stand here and read some of them to you. Not because I'm a glutton for punishment, I'm not, but because I believe there is a lesson to be learned from all this invective. With the pressure of having to come up with a D'var Torah every week, I've learned there is a lot of value in making lemonade when someone hands you a bunch lemons. So here is this week's crop of lemons.

The negative responses came in a couple of different categories. First were the ones that were straight invective – nothing more than unsophisticated name calling, such as:

> ""Rabbis for Human Rights" my ***. Stay in Toledo, Mr. Leff. You're no "spiritual leader" -- you are a defeatist who is more worried about the enemy than about your own people."

Of course, nowhere did I say I was MORE concerned about the enemy than my own people.

> "Leff's drivel has to be one of the most stupid pieces JP has ever published -- stupid and smug pseudo-moralistic superiority."

Well, if you're going to be bad, you might as well go for being the worst. Another person wrote

> "No, that's not gonna work, Mr. rabbi or not rabbi. We just don't have enough Jews left on earth to implement your kind but silly ideas."

He didn't seem to notice that they weren't my kind but silly ideas – they were ideas that had been adopted by the Israeli Defense Forces years ago, ideas that were praised by Rabbi Shlomo Goren z"l, the late chief rabbi of the IDF who also served as chief rabbi of Israel. Rabbi Goren, a noted right-winger who reportedly favored tearing down the Dome of the Rock and building the Third Temple. Rabbi Goren said "Human life is undoubtedly a supreme value in Judaism, as expressed both in the Halacha and the prophetic ethic. This refers not only to Jews, but to all men created in the image of God."

Another invective hurler wrote "The author of this ridiculous contention fails to understand the difference between being moral and being suicidal."

As if those are the only choices – to be moral means to be suicidal.

A similar "either/or" approach is found in this one:

"For certain the moral lectures we are getting from Barry Leff are no representation of genuine Judaism. He is a fit candidate for an Imam. Imams are the ones who are under obligation to preach heresy, confusion and self deception. Some people have no love for Israel. What kind of a state do people have in their minds? Does he mourn the recent death of IDF members? This article is offensive and an excessive abuse of free speech. War is war and should be understood as such. Is Leff lecturing about holy war? Then he should quote the Qu'ran not Jewish religious literature."

Again the either / or ... if you are concerned about the death of innocent civilians on the other side, it must mean you are not concerned about the death of Israelis.

This one at least made me smile: "Is Rabbi Leff afraid that if Israel gets tough he might have a tougher time at interfaith gatherings?"

Oh yes, there's a good reason to want Israel to act morally.

Now some people weren't content to simply dis me, they had to dis the Conservative movement, as in this one:

"But we cannot accept the fraudulent radical goyish "theology" of Conservative Judaism-- specifically its Man-Made Written and Oral Torah, rejection of the binding obligation of the Written and Oral Torah (since they claim it's Man-Made), rejection of rabbinic laws, non-halachic davening (Christian style-mixed seating), removal of portions of the shemoneh esrei, total disregard for the shabbos malachot, disregard for scholarship, etc."

Wow. That one certainly had a lot to do with what I wrote. I wasn't even identified as a Conservative rabbi – he must have gone to the effort of looking me up on the internet.

Another one who looked up my Conservative background wrote

"Foolishness like this is precisely what you can expect if you allow the Masorti movement [Conservative Judaism] to grow stronger in Israel. It's basically just a slightly more knowledgeable version of illiterate Judaism than the Reform but with all the liberalism that Reform has (that sentence is certainly one to speak of "illiterate!"). Leff is a great example of it but he's far from the only one. The movement thrives on being liberal and misquoting Talmud and Text to bolster their silly views that are not based on Torah Judaism."

This also is absurd – obviously there are some very right wing Conservative rabbis, and some liberal Orthodox rabbis.

And then there were the ones who picked up on the note that I was planning to make aliyah next year, and couldn't resist picking on that. "Please do Israel a big favor, rabbi. Do not make aliyah." And one who wrote "While I'm all for everyone making Aliyah, in this author's case I would make an exception. We have enough fuzzy thinkers and nut jobs here as it is. Stay where you are, and make your asinine comments from afar. Very afar! Have a nice day!"

Yes, Israel is home for all Jews – as long as you think like I do. But someone came to my defense in response to this one, and wrote "We have enough simple-minded, belligerent people like you -- I'd rather you go back in exchange for Rabbi Leff."

There was also a category of posts which focused on my service to Rabbis for Human Rights and spent themselves denigrating the work of that organization. I won't bother quoting them, because I think by now you get the idea.

As I read this stuff, I felt very uncomfortable, not because they were picking on me, I can handle that, but because of a concern about what it said about Israeli society. This is where I want to take my children? One of my few fans on the talkbacks put it nicely:

"Reading many of the responses to Rabbi Leff's article, I'm left with a sense of growing dread. The Talmud teaches us that God allowed the first temple to be destroyed because of Avodah Zarah, idol worship, and the second temple was destroyed because of Sinat Chinam, sense-less hatred. Both times prophets and rabbis tried desperately to warn us to turn from our path of self-destruction and find our way back to God. We were stiff-necked and too convinced of our own righteous-ness. Our punishment was a near 2000-year exile at the mercy of the other nations. Did we learn our lesson? Were two millennia enough to turn our hearts of stone into hearts of flesh? Judging from the responses of these "dedicated" Jews, it doesn't seem like it. Once again religious leaders make desperate attempts to wake us out of our delusions of infallibility. If we don't listen, I fear our children will soon face another exile and only the Almighty knows when it will end."

So where does all the negativity come from? Why do some people insist on attacking anyone who disagrees with them?

I believe the problem is that most people are uncomfortable with ambiguity. We like to have things settled. We like things to be black and white. We like to know who the good guys are and who the bad guys are. We like our good guys really good and we like our bad guys really bad.

Even though Judaism often seems comfortable with ambiguity – the Talmud will carry an argument for two pages without reaching a conclusion – there is also a tendency to try and make things black and white. This week's Torah portion serves up an example: the blessings are really wonderful blessings, and the curses are really horrible curses. There's no middle ground.

What's more, if you read the stories in the Bible "straight up," without looking at the commentaries, what you read are the stories of some very flawed human beings—complex and interesting characters. To take just one example, look at the life of Abraham. He has many fine moments – like when God tells him *lech lecha*, go, leave, head out and trust me, and he does. What I believe to be one of the finest moments in the Bible, Abraham arguing with God – imagine the chutzpah, arguing with God – that the cities of Sodom and Gomorrah should be spared if there are righteous people living there. But this same righteous hero passes his wife off as his sister to the Pharaoh, doesn't argue with God when God asks him to sacrifice his son, and he lets his wife badger him into sending his son from another woman off into the desert to die. So read the text and Abraham comes across as an incredibly inspirational, and an incredibly troubling figure.

There are many other examples of ambiguous characters in the Bible: David the sinner, Bilam who wants to curse the Jews but listens to God and doesn't. Esau, Jacob's brother, who doesn't come across as wicked in the plain text reading of the Torah--if anything he comes across as taken advantage of.

But with many of these figures the commentators, especially Rashi, go to great lengths to whitewash the not nice things the good guys did, and if there were such a word "blackwash," paint in a more negative light, the things the bad guys did. You read Rashi's commentary and it's as if he's trying to increase the contrast between good and evil. If the good guys did something that seems morally questionable, it's because there's more to the story that we don't understand, and what they did was actually OK. If a bad guy does something nice, he finds a way to make it negative. My favorite example is when Jacob and Esau have their reunion after having been separated for years. The Torah tells us "And Esau ran to meet him, and embraced him, and fell on his neck, and kissed him; and they wept." Makes Esau sound like a decent guy. But since Esau was the designated bad guy in the Jacob – Esau struggle, Rashi says the reason Esau cried is because he was going to bite Jacob in the neck, but a miracle turned Jacob's neck to marble, and Esau hurt his teeth. Wow! That's certainly not what's written there. Similarly Jacob and his mother Rebecca's deceitfulness gets whitewashed away as being OK because they were doing it to fulfill God's will that he be the father of the Jewish people. God's will couldn't come about some other way?

We like things black and white. We like our good guys good, so some people will come along and make everything that Abraham did good, and we like our bad guys bad, so some people will interpret everything that Bilam or Esau did in a negative light.

So some people did to me what Rashi did to Esau. They decided that if I thought we should be concerned about killing innocent Arabs, I must not be concerned about the death of Jewish soldiers. Which of course is nonsense.

Obviously I am more disturbed about the death of a Jewish soldier than an Arab civilian. The Jewish soldier is family, it's very painful. The closer you are to someone, the more you mourn. You sit shiva for your family, not for strangers. But that doesn't mean you have to be completely immune to feeling that the death of a stranger is a tragedy.

Nowhere in my article did I say that we shouldn't strike our enemies strongly. I believe the IDF should have hit Hezbollah harder than they did earlier than they did with a ground attack that would have really rooted out the weapons. Such an attack could have been conducted while still operating within the guidelines of the Code of Ethics. The Code of Ethics says you have to work to minimize civilian losses. It doesn't say you have to turn the other cheek, and it doesn't say there will never be any civilian losses.

Life is not black and white. It comes in shades of gray. Good guys sometimes do bad things, and there are often some redeeming features to people we've designated bad guys. War confronts us with difficult ethical decisions. One colleague was involved in the first Lebanon war, and his commander told him not to shoot when Palestinians with rocket propelled grenades had civilians in front of them. Two of his Army buddies got killed. To this day he doesn't know whether they did the right thing or not.

I don't know whether they did the right thing or not, and I certainly would not criticize them if they fired in self defense even if there were civilians in the area. But I think to fail to consider the fact that civilians were there would be to lose our humanity. It is appropriate we agonize over decisions like that, regardless of which way the question is answered in a particular case.

One of the other people who wrote in said "Rabbi Leff is right in supporting human values even in wars. As a soldier and officer in the artillery of the IDF I remember I participated in committing war crimes in the past, shelling civilians. To this day it gives me bad feelings to remember that."

No soldier should leave the field of battle feeling dirty, like they did something wrong. Sticking to the Code of Ethics is not easy. The battlefield presents ambiguous situations, and the answer is not "never shoot when civilians are present" and the answer is not "who cares if there are civilians present."

This is not just an abstract lesson. We all have to deal with ambiguity in our lives. In a few weeks it will be Rosh Hashanah, the Day of Judgment, the day when the imagery of our tradition tells us there are three books open, one for the completely righteous, one for the completely wicked, and by far the largest volume, the volume where 99% of us are found, one for the in between. If we can't be completely righteous, we need to strive to be as righteous as we can, so as to merit a place in the Book of Life.

On Friday the Rabbi Got Gassed

Usually my volunteer work with Rabbis for Human Rights goes pretty smoothly...then there was the time I got tear gassed! From my blog, July 10, 2006.

Today I got a good whiff of tear gas for the first time in 33 years. I will be quite content to wait another 33 years before a repeat experience.

Accompanying me on this morning's adventure were Rabbi Arik Ascherman, executive director of Rabbis for Human Rights, and a woman named Ruth who described herself as a "human rights activist" from LA. I must admit I don't really think of myself as an "activist," but I suppose getting tear gassed and serving on the board of Rabbis for Human Rights probably is sufficient to qualify me as a "human rights activist."

So how did I come to get gassed? We were going to a Palestinian village called Beit Ummar in the West Bank, not far from Efrat and Hebron. Some of the residents of Beit Ummar own agricultural land that is right next door to the Jewish settlement of Karmei Tzur. The settlement is building a security fence outside the fence of the settlement itself. A fair amount of Palestinian farmland is being confiscated for this buffer zone. While in theory the Palestinians would be allowed to farm the land, as a practical matter they wouldn't be, because when they go there settlers from Karmei Tzur threaten them, and on occasion have beat them.

To be fair, the settlers have a valid reason why they want a security buffer zone surrounding their settlement. In 2002 three residents of Karmei Tzur were murdered by a terrorist infiltration.

The fence under discussion is NOT part of the famous "security barrier" being built between Israel and the Palestinian territories. This settlement is on the Palestinian side of the security barrier. They are building this fence just around their own settlement. The exact routing is under review by Israeli courts.

The purpose of our visit was to go to the fields with Palestinian far-mers, in essence to shield them from the settlers. We were told after they did some work on their trees, they were planning to hold afternoon prayers at the location, as a sort of peaceful protest.

When we arrived, the Palestinians were a little disorganized. Besides us, there were representatives from the International Solidarity Movement and the Ecumenical Accompaniment Program of the World Council of Churches, altogether about a dozen Israelis and foreigners. Each of us had been given a slightly different story as to the plan for the day. We arrived at 10:30, sat around and had tea and visited with the locals. We never did go out to work on the trees; around noon we joined a crowd from the village that was heading down to the field (near the settlement) for afternoon prayers.

Everything started peaceful enough. There was an Israeli military pres-ence, and there was one slightly tense moment when an Israeli soldier got on the hood of his jeep and started waving his gun around. One of the Israelis in our group convinced him that wasn't a good idea and he got down. The afternoon prayers proceeded uneventfully, about 100 yards from the settlement, under the watchful eyes of a group of about four IDF soldiers.

As the prayers finished and things were breaking up and people were starting to walk back to town, a small group of teens looked like they were getting ready to throw rocks at the soldiers. Rabbi Ascherman did a quick intervention and got them to stop. I breathed a momentary sigh of relief as a potentially bad situation was averted. One of the soldiers started unnecessarily pointing his rifle right at people in the crowd who were acting peacefully -- Arik once again yelled at soldier to put his gun down, and after a few sessions of yelling the soldier eventually complied.

It turned out I breathed my sigh of relief somewhat prematurely. A few minutes later a settler came running down the hill screaming, waving a gun. Fortunately, the soldiers intervened and made him leave, but his presence undoubtedly helped inflame the already hot-headed Palestinian teens, and a few minutes later they got out slings and started hurling rocks in the direction of the soldiers. The effort was totally ineffectively as they were too far away, but it was still enough to get the soldiers attention.

I now have a much greater appreciation for why soldiers have responded with live rifle fire to these kids hurling stones. We're not talking about little kids throwing pebbles. They are using slings that look like they are made of cloth, twirl them over their heads rapidly, with some pretty good sized stones, and when they let fly, those big rocks go quite some distance and can do some serious damage. In addition to slinging stones at the soldiers, the kids used the slings to destroy the bulbs in some big streetlights that had presumably been setup for security purposes, and they started a small grass fire.

At first some of the kids parents' did try and stop them, but the kids outnumbered the parents who were engaging them, and they just kept doing their thing. We started heading for higher ground when the IDF started firing tear gas canisters at the kids. I thought the tear gas was a reasonably restrained response considering what was going on. But I can certainly see how the situation had the potential to get very ugly—there were only four soldiers and about two dozen kids acting very rowdy—and 200 more Palestinians and others nearby. Not an easy situation for crowd control.

At first the tear gas didn't get anywhere near me; but then either one of the canisters went astray, or the soldier intentionally fired higher up the hill and I caught a good whiff of it. My eyes stung and watered like crazy. It definitely would have taken a lot of the fight out of me. The last time I was exposed to tear gas was in the US Army's Basic Training, when I had to momentarily lift my gas mask in a chamber filled with tear gas—both so we'd know what it's like, and so we'd take instructions to put our gas masks on seriously.

As we were walking back to the car, I was furious, and not because the gas bothered me that much. The whole situation was just so completely stupid and unnecessary.

There was stupidity all around: there was the stupid soldier pointing his gun at people who were being peaceful, there was the stupid settler running toward a crowd of Palestinians waving his gun (how did he know one of them didn't have a gun, too?), the stupid, very stupid, Palestinian teens who turned a peaceful demonstration into a violent confrontation, and the stupid parents and crowd who didn't stop the kids.

And I felt like a stupid American who got taken advantage of. I will gladly go out and defend anyone's right to have a peaceful demonstration. I will NOT defend someone's right to go out and throw stones, engage in vandalism, and start fires.

There are all sorts of reasons given why the kids do these things, and reasons are given why the parents don't stop them. Maybe it's all just a game, as the kids did stay pretty far away from the soldiers. But it is so totally self-defeating! When the court case comes up, the Palestinians have just given the settlers proof for why they need a larger area for their security fence.

The whole experience struck me as a metaphor for why there are such problems in the Middle East today. I don't know if it's something in the water or what, but there sure is a lot of stupidity in this part of the world. All the trouble was caused by a small group—less than 10% of the Palestinians present. The vast majority I believe really did want a peaceful demonstration. But they weren't willing to stop the hot heads. The same principle is at work for Palestine as a whole: the problems are caused by a relatively small group that really wants to engage Israel violently. The majority of Palestinians have said in polls that they would happily live in a Palestinian state at peace with Israel. But that majority is not willing to stand up to the "hot heads."

We won't have peace until the calmer heads prevail over the hotter heads. Israel has its hot heads, but compared to the Palestinians they are under the control of grownups. We won't have peace until the Palestinians who want peace—and I believe they are the majority—are willing to really step up to and control the ones who don't.

Last week's Torah portion, when all this happened, was Balak. At the end of parshat Balak, the Israelite people go crazy, abandon the rules, and go whoring after Midianite women. A plague breaks out which killed 24,000 people.

The plague was only stopped when Pinchas made a show of killing Zimri and Cozbi, which got the people's attention and turned them away from their whoring ways. Note that I don't think this would have worked if Pinchas was a Midianite—if a Midianite killed a Jew, they would have just kept right on going. The fact that it was a Jew who killed Zimri—a reminder to the Jews that what they were doing was not acceptable—is what made the message take hold.

I certainly don't advocate anyone killing anyone, but I think there is a parallel here. Israelis killing Palestinians is not what will ultimately lead to peace. It's going to have to be the Palestinians who recognize that violence is destroying their lives, not improving them. And while we wait for that glorious moment, Israelis need to do what they can to try to avoid inflaming more violence by waving guns at people who are acting peacefully, or by denying Palestinians the right to farm their fields. We should be leading them in the direction of peace, not the direction of hate.

I was only slightly disillusioned by my experience. We have a responsibility to treat Palestinian non-combatants as humanely as possible, while at the same time we aggressively go after the ones who would destroy us. I say "*kol hakavod*"—I honor—those people who can go out and try to help the Palestinians and be exposed to this kind of foolishness without getting totally disgusted. And that really is the test—to be nice to people who are compliant, do whatever you ask, make no trouble, that's not such a big mitzvah. But if you can continue to remember to honor the rights of people who aren't acting so nice—well, that's to really do the mitzvah credit!

Quite a day indeed. Tear gassed, disillusioned, and to top it all off a mild sunburn. Thank God I had a wonderfully restful Shabbat right after to regain my equilibrium. Despite it all, I continue to believe it is incredibly important for us to continue to work to defuse the situation, to continue to talk with Palestinians, and to support them when their rights are being abused. We'll never have peace if all we do is fight.

Competing Narratives

This is an op-ed I wrote that was published by Common Ground News Service on October 2, 2009. It describes how we need to live with the contradiction inherent in different ways Israeli Jews and Palestinians tell their stories.

JERUSALEM - How do you make peace with someone whose entire view of recent history is completely different from yours?

For Jews, 1948 stands out as one of their finest hours—tiny, beleaguered Israel heroically stood up to vastly superior Arab forces in the War of Independence, which gave birth to a dream of 2000 years, an independent Jewish state in Palestine.

Palestinians call the 1948 war "Al-Nakba", "The Catastrophe", a time when the colonising Zionists, with international support, expelled hundreds of thousands of Arabs from their homes and turned them into refugees.

The way that the Jews tell their story, they have been in Israel continuously since the days of Joshua, 3,400 years ago, sometimes fewer in number, sometimes greater. When Jews started returning in larger numbers, in the late 1800s, Israel was an empty place, swampy and desolate. They came home and made the desert bloom. Arabs from around the region started moving in when the Jews created a functioning economy.

The Palestinians say they have always lived here. In the late 1800s they were peacefully minding their own business when imperial colonisers bought up land from absentee landlords, driving the local inhabitants off land they had worked for generations. Zionists, people who came from Europe and knew little about Palestine or its people, took the land away from its rightful inhabitants.

How can people with such completely different views of history reconcile their perspectives sufficiently to make peace with each other?

By accepting that different people will see the same facts in a different light. The Jewish tradition teaches "*shivim panim batorah*", there are 70 faces to the Torah (Midrash Bamidbar Rabbah 13:16). Jews will always see their return to Zion as the fulfilment of a 2000 year-old dream. Palestinians will probably have a hard time ever seeing the same facts as anything but a colonialist imposition.

My volunteer work with Rabbis for Human Rights affords me the opportunity to meet Palestinians from the West Bank and to hear their stories. It's one thing to read about the problems facing farmers in the West Bank in the newspaper; it's another thing completely to hear it first hand, or even more powerfully, to experience the problems in real time, or to share the experience of being tear-gassed, as I have.

What I have found is that hearing their story does not invalidate my story. We need to become comfortable with contradiction. F. Scott Fitzgerald said "the test of a first-rate intelligence is the ability to hold two opposed ideas in the mind at the same time, and still retain the ability to function". We need to be able to live with the contradiction that what the Jews see as their finest hour, the Palestinians see as their "Nakba".

For peace to come, each side needs to appreciate the core perspective of the other:

Jews need to appreciate that Palestine was not "a land without a people". For too long Israel has ignored the fact that Palestinians also have long-standing and deep ties to this land.

Palestinians need to appreciate that Zionism is not colonialism. Many Palestinians think of the arrival of Jews in Israel as a colonial phenomenon, like the Belgians going into the Belgian Congo. It's not. The Jews are not "going back where they came from". They are back where they came from.

A few weeks ago I was at a joint Israeli-Palestinian retreat, and was very surprised to hear one of the Palestinian participants, Dr. Taleb Al-Harithi, proudly describe how he was descended from Bar Kochba, the great 2nd century Jewish rebel who was crushed by the Romans. Surprised, but it makes perfect sense that the Palestinians are descendants of the Jews who stayed—many of whom converted to Islam—just as many of the Jews who left converted to Christianity.

To make peace in Israel we need to make peace with contradictions; contradictions such as a Palestinian descended from a Jewish rebel, Jews being "home" after 2,000 years of wandering, and how one nation's "finest hour" is another nation's "catastrophe". We need to stop fighting about who is right. We both are.

Chapter Eleven

Conservative Judaism

"Yafe Talmud Torah v'derech eretz," "Studying Torah combined with a worldly occupation is a beautiful thing"

Rabban Gamliel, Mishnah Avot, 2:2

Judaism comes in a variety of different "flavors:" Orthodox in its many varieties, Conservative, Reform, Reconstructionist, Humanist, non- and/or post-denominational. In terms of finding the right balance between fidelity to tradition and being a part of the wider world, the Conservative approach is the one that resonates with me the most, at least intellectually. That's why I became a Conservative rabbi. However, I also appreciate the passion and commitment (especially to learning) that is more often found in Orthodox circles. Hence, at the time I am writing this, I belong to two synagogues here in Jerusalem: Conservative Kehilat Moreshet Avraham, and Orthodox Mizmor L'David (a.k.a. the Arnona Carlebach Minyan).

A Short Definition of Conservative Judaism

This was originally written as an email reply to a colleague who was looking for a definition of Conservative Judaism.

We believe mitzvah means commandment, and that there are things that God (and the Jewish tradition) calls on us to do.

We also believe in living in and being part of the modern world, not excluding ourselves from the modern world. We believe to be *"ohr legoyim"* means we have to interact with the nations.

Hence we adapt our understanding of what it means to be commanded to the modern world we live in—acknowledging the changing role of women, for example.

We believe that at the heart of the Torah there is a message from God, even though we acknowledge that the Torah was also edited by different people over a thousand year period. Torah is in a sense a partnership between Man and God, and that partnership continues today.

For most of us the translation of "*yirah*" (as in *yirat shamayim*) emphasizes awe, not fear. We don't believe God is obsessed with minutiae (separate dishes, yes; two dishwashers, no). We are the "Hillel's" of the modern world. If the halacha could reasonably be *makil* (lenient) or *machmir* (strict), we tend to prefer to be *makil*—it's hard enough to be a Jew. Or, as the Ben Ish Chai (chief rabbi of Baghdad in the mid-19th century) put it, the Torah forbids enough stuff, we don't need to go looking for more.

It may be a slogan, but for most of us Conservative Judaism does represent the perfect balance between fidelity to tradition and openness to change.

The State of the Conservative Movement

A report on the state of the Conservative Movement in 2005, based on observations from the Rabbinical Assembly Convention that year. Parshat Pekudei, 5765.

"This is the accounting of the Tabernacle, the Tabernacle of the Pact"...Exodus 38:21

This week's Torah portion begins with an accounting of the gold, silver, copper and other valuable things that were used in constructing the Mishkan, the Tabernacle, which represented God's presence among the people of Israel.

Like any good leader, Moses knew that after the contributions have come in and the work has begun, you need to take an accounting – both so that the donors will know how the capital campaign went, and so that you'll know what you have to work with in the next phase.

You can see our accounting for the results of our capital campaign every time you come in the door of the synagogue, where our "thermometer" showing funds raised to date is prominently posted.

The Hebrew word normally used for accounting is *roeh cheshbon*, literally, to "see the accounts." But beyond the accounting for the physical assets—the gold, silver, copper, money, etc.—we occasionally need to take what the tradition calls *cheshbon hanefesh*, a spiritual accounting.

Last week I was in Houston, Texas, participating in a *cheshbon hanefesh*, a spiritual accounting, of the Conservative movement. I was at the annual meeting of the Rabbinical Assembly, the worldwide organization of Conservative rabbis. Our conference was titled "Reinventing Conservative Judaism: Redefining Our Mission for the Twenty-First Century." As one Jewish paper described our meeting, "At a time when some say the Conservative movement is at a crossroads, and perhaps suffering an identity crisis as its membership dwindles, some 300 rabbis are scheduled to "ponder the future" at the 105th

Rabbinical Assembly convention." Rabbi Ehud Bandel started his remarks with "Houston, we have a problem!"

The very short answer is that in many ways, the movement is much like our synagogue. B'nai Israel is facing big demographic challenges: as the Jewish population of Toledo shrinks, our membership base has been shrinking. Our congregation is aging. But there is good news as well: there are a lot of exciting things going on at B'nai Israel, our capital campaign is off to a great start, we are designing a new building, and we have lots of well attended, exciting programs.

The Conservative movement as a whole is in almost exactly the same situation. Several speakers in Houston talked about the demographic challenges facing the Conservative movement. The most recent survey of American Jews showed that the Conservative movement is losing market share—we were once the largest movement, now Reform is larger.

Many of the reasons for our losses are things we can't do anything about. Conservative Judaism is middle of the road, centrist. Back in the heyday of the movement, in the 40s, 50s, and 60s, society valued being a centrist. Radicals were shunned. But since the convulsions of the late 60s and the war in Vietnam, our society has become increasingly polarized. People are moving to extremes. One speaker gave an example of a marriage: if one partner wants to live in New York, and one partner wants to live in California, compromising by living in Kansas is not going to please anyone! People are gravitating toward one or the other of the extremes, and there's not much we can do about that.

Another demographic fact is that intermarried Jews who choose to raise their kids Jewish mostly choose to affiliate with the Reform movement—and with 31% of all adult Jews intermarried, that's a lot of people.

There are other factors in the decline that represent conscious choices we have made. In addition to the intermarriage angle, the Reform also have made inroads because in many cases they don't require as many hours a week of religious instruction for kids to have a bar or bat mitzvah. For many parents who consider Judaism just another activity, to be scheduled somewhere in between soccer and music lessons, the reduced time demand is a big consideration. The Conservative movement has, rightly in my opinion, insisted that six hours a week of religious instruction should really be the minimum.

It's unfortunate that we are losing the least connected and committed Jews to Reform, but what's more troubling to me is that we are losing some of our most committed and knowledgeable young Jews to Orthodoxy.

Why are we losing some of our most committed to Orthodoxy?

It's because it is where they find communities of serious Jews, committed to living a Jewish life.

The nationally syndicated radio talk show host Dennis Prager spoke to us. He spoke about the importance of faith, the divinity of Torah, Israel's Christian supporters, and gay marriage—all of which are topics for another time. What he shared that I want to focus on is how people assume he's Orthodox when he says he won't do a show on Shabbat or Yom Tov. People in LA were amazed that he turned down an invitation to be on Larry King because it was a Friday night, and he's not Orthodox.

Dennis Prager's problem – people assuming he's Orthodox, when in fact he identifies himself as a "non-Orthodox religious Jew"—highlights what some rabbis think is a big problem for the Conservative movement. No one knows what we stand for. Many Conservative rabbis feel they cannot clearly articulate what the Conservative movement is about. The Orthodox speak of "Torah-true" Judaism. The Reform speak of "Tikkun Olam," repairing the world. The closest the Conservative movement comes to a similar slogan is "Tradition and Change" but somehow that doesn't tell you much and isn't very compelling. One of my colleagues suggested "Honest-to-God" Judaism, which at least has nice ring to it even if I'm not sure what it means.

Some of my colleagues think the Conservative movement has a marketing problem, which they define as meaning we have a great product, but we are not promoting it well. To them, we just need a great slogan for a billboard and all will be well. The President of the RA, Rabbi Rafi Rank, said we should be promoting not just Judaism, but specifically Conservative Judaism—he gave an example that if he were a manager for the Fuller Brush company, he would want his salespeople out there promoting Fuller brushes, not just any old brushes.

As a former marketing guy, I can tell you the first thing you have to do in marketing a product is to pay attention to your product, not your advertising slogans. So, let's look at our product: why do people join Conservative synagogues?

Fidelity to Conservative ideology is NOT a big reason. Chancellor Schorsch of the Jewish Theological Seminary, said ideology is not important to most Jews. This is absolutely correct. Therefore, a clever marketing slogan that focuses on ideology—a better way to describe what we are about—is not going to make any difference whatsoever.

The Chancellor also said that one problem is the seminary is training rabbis as managers, and what we need is more entrepreneurs. What I read into his remarks was an implication that he thought this problem could be solved by changing the curriculum at JTS to be more entrepreneurial.

If he does think that would fix it, I disagree. A few college courses on entrepreneurship are not going to create entrepreneurs.

Who are the real entrepreneurs in the Jewish world today? Why?

The big entrepreneurs are Chabad—there are a lot of them, and they get pushed out into the world as *shluchim* with a small stake to get them started. Then it's sink or swim. THAT's what breeds entrepreneurs. One of our problems is our rabbis are a very elite group: you have to have a college degree to start the program, and then you spend five or six years studying—longer than law school, comparable to medical school. Rabbis today graduate with a ton of debt, so they can't afford to be entrepreneurs—they have to get a high paying job to pay off the loans. So we have mega-shuls with four rabbis and multi-million dollar budgets in big cities, and we have small communities who don't have a rabbi because they can't afford to pay $80k or $90k starting salaries. We're also not starting new synagogues—young Conservative rabbis are not moving to places where Jews are moving to and starting new shuls because they can't afford it and no one encourages them to. If a community can't bootstrap itself to 100+ members and financial viability they will never have a Conservative rabbi come serve them. And we certainly don't have young Conservative rabbis going to places like Ukraine and trying to set up shop simply because there are Jews there who need to be connected to Judaism. The system is not set up in a way that encourages this.

If my accounting of the Conservative movement seems a little pessimistic, let me share some good news as well. There are some things the movement does a great job with—Camp Ramah and USY among them. There are now 50,000 kids affiliated with the Conservative movement going to Jewish day schools. There are some amazing teachers affiliated with the movement—I learned some incredible Torah from Rabbis Brad Artson and Alan Lew during my days in Houston.

And there are some Conservative rabbi entrepreneurs: Rabbi Howie Siegel in Houston has started what you might call a Conservative Chabad House: he offers Talmud classes at Borders, Introduction to Judaism classes at the offices of his wife's dental practice, Shabbat services at a branch of the JCC, charges no membership fees and offers free High Holiday services, by donation.

We have several entrepreneurs in Israel: Rabbi Yonatan Rudnick is bringing something brand new to Israel—he is the first real hospital chaplain in Israel. Many Israeli hospitals have rabbis on the staff: who supervise the kashrut of the kitchen and go around before Yom Kippur with a doctor to figure out which patients are capable of fasting (I kid you not), but not talking with them about spiritual issues. Rabbi Rudnick doesn't introduce himself as "rabbi" because too many secular Israelis get the heeby jeebies around rabbis. So his ID card says "*tmicha ruchanit*," spiritual support. He tends to the needs of Haredi Jews, secular Jews, Muslims and Christians.

Rabbi Uri Ayalon has started a community, Yotzer Or, based on serving a low income community with what they need. They provide tutoring for kids, classes for adults. As yet, they do not offer regular prayer services, which has a lot of rabbis wondering "what the heck kind of community is that?" But he's starting with what the community needs, not a preconceived idea of what a community should be. He hopes that eventually prayer will be part of the mix, but doesn't feel the time is yet ripe.

What's important about these three is they are not selling "Fuller brushes" – they are not making a big deal that they are capital C Conservative – but rather they are just out there serving the Jewish people. And the way they serve them of course reflects who they are – Conservative rabbis. They are not preaching about the glories of our ideology – rather they are out there living it, and being examples to others.

So to summarize, the state of our movement is like the state of our shul—demographically challenged, but with some real exciting things going on. My prescription for fixing things:

- Our synagogues don't need to focus on ideology. They need to focus on having prayer services that move people and learning that challenges people. They need to instill our values in our young people.
- We need a lot more Jewish entrepreneurs who follow our approach to Torah. If instead of graduating 30 or 40 new rabbis a year, almost all of whom carry a huge debt load, we graduated 100 new rabbis who had no student loans to pay off, and who could each be given a stake to start something new, we could change the Jewish world—and seriously promote our approach to Judaism, which truly does resonate with many Jews. Rabbi Ehud Bandel, president of Masorti, the Conservative movement in Israel, said most Israelis are Conservative Jews—they just don't know it yet!

We don't need an improved central organization, better strategic planning, and more direction. We need the opposite. We need the chaos of a real entrepreneurial environment, with more organizations serving Jews all over the world in all kinds of ways—united not by being officially part of the Conservative movement as defined by our institutions, but being united by following our approach to Judaism: committed to halacha, adapting to the world around us, and driven by the core values of Judaism including *tzedaka* and *gemilut chesed*.

Maybe one of these days I'll hit you all up for donations so I can start a yeshiva!

Shabbat Shalom

Chapter Twelve

Interfaith

"And Melchizedek king of Shalem brought forth bread and wine; and he was the priest of the most high God."

Genesis 14:18

Melchizedek was not Jewish: yet as we see in the quote above, he was "a priest of the most high God." Jews have never claimed that God is ONLY our God; He's God to the whole world. Being open minded about that certainly simplifies interfaith relations from our standpoint.

Especially for a religion with as few adherents as Judaism, having good relations with people of other faiths is essential. Ever since ordination (and even before, when I was a student) I have been active in interfaith work. One of the key principles in interfaith work is respecting other faiths – hence the following op-ed on Christmas trees.

Yes, Virginia, it really is a Christmas tree
Originally published as an op-ed piece in the Toledo Blade, December 17, 2005.

A few weeks ago there was a flurry of news media attention about House Speaker J. Dennis Hastert's decision to go back to calling the U.S. Capitol's holiday tree a "Christmas" Tree.

And then there was the Nova Scotia logger indignant that the 48-foot spruce he'd donated to the city of Boston was labeled a "holiday tree."

The controversy has reached Toledo as well. As reported in The Blade on Dec. 3, Bowsher High School principal Larry Black corrected himself when he slipped up and said the school had erected a Christmas tree. He said it's really a "holiday tree."

"We try to respect everybody's beliefs," he said. "The music department does a Christmas concert. Well, actually it's a holiday concert."

I took a survey of my Jewish sixth grade Sunday school class. The sixth graders and their parents joined me in agreeing that calling those pointy green things laden with ornaments "holiday trees" is silly.

Jews are a very small percentage of the population in Toledo. Statistically, if you filled a room with 75 people randomly picked off the streets, only one would be Jewish.

Jews often feel a little out of sync with the mainstream culture this time of year when you can't turn on the radio without hearing Christmas carols, when the clerks in the stores are all wishing everyone a "Merry Christmas," and our homes are often the only ones on the block without an impressive display of reindeer and electric icicles.

But talking about "holiday trees" does not help make us feel more included: there's no such thing as a Hanukkah tree. The tree is a Christmas tradition. It's not a generic symbol of all winter holidays. The first family lights a Hanukkah menorah at the White House, which I think is wonderful, but I would be offended if they decided to call it a "holiday candelabrum."

Christmas concerts at public schools are a completely different issue, especially when the carols make overt references to Christian beliefs. One of the kids in my class asked, "Why can't they stick with neutral stuff, like Frosty the Snowman?"

In this instance, including a few Hanukkah songs and calling it a "Holiday Concert" actually is a nice statement of inclusiveness.

My 7-year-old daughter takes jazz dance lessons, and when they started learning some dances set to Christmas music, she said, "I'm Jewish. Don't you have any Hanukkah songs?" The teacher said no. I'll send her a CD.

Most Jews I know aren't offended by Christmas trees. In fact, we enjoy looking at them. I take my kids to the zoo to see the lights, and we drive around our neighborhood to admire the decorations. It's not "our" holiday, but that doesn't mean we can't share in others' enjoyment of it.

Some Jews find themselves humming Christmas carols this time of year because the tunes are very catchy. What the heck, many of them, like "White Christmas," were written by Jews!

So call a Christmas tree a Christmas tree. Call a Hanukkah Menorah a Hanukkah Menorah. But please, have a "holiday concert" or dance program that includes songs from other traditions like Hanukkah or Kwanzaa.

Have a Merry Christmas, a Happy Hanukkah, a Joyous Kwanzaa, a Happy Winter Solstice, a Blessed Bodhi Day.

May whatever holiday you celebrate cast a little light in the cold and dark nights of December.

Pope John Paul II

The Pope is the most powerful spiritual leader in the world—leader of one billion Catholics, half of the world's two billion Christians. It is Catholic doctrine that the Pope is infallible: according to Catholic doctrine, things he says in his role as Pope are guaranteed to be correct because he is assisted by God in his role.

Non-Catholics might have reservations about the idea of papal infallibility, but there is agreement among people of all faiths that Pope John Paul II was a truly remarkable individual. Many Jews remember the Pope for his famous visit to Israel. What makes his visit to Israel so special is not that he was the first Pope to visit Israel—he wasn't. Pope Paul VI visited Israel in 1964. When Paul VI visited Israel, however, he never called Israel "Israel," he avoided even mentioning "Jews," and he did not visit a single Jewish site. In those days the Vatican did not consider Israel a country. There were no diplomatic relations between the Vatican and Israel.

A year later, Pope Paul VI did confirm a groundbreaking statement in Jewish-Catholic relations, Nostra Aetate, which was part of the Vatican II process started by his predecessor, Pope John XXIII. Nostra Aetate includes a remarkable statement: "Nevertheless, God holds the Jews most dear for the sake of their Fathers; He does not repent of the gifts He makes or of the calls He issues-such is the witness of the Apostle. In company with the Prophets and the same Apostle, the Church awaits that day, known to God alone, on which all peoples will address the Lord in a single voice and "serve him shoulder to shoulder." Which almost sounds like a quote from Aleinu, the prayer that closes every Jewish worship service, when we pray for the day when "all who live will know that to You (God) every knee must bend, every tongue pledge loyalty."

In Nostra Aetate the Catholic Church condemned anti-Semitism, and acknowledged that the Jewish people still have a covenant with God. But the

326

implementation of many of the concepts of Nostra Aetate really fell to Pope John Paul II.

John Paul II recognized Israel as a country. He established diplomatic ties with Israel in 1993. When he came to visit Israel in 2000 he visited many Jewish sites including the Western Wall and Yad Vashem, the Holocaust Memorial.

We are all familiar with the custom of leaving a note at the Western Wall with a prayer on it. When the Pope visited the Western Wall, he too left a note; his read: "God of our fathers, you chose Abraham and his descendants to bring your Name to the Nations. We are deeply saddened by the behavior of those who in the course of history have caused these children of yours to suffer and, asking your forgiveness, we wish to commit ourselves to genuine brotherhood with the people of the Covenant."

This Pope walked the talk. In February, 1945 he saved the life of Edith Zirer, then a 13 year old Jewish girl, starving and confused after being liberated by the Soviets from the Hassak concentration camp.

When he visited Yad Vashem, Ehud Barak, then Prime Minister of Israel told the Pope "You have done more than anyone else to bring about the historic change in the attitude of the Church towards the Jewish people, initiated by the good Pope John XXIII, and to dress the gaping wounds that festered over many bitter centuries."

Pope John Paul II is deserving of the highest praise in the Jewish tradition: to be called a mensch.

Our prayers go out to Catholics everywhere as they mourn the loss of this courageous leader. May his memory be a blessing.

Judaism and Islam

Most people don't know it, but if you compare Judaism, Islam, and Christianity, Judaism and Islam are the two that are most similar: Christianity is definitely "the odd man odd." This was a talk I gave at Moreshet Yisrael in Jerusalem, parshat Vayishlach 5769.

In this week's Torah reading, Yakov (Jacob) is reunited with his brother Esau. Despite the fact that they were brothers—or perhaps it's BECAUSE of the fact that they were brothers—Yakov is afraid for his life. He's afraid that at this fateful family reunion, Esau is going to try and harm him.

What happens when the much anticipated reunion occurs? The Torah tells us "And Esau ran to meet him, and embraced him, and fell on his neck, and kissed him; and they wept."

Despite the plain meaning of the verse, Midrash Tanchuma says the reason Esau cried is because Esau wanted to bite Yakov on the neck, but Yakov's neck turned to marble, so Esau hurt his teeth and cried. Yakov cried because he was afraid Esau was going to bite him. Tanchuma even brings proof texts: Jacob's neck turned to marble, as in a verse from Song of Songs: "Your neck is as a tower of marble." Esau's broken teeth are predicted in Psalm 3: "You have broken the teeth of the wicked."

Why does the midrash paint Esau in such a negative light? Likely because Esau is Edom, which came to be associated with Rome, and Rome with Christianity. Tanchuma is a late midrash – post-Talmudic, so it was likely written during a time of Christian persecution. Perhaps it would have been hard for the author to find nice things to say about Christians.

Nowadays, however, in the wake of Vatican II and evangelical support for Israel, throughout Christendom, relations between Christians and Jews are generally good and improving. Yakov and Esau have had a peaceful reconciliation at last. So we would not be so likely to cast aspersions at Christians. But what about our other cousins? What about Muslims? Unfortunately relations between the descendants of Yakov and the descendants of Yakov's uncle Ishmael are not so good. Ishamel, brother of Yitzchak (Isaac), is considered by both Jews and Muslims to be the ancestor of the Muslims.

A few weeks ago I had the opportunity to attend a conference sponsored by the Interreligious Coordinating Council in Israel on the theme of "Teaching Islam to Jews and Judaism to Muslims." At the conference, Rabbi Ron Kronish, head of ICCI, said "We believe that if there will be more knowledge about Islam among Jews and if Israeli Muslims know more about Judaism this would have a positive effect on social relations." Not surprisingly, one speaker said that Arab Muslims in Israel know a lot more about Jewish culture than Jews know about Islam or Arab culture.

I agree with Rabbi Kronish. I believe the more we know about each other's religions, the more progress we can make toward peace. For one thing, we can learn to use religion as a way to come together, instead of as a way to sow hatred. The truth is, if you look at the three Abrahamic faiths, Judaism, Christianity, and Islam, Judaism and Islam are very similar – Christianity is the "odd man out" with the greatest variation from the other two. So to further that goal, this morning we're not only going to study some Torah – we're going to study some Koran.

The first similarity that even a casual examination yields is in language. Since Arabic is a Semitic language as is Hebrew, it should come as no surprise that we share many of the same words. A few examples:

Arabic = translation = Hebrew = translation

Abd = servant = eved = slave
Amin = trustworthy = emunah = faith
Al-Kitab = the book, the Koran = catav = writing
Allah = God = El = God (Elohim)
Rachman = compassionate = rachamim = compassionate
Amr=decree = amar = spoke
Jahannam = Hell = Gehinnom = Hell
Khatimah = seal, Muhammad's prophethood = khatimah = seal or signature
Mala'ikah = angels = malakh = angel

Tsadaka = charity = tzedaka = charity, righteousness

But far more than similar terminology, Judaism and Islam share a very similar theology—very similar beliefs about the nature of God and what's more, the role of religion. Muslims believe that all the prophets we consider prophets, especially Moses, were prophets. They also believe that Jesus was a prophet, but not divine. From the Islamic perspective, Mohammed came to expand the audience for the message of the one God, and to correct what they believe to be deviations from the true text or true story. So for example, the Muslims also believe that Avraham bound one of his sons on an altar. The Koran just says Avraham (Ibrahim in Arabic) bound one of his sons, but it doesn't say which one. Mainstream Muslim thought now considers the bound son to be Ishmael, but you can find medieval Muslim scholars claiming it could have been either, or even that it was Yitzchak.

Jews and Muslims both share a firm belief that the essence of the universe is the oneness of God. We both reject Christian notions of God incarnate in human form. I'm going to share two sources and I challenge you to tell me which is the Jewish source and which is the Islamic source. Source #1:

> "It is the most basic of basic principles and a support for wisdom to know that there is something [namely God] that existed before any-thing else did and that He created everything that there is. Everything in the skies, on the ground and in between exists only because of the fact that He created them. Let it be known that if the Creator did not exist then nothing else would, for nothing can exist independently of the Creator. Let it further be known that if everything ceased to exist, the Creator alone would exist and would not have ceased to exist like everything else had. All things in creation are dependent upon the Crea-tor for their continued existence, but He does not need any of them [for His continued existence]. Therefore, the reality of His existence is not like the reality of the existence of any creation."

Source #2:

"God is one; He has no partners; Singular without any like Him; Uniform, having no contrary; Separate, having no equal; Ancient, having no first; Eternal, having no beginning; Everlasting, having no end; Ever-existing, without termination; Perpetual and constant, with neither interruption nor ending."

Source #1 was Maimonides, the great rabbi of the 11th century. Source #2 is a description of the Sunni Muslim conception of God from a book on Islam. Yet they describe very much the same God.

When it comes to understanding the beliefs and motivations of others, we often get it wrong.

Judaism has a system called *halakha* that is designed to regulate our conduct. A common categorization of the *mitzvot* (commandments) is between those that are *"bein Adam l'makom,"* between man and God, and those that are *"bein Adam l'chavero,"* between people. Islam has a similar system, called *sha'riah,* which also is divided into laws regulating conduct between man and God, and those regulating conduct between people. Both Judaism and Islam have dietary restrictions—as is well known, neither group eats pork, and both require slaughter to be performed in a certain way, with a blessing. Muslims pray five times a day; Jews also have five obligatory prayers a day: the Shema twice a day, and the Amidah three times a day. Muslims and Jews are both commanded to give charity and to take care of the poor, especially widows and orphans.

The Ten Commandments can be found in the Koran as well as in the Torah – they are not organized in one section like the Ten Commandments, but the concepts are all there.

(Thanks to http://www.submission.org/quran/ten.html where I found the listing of the Koranic sources for the Ten Commandments).

Torah	Koran
I am the Lord Your God	He is the one God (28:70)
You shall have no other Gods before Me	There is no other god beside GOD (47:19)
Do not take the name of the Lord, your God, in vain	Do not subject GOD's name to your casual swearing, that you may appear righteous, pious, or to attain credibility among the people. (2:224)
Remember the Sabbath day, to keep it holy.	O you who believe, when the Congregational Prayer (Salat Al-Jumu`ah) is announced on Friday, you shall hasten to the commemoration of GOD, and drop all business. (62:9)
Honor your father and your mother; that your days may be long upon the land which the Lord your God gives you.	. ....and your parents shall be honored. As long as one or both of them live, you shall never say to them, "Uff" (the slightest gesture of annoyance), nor shall you shout at them; you shall treat them amicably. (17:23)
You shall not kill.	...anyone who murders any person who had not committed murder or horrendous crimes, it shall be as if he murdered all the people. (5:32)
You shall not commit adultery.	You shall not commit adultery; it is a gross sin, and an evil behavior. (17:32)
You shall not steal.	The thief, male or female, you shall mark their hands as a punishment for their crime, and to serve as an example from GOD. GOD is Almighty, Most Wise. (5:38 - 39)
You shall not bear false witness against your neighbor.	O you who believe, you shall be absolutely equitable, and observe GOD, when you serve as witnesses, even against yourselves, or your parents, or your relatives.
You shall not covet your neighbor's house, you shall not covet your neighbor's wife, nor his manservant, nor his maidservant, nor his ox, nor his ass...	And do not covet what we bestowed upon any other people. Such are temporary ornaments of this life, whereby we put them to the test. What your Lord provides for you is far better, and everlasting.[20:131]

As you can see, there are many similarities between Judaism and Islam. A few years ago when I was serving as a congregational rabbi in Toledo, Ohio, I gave a lecture on Judaism at the main mosque in Toledo. A couple of hundred people stayed to hear my hour-long talk, and they had a lot of good questions. Yet at the end of the presentation, there was one question that stumped me: "If our religions are so similar, why do we have so many problems?"

Now I suspect some people may be thinking, OK, there are lots of similarities, but maybe the problems come from those verses in the Koran that call Jews the "sons of pigs and monkeys," who distorted God's teachings, and have been cursed and are inheritors of Hell?

Of course we have some ugly passages in the Torah as well, that can be tough to explain; like when we went to war against Midian, and Moses commanded "Now therefore kill every male among the little ones, and kill every woman that has known man by lying with him." Or "Therefore it shall be, when the Lord your God has given you rest from all your enemies around, in the land which the Lord your God gives you for an inheritance to possess, that you shall blot out the remembrance of Amalek from under heaven; you shall not forget it." Or the politically incorrect these days "And you shall dispossess the inhabitants of the land, and live in it; for I have given you the land to possess it. And you shall divide the land by lot for an inheritance among your families."

Both the Koran and the Torah contain hateful war-like messages. A Torah of Hate and a Koran of Hate.

But, thank God, neither of those teachings is the whole story. There is also a Torah of Love and Koran of Love.

In the Torah we have our well known teachings like "Love your neighbor as yourself," and "there shall be one law for the citizen and the resident alike."

The Koran wisely points out that not everyone of a different faith is alike. It teaches "Not all of them are alike: of the People of the book are a portion that stand (for the right); they rehearse the signs of Allah all night long and then prostrate themselves in adoration. They believe in Allah and the Last Day; they enjoin what is right and forbid what is wrong; and they (hasten in emulation) in (all) good works; they are in the ranks of the righteous. Of the good that they do nothing will be rejected of them; for Allah knoweth well those that do right."

As fellow descendants of Abraham, we are included in another teaching from the Koran "Who is better guided in his religion than one who submits totally to GOD, leads a righteous life, according to the creed of Abraham: monotheism? GOD has chosen Abraham as a beloved friend."

The Koran shares with Judaism the universalistic notion that we were all created from Adam and Eve and should act accordingly: "Mankind! We created you from a single (pair) Of a male and a female, And made you into nations and tribes, that Ye may know each other (Not that ye may despise each other)."

Just as Judaism has a written Torah – the Torah – and an oral Torah, the Talmud – Islam has the written Torah from Mohammed, the Koran, and a record of sayings attributed to him, an "oral Koran" so to speak called the Hadiths. In the Hadiths we find teachings against killing women and children – which would certainly preclude most acts of terrorism. One Hadith states: "It is narrated on the authority of Abdullah that a woman was found killed in one of the battles fought by the Messenger of Allah (may peace be upon him). He disapproved of the killing of women and children." And the other says "It is narrated by Ibn Umar that a woman was found killed in one of the battles; so the Messenger of Allah (may be peace be upon him) forbade the killing of women and children."

Yes, sadly there are Muslims who are terrorists on a large scale, bent on hate and destruction, as we witnessed tragically in the recent events in Mumbai. And there are Jews who shoot and harass Palestinians, as we recently witnessed the violence in Hebron. NOTE: Even though I refer to those two events in the same paragraph, I am in no way saying they are equivalent! When I presented this d'var Torah, a few people came unglued because they thought I was comparing the two. I'm not. But we can't ignore the fact that there are also Jewish terrorists, and the ongoing occupation of the West Bank, and situation in Gaza all cause a lot of suffering to many Palestinians. Not as much death and destruction as has been caused Muslim terrorists, but we are not in a contest to measure suffering here.

A very important thing to remember is that there are also Muslims who condemn terrorism. The headlines from Mumbai about the terrorists were all front page news; buried in the back of the paper was the news that Muslims in Mumbai organized a demonstration after the attacks proclaiming very publicly that Islam opposes terrorism. Just as there are Rabbis for Human Rights, there is now a group called Imams for Human Rights.

I don't think there is much point in arguing over whose terrorists are worse or whose peace lovers are more numerous. The important point is that moderate peace loving Jews should join forces with moderate peace loving Muslims. For Jews to condemn suicide bombers and Muslims to condemn violent settlers does little to help bring peace closer. We each have to work to get our own houses in order. Jews need to condemn violent settlers and to seek an end to the occupation of the West Bank and the conflict in Gaza, and Muslims need to condemn those who would kill innocent people in the name of Islam.

I believe the more Jews and Muslims know about each other, the likelier we are to see the common ground and the humanity in the other, the likelier we are to find real peace. In Jerusalem organizations like the Interfaith Encounter Association and the Interreligious Coordinating Council of Israel provide frequent opportunities to learn with and interact with Muslims.

The midrash about Esau crying because Jacob's neck was marble is not the only way to read the story in this week's parsha. HaEmek Davar, a 19th c. Lithuanian commentator said "Both wept, implying that Jacob's love too was aroused towards Esau. And so it is in all ages. Whenever the seed of Esau is prompted by sincere motives to acknowledge and respect the seed of Israel, then we too, are moved to acknowledge Esau: for he is our brother. As a parallel we may cite the true friendship that existed between Rabbi Judah Hanasi and the Roman emperor Antoninus, and there are many similar instances."

In these trying times, Yakov and Esau – Jews and Gentiles – are both weeping and crying out for peace. May God's compassion be aroused and may the Holy One help us find a way to peace and reconciliation with our neighbors and cousins.

Amen.

I Swear: But by What Book?

In December 2006, there was a big flap because the first Muslim elected to Congress, Keith Ellison, announced his plan to take his oath of office on a Koran. I was astounded by the foolish opposition to his plan. This was my blog entry on the topic.

Cyberspace is abuzz with a brouhaha initiated by Dennis Prager's bigoted rant against Congressman-elect Keith Ellison of Minnesota, the first Muslim to be elected to Congress. Prager is outraged that Ellison plans to take his oath of office on a Koran:

> "Forgive me, but America should not give a hoot what Keith Ellison's favorite book is. Insofar as a member of Congress taking an oath to serve America and uphold its values is concerned, America is interested in only one book, the Bible. If you are incapable of taking an oath on that book, don't serve in Congress. In your personal life, we will fight for your right to prefer any other book. We will even fight for your right to publish cartoons mocking our Bible. But, Mr. Ellison, America, not you, decides on what book its public servants take their oath."

Prager is wrong on so many levels I hardly know where to start. First of all, he is wrong on the Constitution. As pointed out by Religion Clause, it would be unconstitutional to insist that everyone be sworn in on the Christian Bible:

UCLA Constitutional Law Professor Eugene Volokh responded at National Review Online, saying that Prager "mistakes the purpose of the oath, and misunderstands the Constitution." He continued, "If Congress were indeed to take the view that 'If you are incapable of taking an oath on that book [the Bible], don't serve in Congress,' it would be imposing an unconstitutional religious test.... Letting Christians swear the oath of office, while allowing members of other denominations only to swear what ends up being a mockery of an oath—a religious ceremony appealing to a religious belief system that they do not share—would be [religious] discrimination."

Not only that, but Prager has his facts wrong. There are Presidents who did not take an oath on the Bible, and there are Jews who have taken the oath on the Torah, as reported by Minnesota Monitor:

In our country's history, four presidents have been inaugurated without swearing an oath on the Bible. Franklin Pierce was affirmed, and swore no oath, Rutherford Hayes initially had a private ceremony with no Bible before his public ceremony, Theodore Roosevelt had no Bible at his ceremony, and Lyndon Johnson used a missal during his first term.

Despite Prager's insistence that "for all of American history, Jews elected to public office have taken their oath on the Bible, even though they do not believe in the New Testament," it is clear that he is wrong. Linda Lingle, Governor of Hawaii, took the oath of office on a Torah in 2001. Madeleine Kunin, a Jewish Immigrant and Governor of Vermont "rested her left hand on a stack of old prayer books that had belonged to her mother, grandparents, and great grandfather" as "a physical expression of the weight of Jewish history."

And no, I don't know what book Joe Lieberman used.

The other bloggers miss the religious angle. If I were to be elected to office, there is no way I would ever take an oath of office on a Christian Bible. That would be a mockery of my faith, and disrespectful to the Christians. When we take an oath with our hand on a sacred book, we are swearing by that which is most sacred to us. Since I don't believe in the New Testament, what kind of oath would it be for me to swear by it? It would be utterly meaningless. On the other hand, if I were to swear on a Hebrew Bible, on the Torah, THAT would be a real oath.

In fact, not only would I "allow" Mr. Ellison to take his oath on the Koran, I would insist on it. If he were to take his oath on a Christian Bible, I might be afraid he wasn't sincere, it wasn't really an oath. But if he were to swear by the Koran—well then I would know that it was a real oath to him.

Acknowledgements and Eulogies

It may seem odd to put a small collection of eulogies together with my acknowledgements, but the eulogies included here are of people who were my teachers in one or way another, so it is fitting they be part of my acknowledgements. In the opening passage of parshat Noah, Noah is called *"ish tzaddik v'tamim b'dorotav,"* a righteous and pure man in his generation." A little further on in the story of Noah, God talks to Noah and says "I have seen you are righteous in this generation." The *"tamim"* "pure," is left out when God is speaking directly to Noah. Rashi says that this is to teach us that we may praise a person in his presence, but we only praise him fully when he is NOT present. Hence my praise for those who are "no longer present" is fuller than my praise and acknowledgement of my teachers who ARE still present.

I have had many teachers who have contributed to forming my world view, and hence the ideas expressed in this book. The list is incomplete: it would be impossible to acknowledge ALL of my teachers; we learn from King David that someone who teaches you one thing merits being called "teacher." My apologies to my many teachers not listed here:

- Rabbi Elliott Dorff helped me develop my personal Jewish philosophy, which is heavily influenced by his. He has also has been a big influence in my approach to halacha. Rabbi Dorff is truly a "rabbi's rabbi." Like many of my colleagues, if I have a halachic question that seems beyond me, I turn to Rabbi Dorff.
- My chavruta, Rabbi Alana Suskin, has been the foil against which I sharpened my learning. Rabbinic texts are so male-dominated I found it very helpful having an ardent feminist for a study partner.
- From Rabbi Dan Shevitz I learned when in doubt to err on the side of being kind. This is a hugely important lesson, and not so simple. The easiest halachic answer is often not the kindest.
- Professor Walter Herzberg taught me to start studying a text by asking very detailed questions. It's a beautiful way to learn and one I use with my students to this day. We spent one complete classroom session debating the meaning of the word *"tov."*

- Rabbi Ed Feinstein taught me that the role of the rabbi is to connect the wisdom of the Torah to the lives of today's Jews. He also helped show me how to do that.
- Dr. Alan Morinis introduced me to the wisdom of Mussar.
- Rabbi Nat Ezray has been a friend and mentor practically since I started on my "Jewish journey." His advice has always been excellent.
- From Rabbi David Hartman I learned to become comfortable struggling with uncomfortable texts and with uncomfortable passages in the siddur.
- Professor Phil Racicot showed me that smart, thoughtful people can have faith in God. At the time it was a revelation; since then I've been blessed with knowing many smart, thoughtful people who believe in God.

I am grateful to all my teachers, not just those mentioned above, both from the Ziegler School of Rabbinic Studies and elsewhere. The Talmud teaches that your parents may give you life in this world, but your teachers lead you to eternal life in the world to come.

When I visit someone's home, one of the first things I do is look at their bookshelves. I think you can tell a lot about a person by what he reads. I have had several teachers who have influenced me primarily through their writings: Rabbi Abraham Joshua Heschel (z"l), from whom I learned that God needs Man, and that the path to faith is through awe; Rabbi Joel Roth, whose book on the halachic system is a "how-to" manual for poskening halacha; and Rabbi Aryeh Kaplan (z"l) whose works on Jewish meditation have deepened my personal prayer practice. Will and Ariel Durant's book, "The Lessons of History" has helped me learn to take a longer term view of seemingly immediate issues.

Any parent knows that you learn an amazing amount of Torah from your children, and Kiri, Heather, Katherine, Lizzy, and Devorah have all taught me much—they also forced me to learn certain lessons, whether I was fully prepared to learn them or not! And *"acharon acharon chaviv,"* "the last is most precious:" if my wife Lauri Donahue hadn't gotten interested in Judaism when we married, my own interest may have remained dormant. She has been the perfect partner for life's adventures, ready for crazy things like quitting Silicon Valley for rabbi school, or the even crazier adventure of immigrating to Israel. She's also the best editor I know—if the high holiday sermons in this volume read better than the other material in this book, it's thanks to her editing.

Bertha Leff, z"l

My grandmother passed in June, 1998, just as I was starting rabbinical school. In many ways she was my first Jewish role model.

We are here to celebrate the life of my Grandmother, Bertha Leff, Basha Bat Chaya.

Whenever a loved one goes on to *Olam Haba*, the world to come, we're not ready for it. We all had more things we wanted to share with Grandma; I wanted her to see my daughter's Bat Mitzvah in two years, I wanted her to see me graduate from rabbinical school in four years, I wanted my youngest children to get to know her. However, since she did have almost 92 very good years, I feel almost selfish to say "but I wanted more." It was time for her to rejoin her beloved Louis and Natie, and wait for the rest of us who will inevitably follow. She died peacefully, at a ripe old age, surrounded by people who love her. What more could one ask for?

I'm a *baal teshuvah*, a returnee to Judaism, after many years of being a typical secular Jew dabbling with Eastern religions. As soon as I learned about the importance of *gemilut chesed*, acts of lovingkindness in Judaism I realized my Grandma was overflowing with it; it was the trait that defined her. She had a heart that was bigger than she was.

Acts of chesed are among the greatest of mitzvot a person can perform. In Proverbs it is written that doing deeds of charity (tzedaka) and justice is greater than offering all of the sacrifices, and in the Talmud it says that *gemilut chesed*, deeds of lovingkindness, are greater than tzedaka. (Ask me later if you want to know why).

The Shaloh HaKodosh writes: "Therefore, one should be extremely careful to observe the mitzvah of *gemilut chasadim*, and should see to it that not a single of the days of his life goes by without performing some deed of *gemillus chesed* with his body, his money, or his soul." If anyone I know came even close to fulfilling this, it was Grandma.

In my application to rabbinical school, I had to write a lengthy essay describing my background and why I thought I'd make a good rabbi. In it I wrote: "Even though none of my grandparents or aunts and uncles, let alone my immediate family, were regular shul goers or observant, there was a very strong sense of Jewish identity. It was taken for granted as a part of who we were. All the children made B'nei Mitzvah. The holidays were special times for us. My grandmother is the archetype of the Jewish grandmother: warm, loving, a fantastic cook, her life totally dedicated to her children, grandchildren, and great-grandchildren. Thankfully she is still alive and well at the age of 91, and she serves as a real inspiration to me with the *gemilut chesed* she displays not just for family, but for friends and people in need."

Muriel, Karen, and I stopped by Grandma's place on Sunday. Her neighbors at the assisted care facility she lived in all came by to tell us how much they were going to miss her. One woman said she was the best friend she ever had; another said she was the sister she never had; another talked about how Grandma was there for her in difficult times when no one else was there for her. Another one said that she always always talked about her grandchildren. She said "I have grandchildren too," letting us know she rarely got a chance to talk about them as Grandma was so enthusiastic about all of us.

Last Friday night, we made Shabbos dinner in Grandma's hospital room. I think the hospital staff were taken slightly off guard as we borrowed a table from their break room and brought it into Grandma's room, and set the table with kosher takeout, challah, wine, all the trimmings, and started singing songs and niggunim and saying the blessings. The only thing we didn't do was light candles: since Grandma was on oxygen, candles would not have been a good idea. Grandma joined in the singing of a niggun from her bed. She knew what was going on.

Saturday night, in the hospice, we all sat around Grandma's bed, taking turns holding her hand and telling our favorite Grandma stories, and wonderful stories they were. When Robin was a baby, Grandma reading by a flashlight, waiting for Robin to wake up so she could feed her; throwing a dirty, emaciated,19-year-old Mitchell, straight off a plane from Panama, into a bathtub and scrubbing him clean and feeding him and taking care of him. Sitting in bed with 15-year-old Karen, telling her stories of her younger days. How she used to drag my father, Mickey, by the arm on vacations. Muriel sharing how she used to only cook the vegetables that Grandpa liked. Judy told us how Ivan would run into bed with them during summer storms. I tend to think of sitting at the kitchen table with Grandma, her always encouraging me to eat a little more, no matter how much she had just fed me, while we just sat and were together, not talking about anything important, but just being together.

Grandma wasn't responding while we told the stories, but I feel she heard us, and was comforted, and it made it easier for her to go. It is said in the Talmud that being with someone when she or he dies is a great deed of loving-kindness, for a soul in transition is comforted by a soul in a peaceful state. I feel honored that I was able to join my family in doing this mitzvah for Grandma.

We have been taught that if a person acts kindly here on this earth, this arouses kindness above. The angels sing on that day, and the day is crowned because of him. The angels had nearly 92 years of singing thanks to Grandma.

I close with a thought from Reb Aryeh Levin: "When a child is born and comes into the world, all are rapturous with joy—and the child itself cries and wails. When someone dies and his life-spirit leaves the world, all mourn and grieve—but that living spirit itself exults and rejoices. It has gone from a world of darkness to a world of light." Grandma has gone to a world of light. And we will all miss her terribly.

Rabbi Alan Lew, z"l

Rabbi Lew passed away in January, 2009.

One of my teachers, Rabbi Alan Lew, passed away in January. As I was re-reading his awesome book about the transformative power of the High Holidays, "This Is Real and You Are Completely Unprepared" I was reminded of how much I miss him, and how much the world has lost with his passing.

I don't know why I didn't write something about Rabbi Lew earlier, right when he died; probably because I was too shocked and surprised.

Rabbi Lew was a fascinating character: he was in line to be the head of the San Francisco Zen Center when he changed gears and decided to become a rabbi. He was a great author, teacher, and social activist.

I first met Rabbi Lew in the San Francisco Bay Area, it must have been around 1996, before I even thought about becoming a rabbi. He taught a Jewish Meditation class at the synagogue I belonged to, Temple Beth Jacob, as part of the Bay Area's adult Jewish learning consortium. Considering how I was making my way back to Judaism -- after a period of time exploring other religions, like Buddhism -- his teachings had a profound impact on me. I had meditated in the past, and at that time I was starting to get into Judaism, and Rabbi Lew's teachings very much helped me connect these two seemingly disparate disciplines. He opened my eyes to the ancient Jewish meditative tradition, which got me started on reading a lot of books on the subject (such as his spiritual memoir, "One God Clapping: The Spiritual Path of a Zen Rabbi" and Rabbi Aryeh Kaplan's excellent books "Jewish Meditation," "Meditation and the Bible," and "Meditation and Kabbalah"). Jewish meditation has become an important part of my spiritual practice, and I am forever indebted to Rabbi Lew for introducing me to the subject.

I've been to a lot of classes, lectures, etc. I'm hard to please -- there are not many teachers who inspire me to pull out my pocket PC and start taking notes. Rabbi Lew was one of those who did. One of the things I wrote down from studying with him is especially applicable to this time of year. He spoke about the High Holiday period as beginning with Tisha b'Av, the holiday in August when we commemorate the destruction of the Temple, and culminating with Sukkot, the holiday in October when we remember our ancestors wandering in the desert by taking our meals and spending time is Sukkot, in booths, in flimsy structures that a strong wind is supposed to be able to blow over. He talked about how this time is a journey from one broken house to another -- in one, the destroyed temple, we are sitting and crying. In the other, the sukkah, the flimsy "booth," we are sitting in rejoicing, commanded to be happy. In "This is Real" he describes the idea very eloquently:

So this concatenation of ritual -- this dance that begins on Tisha B'Av and ends on Sukkot, that begins with the mournful collapse of a house and ends with the joyful collapse of a house, this intentional spasm that awakens us and carries us through death and back to life again -- stands for the journey the soul is always on.

Another teaching of Rabbi Lew's that I wrote down was one he gave over at the Rabbinical Assembly convention in 2005. Here's what he taught, and I think you'll be able to see from my comments why I felt he was a "kindred spirit:"

At the RA convention, Alan Lew shared a beautiful piece of Torah from the Zohar, with Torah portrayed as a beautiful woman hidden away in a palace, and the serious student hangs out outside the palace all the time, just getting an occasional glimpse of the beautiful princess; others don't even notice the beautiful princess because they are not prepared and are not looking. Alan asked whether we related to this teaching or not. I did: I said it was how my daf yomi experience was, hours of hanging around outside, maybe a little bored, and then a glimpse of something really cool and exciting. One colleague (female) couldn't get into the whole metaphor because of the male oriented sexual metaphors; another didn't get the "passion." He said he likes Torah, but if he didn't study Torah for a week he wouldn't "pine away" as the Zohar model seems to imply. To me, that lukewarm response to Torah is one of the problems we have. I don't mean to sound immodest or overly pious, but I would feel that pining away--I couldn't imagine going two days, let alone a week, without studying Torah.

I have to admit to having kind of a weird relationship with books. I like buying books. I'll spend $15-20 to buy a book and have it on my shelf, rather than borrow it from a library. Even though the vast majority of books on my shelf are books I just read once. And maybe refer to later. Maybe. If it was good. As a result, when we move we have about 50 boxes of books that go with us. Maybe it's a rabbi thing. "This is Real and You Are Completely Unprepared" is an exception to my "read once" custom. It's a book I reread every year at this time. Unfortunately, Rabbi Lew is no longer with us -- God called his soul home while he was out for a jog -- but, fortunately his teachings endure forever in his books. "This is Real" is a book that can completely transform the way you look at the High Holidays...and it's beautifully written, to boot!

I think of Rabbi Lew as a spiritual guide in the style of the Peshischa chasidim—not one who sought to be a rebbe with followers, but rather one encouraging you to be authentic, helping by giving you some tools for your own spiritual journey.

May his memory be a blessing.

"Doc" Ron Rosen, z"l

Ron was a good friend for thirty years. He was just a few years older than me; I was shocked when he died unexpectedly. This was written on the occasion of his unveiling, a year after his untimely death.

7 Tammuz 5769 / July 11, 2008
Jerusalem

Psalm 116 tells us *"yakar b'einei Hashem hamavta l'chasidav,"* "Precious in the sight of the Lord is the death of his pious ones."

I admit to being very troubled by this Psalm. Why should the loss of a pious man to this world be precious to God? God may get to enjoy the pious man's company on a more intimate basis, but how pious can a person be in heaven where you can't do any mitzvot?

When I met Ron back in 1976, the fact that we were both Jewish was very incidental and strictly coincidental. I certainly would not have predicted that either one of us would one day be considered "pious." Neither of us had any real connection to Jewish life, the Jewish community, or the Jewish tradition at that point in our lives. Ron had a Kung Fu studio on Denver's Capitol Hill, and I was teaching a Tae Kwon Do class in the neighborhood. We became buddies – Ron introduced me to sushi – and colleagues. Ron got me a job working with him as a bouncer at a gay disco. His sales pitch was very straightforward – they pay us double what they pay big bruiser bouncers, since they preferred people who looked "normal," and all we had to do was stand around and drink grapefruit juice until 4am.

Ron and I both had lengthy periods when we sought religion every-where EXCEPT in Judaism. Everyone knows the idea of running around all over the world, and then falling in love with the girl next door. There is a Chasidic story that illustrates the journey Ron and I both went on – about a man from the boonies in Poland who goes to Warsaw seeking a treasure he saw in a dream, only to discover it was hidden in his own home. I don't know if he shared it with you, but I found the story of how Ron came to return to Judaism a fascinating tale.

One night about ten years ago, Ron and I went out for sushi and sake, and he told me how performing a particularly grueling Native American ritual helped lead him back to Judaism. He participated in a sun dance or something like that, which involved fasting for four days and nights, no food or water. Towards the end of the ceremony, he had a vision where he saw a line of grandfather types welcoming the people going through the ceremony, and he realized that none of them was HIS grandfather; they were all obviously Native Americans. He decided he should look in places where he would find his grandfathers, in Judaism.

So although it would be a while yet before he reconnected with Judaism, in those days when I first met Ron, over 30 years ago, an astute observer could have picked up on Ron's "piety," and righteousness. When I think of the way Ron was pious, I think of the way Abraham was pious – not quiet, not demure, but rather an iconoclast. Just as Abraham smashed his father's idols, Ron was quite ready to smash other people's idols, assumptions, and expectations. Some people are pious in their observance of the ritual commandments – however you can be equally pious in the observance of the commandments that are between people, especially the commandment to love your neighbor as yourself.

R. Nachman of Breslov taught that when we say in our prayers *"m'lo kol ha'aretz k'vodo,"* the whole world is full of God's glory, it is meant quite literally – there is no place that is devoid of God's presence. In fact if you want to do some good elevating spirits that have fallen to a low level, you have to go down to where they are.

All of which can make me feel better about the kind of bars Ron and I used to visit back then! But here's where an astute observer could have picked up on Ron's righteousness – even though Ron and I occasionally visited some pretty disreputable places, he would bring cheer to the people working there – and he was much more interested in the people working there than in the patrons – doing things like magic tricks. Although he was always careful to tell people he did illusions, not tricks. And his generosity of spirit was obvious in the way he was always ready to reach out to people who were in need, people who may have been battered by the vicissitudes of life.

Ron was always ready to make financial sacrifices to hop on a plane to help others who were worse off than he was. Guatemala, Thailand, makes no difference, no location was too remote, no people living in conditions too primitive, he was ready to go make a difference helping when he could, regardless of the personal cost and loss of income. He was driven to make a difference. Figure out the finances later.

The Talmud teaches that he who saves a life is as if he saved a world. Ron's dedication to healing and helping has surely earned him a worthy place in *Olam Haba*, the world to come.

The Psalm I quoted at the start, Psalm 116, could be translated differently – "*yakar*" can mean not only precious, the usual translation in books of psalms, but it can mean expensive. Instead of reading the verse "Precious in the sight of the Lord is the death of his pious ones," I suggest we read it as telling us the loss of His righteous ones is expensive in the sight of the Lord – it's a heavy cost, even to God, to lose a righteous soul from the world where it can do good.

May Ron's memory be not just a blessing – may it be an inspiration to us, a reminder to stretch ourselves to do God's work by helping others.

Amen.

Rabbi Mickey Rosen, z"l

I was saddened today to learn of the passing of Rabbi Mickey Rosen.

Rabbi Rosen was the founder of Yakar, an institution that was one of the influences that helped me fall in love with living in Jerusalem. When I first arrived in Jerusalem in the summer of 2000, Yakar was THE "in" place for the "observant hip Anglo" crowd. Rabbis like David Hartman, Danny Gordis, Levi Lauer, were all regulars. It was the first of the many "Carlebach minyans" in the English speaking regions of south Jerusalem. The Friday night service, with a room packed with hundreds of people singing Carlebach tunes in harmony, moved my soul in a way nothing else had until then. The focus of Yakar was, and is, learning. On Saturday morning, they take a break in the middle of the service, after the Torah reading and before Musaf, and break into a couple of different groups to study the weekly Torah reading—to study, not just to sit and listen to a sermon. It's a great model.

I was in Jerusalem to study at Machon Schechter in the summer of 2000. We arrived in the summer, but classes didn't start until after the High Holidays. So I started out by studying in the month of Elul program at Yakar, where I had the *zchut* to study with Rav Mickey. A couple of times a week for the month of Elul, we studied Rambam's (Maimonides) famous teachings about teshuvah, repentance. Rambam teaches that repentance involves first admitting to the sin, fixing any damage you did, and then asking for forgiveness from the other person. Rav Mickey's central thesis—which I very much agree with, and which has stayed with me 8 years later—was that Rambam's model is inadequate. It doesn't go far enough. If your spiritual preparations for the High Holidays consist of doing teshuvah ala Rambam, all you do is fix bad stuff you did, but you have not made any real improvement in yourself. I wasn't very familiar with the teachings of Mussar at the time, but he was really teaching us a very Mussar lesson—that you need to work on improving your *middot*, your character traits, not just fixing any damage you had done.

Mickey had certainly done his work on his character traits. He created an institution that in many ways was at the forefront of a whole movement of liberal Orthodox institutions in Jerusalem. He was a dedicated campaigner for peace and human rights. He challenged people to think, to learn, to grow, and to be decent and moral.

On the one hand, the amount of Torah going forth from Zion—coming out of Jerusalem—is diminished with the passing of Rabbi Mickey Rosen. On the other hand, the amount of Torah coming from his students and those whose lives he touched continues to grow, and is the greatest legacy a rabbi could hope for.

May his memory be a blessing, and may his family, friends, and students take comfort in knowing the world is better place for his having been with us.

Emerich Salzberger, z"l

A Short Story of a Long Life is the title of my late friend Emerich Salzberger Stoessl's z"l autobiography.

Emerich was a truly remarkable person. Born in Austria, he learned to fly in Prague and he studied aeronautical engineering in Italy at a very young age. When WWII broke out, he joined the RAF and served as a fighter pilot, and later test pilot at England's legendary Farnborough, where at the end of the war he was the senior pilot and director of flying—and one of the first people (if not the first) to fly a jet aircraft in England, a captured Messerschmitt 262.

During the war he was sent on a secret mission to Czechoslovakia, which failed. He managed to get a job as navigator for a ship heading down the Danube toward Palestine. The ship wrecked, and was captured by the German's allies, the Italians. He was put in a concentration camp in Italy, managed to escape and get back to England, and was sent to North Africa as commander of a squadron of fighter planes.

After the war he took a posting in Palestine where he headed air traffic control for the entire Middle East. His parents had moved to Mexico, and he ended up joining them there. He continued to help the infant Israel, identifying and smuggling surplus WWII planes from America to Israel. He was a block away, and was knocked out of his chair when Jewish terrorists blew up the King David Hotel.

I met Emerich around 1980, when I was working for Geometrics. Emerich had a photogrammetry (aerial photography & mapping) company based in Mexico City. My boss at the time, Sheldon Breiner, suggested I meet with Emerich as they had worked together before. Emerich introduced me to a man who became our sales agent for Mexico. I remember the first time I met Emerich, we sat in his office and he offered me a cigar. He seemed pleased when I accepted; he said "I can't stand a vice-less Jew!" Having at least one vice made one more human.

Emerich and I hit it off, I suppose because we were both part of the fraternity of Jewish pilots. All Jews feel a certain sense of connection with each other as a large extended family; pilots also feel a certain camaraderie that comes with a shared understanding of how amazing it is to fly an airplane. So fellow Jewish pilots makes for a "two-fer."

After our first meeting we would get together whenever I visited Mexico or when he visited the San Francisco Bay Area; we went flying together a few times in the Bay Area. Emerich mapped many of Mexico's airports and railway lines. At his recommendation we tried a visit to Zihuatanejo, and fell in love with the place. Zihua sits on a beautiful horseshoe-shaped bay on the coast about 100 miles north of Acapulco. In the years that followed I often would go to Zihua for a few days and then head to Mexico City for business.

One time when a few of us were in Mexico on a combination of business and pleasure, on the leg from Zihuatanejo to Mexico City, the engine started running rough at 15,000 feet over Cuernavaca. When I landed I asked Emerich if he could recommend a mechanic. He told me to take it to these guys across the field...with the caveat, "they're the best in Mexico, but not very good. I take my planes to Brownsville for maintenance." Not the most encouraging recommendation, but somehow that recommendation captured something of Emerich's attitude and way of dealing with adversity—a sort of resignation and acceptance of the limits of a particular time and place.

Between Emerich and a few other friends I have who were his contemporaries, I feel a connection to an amazing period of history. The events of WWII—including the Holocaust and immediately after the creation of the State of Israel—in many ways created the world we live in today. I envy the opportunities Emerich and his compatriots had to be a part of the creation of a new world and a new country. From today, we look back on that era and it seems like a time when things were clearer. There were good guys and bad guys, and when the war was over the bad guys were done. Today the war on terrorism—

or more accurately, the war against Islamic Fundamentalism—seems bogged down with an enemy that grows two new heads every time you cut one off. With the way they hide among civilians, our ethics are challenged every time we try and stop them because it usually means killing innocent civilians along with the terrorists. I suppose the clarity we project on the world 60 years ago is really just an artifact of hindsight—they had their own moral quandaries, like dropping the bomb on Hiroshima and Nagasaki, or the bombing of Dresden.

Emerich was a gentleman of the old school—I bet he really charmed the ladies when he was young. Heck, he still charmed them when he was old! He had a dry sense of humor, and he was a real mensch. One time he offered to give me his company because he wanted to retire, he hadn't been able to sell it, and he didn't want to simply shut the doors and liquidate the assets because he wanted to make sure his employees, who had been loyal to him for years, were taken care of. I'm adventurous, but I wasn't quite adventurous enough to take over a company that was financially troubled in a business I knew nothing about in a country where I could hardly speak the language. Then again, who knows, that may be what I'll be facing in Israel next year! Emerich eventually did give the company away.

In March of this past year the Rabbinical Assembly had its annual convention in Mexico, so of course I looked up Emerich, and was greatly saddened to learn he was gravely ill. I'm very glad we had a chance to visit before he passed away. One of my great disappointments as a rabbi is that I wasn't able to help Emerich find God. He really wanted to believe in the God of his ancestors, but had trouble getting there. I recommended some books, we talked, we corresponded, but he just was not able to find faith in God. That experience strengthens me in my resolve to finish writing the book I'm working on, which is all about how to develop faith in God.

When I was there I said the *vidui* for him, which is a special prayer recited by people with a terminal illness. It was one of the most difficult things

I've done since becoming a rabbi; I've said that prayer for any number of people, but this was the first time I did it for a friend. I think it helped him feel a little more at peace.

Of course, I see the presence of God just in the fact that after not having been to Mexico for many years, I was able to see Emerich again just a few months before he passed away. Could it have been a coincidence? Sure...but maybe it wasn't.

Even though I didn't speak to Emerich a lot in the last few years, the world feels just a little colder with his passing. I'll miss our visits, usually over a meal.

Emerich's memory is a blessing to all who knew him.

Rabbi Barry Leff

Prayers

Prayer for those who contemplate suicide

El Harachamim, compassionate God

Rofei lishvurei lev, healer of shattered hearts

Grant strength and comfort

to those who struggle with internal demons

Shine your light to the dark corners of their souls

Share your strength with them

to await the dawn that follows the night

Help them to see the love that is around them

Bless them and those who care for them

Amen

Prayer for those affected by Hurricane Katrina

Ribono shel olam, Master of the Universe!

Harachaman, the compassionate One! As you blessed our ancestors Abraham, Isaac and Jacob, Sarah, Rebecca, Rachel and Leah, please bless and heal those affected by Hurricane Katrina.

El Na, Please, God, bring physical healing to those who are sick or injured; bring material support to those who have lost their homes and their jobs; bring comfort to the *neshamot*, the souls, of all whose lives have been disrupted by this catastrophe.

Please God, support the hands of all those who are working to save lives and rebuild in the effected lands. Help us to remember that the poorest have been made poorer, and we are commanded not to turn our eyes from our poor brother. Bring them speedily from darkness to light,

Amen

About the Author

Rabbi Barry Leff was born in Heidelberg, Germany, grew up in New York and Denver, and lived in California for many years. He has lived in Thailand, Iran, and Canada. Now a dual Israeli-American citizen, he makes his home in Jerusalem, where he hopes to finally "settle down" with his wife and as many of his five daughters that will join him there.

He has a Doctorate in Business Administration from Golden Gate University, and received his Master's in Rabbinic Studies and ordination as a rabbi from the Ziegler School of Rabbinic Studies in Los Angeles.

He's a flight instructor, SCUBA Divemaster, black belt in Tae Kwon Do, and enjoys skiing, yoga, running, sailing, and playing the piano.

After a 20 year career as an entrepreneur and executive in Silicon Valley, he had a nine year Sabbatical from the business world as he pursued rabbinic studies and worked as a pulpit rabbi.

Once again a business executive, he has not lost his passion for rabbinic work, which he fulfills as a human rights activist and teacher, engaged in ecumenical activity.

CPSIA information can be obtained at www.ICGtesting.com
Printed in the USA
LVOW060324121011

250137LV00002B/40/P